MODERNISM, SATIRE, AND THE NOVEL

In this groundbreaking study, Jonathan Greenberg locates a satiric sensibility at the heart of the modern. By promoting an antisentimental education, modernism denied the authority of emotion to guarantee moral and literary value. Instead, it fostered sophisticated, detached, and apparently cruel attitudes toward pain and suffering. This sensibility challenged the novel's humanistic tradition, set ethics and aesthetics into conflict, and fundamentally altered the ways that we know and feel.

Through lively and original readings of works by Evelyn Waugh, Stella Gibbons, Nathanael West, Djuna Barnes, Samuel Beckett, and others, this book analyzes a body of literature – late modernist satire – that can appear by turns aloof, sadistic, hilarious, ironic, and poignant, but which continually questions inherited modes of feeling. By recognizing the centrality of satire to modernist aesthetics, Greenberg offers not only a new chapter in the history of satire but a persuasive new idea of what made modernism modern.

JONATHAN GREENBERG is Associate Professor of English at Montclair State University. He has published essays on numerous twentieth-century writers including Chinua Achebe, Salman Rushdie, Evelyn Waugh, Nathanael West, and Ian McEwan. A comedic writer himself, he has also won an Emmy Award for his writing for children's television.

MODERNISM, SATIRE, AND THE NOVEL

JONATHAN GREENBERG

Associate Professor, Montclair State University

CAMBRIDGE
UNIVERSITY PRESS

CAMBRIDGE UNIVERSITY PRESS
Cambridge, New York, Melbourne, Madrid, Cape Town,
Singapore, São Paulo, Delhi, Tokyo, Mexico City

Cambridge University Press
The Edinburgh Building, Cambridge CB2 8RU, UK

Published in the United States of America by Cambridge University Press, New York

www.cambridge.org
Information on this title: www.cambridge.org/9781107008496

© Jonathan Greenberg 2011

First published 2011

Printed in the United Kingdom at the University Press, Cambridge

A catalogue record for this publication is available from the British Library

Library of Congress Cataloging-in-Publication Data
Greenberg, Jonathan Daniel, 1968–
Modernism, satire, and the novel / Jonathan Greenberg.
p.   cm.
ISBN 978-1-107-00849-6 (Hardback)
1. Modernism (Literature)   2. Satire–History and criticism.   3. Emotions in literature.
I. Title.
PN56.M54G75 2011
809.3′9112–dc22

2011009239

ISBN 978-1-107-00849-6 Hardback

One must have a heart of stone to read the death of Little Nell without laughing.

Oscar Wilde

I always find it necessary to burlesque the mystery of feeling at its source; I must laugh at myself, and if the laugh is "bitter," I must laugh at the laugh.

Nathanael West

"If I wasn't real," Alice said – half-laughing through her tears, it all seemed so ridiculous – "I shouldn't be able to cry."

"I hope you don't think those are real tears?" Tweedledum interrupted in a tone of great contempt.

Lewis Carroll

Tears and laughter, they are so much Gaelic to me.

Samuel Beckett

Contents

Illustration

Preface

A 1946 Charles Addams cartoon, "Sad Movie" (see Fig. 1), shows a movie theater full of people watching a film. We don't see the screen, but the faces of the audience members – eyes wide, brows furrowed, tears running down cheeks – tell us that they are watching something distressing, maybe tragic. In the second row of the weeping crowd, slightly off-center, sits a familiar Addams ghoul, the character later named Uncle Fester, his face lit up in a grin. As in so many Addams cartoons, no caption is provided. His smile is the only punchline the joke needs.[1]

By making a spectacle of the audience, showing not the action onscreen but the reaction in the seats, the cartoon diverts attention from the upsetting events of the film to the comic impropriety of Uncle Fester's laughter. Addams's joke hinges on the discord between Fester's cruel pleasure and the heartfelt tears of the crowd. But although it is the deviant reaction that makes the scene a joke, it would be too simple to call Fester the object or the target of *our* laughter. For we are complicit with him; we feel that he shares our emotional distance from the movie, and hence our aesthetic superiority to those moved to tears by the spectacle on the screen. "The mind is complex and ill-connected, like an audience,"[2] William Empson wrote; this audience is complex and ill-connected like a mind. Indeed, I suggest, Addams's audience gives us a picture of the *modernist* mind. Some minds are full of Uncle Festers in the seats of their intrapsychic cinemas, others have only one, but without any we are not fully modern. Call this the Uncle Fester Principle.

The reader's complicity with Fester derives partially from her knowledge of the fictionality of the cartoon, and of the movie within the cartoon. A real man laughing at real suffering might violate protocols of decorum, if not morality or sanity, but he has more latitude if he is laughing at make-believe suffering. This process of accounting for

Figure 1. "Sad Movie" by Charles Addams, *New Yorker*, March 23, 1946. p. 31.
© Charles Addams. Reproduced with permission of the Tee and
Charles Addams Foundation

fictionality in one's emotional response to perceived events, what Freud called "reality-testing,"[3] is always at work in our understanding of representations, and the fact that both movie and drawing fail the reality test makes it easier for us to understand the moviegoer's reaction as funny rather than cruel or lunatic.

But fictionality hardly tells the whole story. For Uncle Fester, judging by his looks, may very well *be* cruel or lunatic; that suspicion is in fact part of his charm. And under the right conditions anyone might laugh at real horrors. Instead of fictionality, the comedy of the cartoon hinges on the question of sensibility. The urbane *New Yorker* reader might well prefer to think of herself as sharing a dark sense of humor with Addams's moviegoer – free to indulge her cruelty, or at least to laugh at the tear-jerker with its tired conventions. Henri Bergson famously claimed that laughter requires a "momentary anaesthesia of the heart," an absence of sympathy with the object of the laughter, and Fester certainly exhibits this anaesthesia.[4] Yet such an insight still prompts the question why some viewers should experience this anaesthesia and not others. There is a social dimension at work: the cartoon, though hardly high culture, belongs to a higher stratum of culture than the movie, if only because it appeals to an audience that is more educated, sophisticated, worldly. Indeed, the best term for the quality of this sensibility might be *modern*. For our ideas both of modernity and of modernism itself are tied up with the ways in which we respond to various works of art and other representations. What saddens us, frightens us, outrages us, amuses us – these are indices of our modernity.

This book is guided by a group of questions concerning such an idea of modernity. How do different kinds of fictional representations of suffering make us feel? What aesthetic and cultural functions do such representations perform? Can ethical and aesthetic responses to a representation be separated, and what happens if they conflict with each other? And to what extent is our capacity to think of ourselves as modern, as fully at home in modernity, contingent on an aesthetic training, an antisentimental education?

My discussion of what I call late modern satire proceeds along both conceptual and historical axes. I attempt to understand the dynamics and the significance of ambivalent affective responses, on the part of both authors and characters, to suffering – responses which often include various combinations of laughter, fear, and pity. At the same time, I want to show how the works in question not only express but also *test* their own sensibility, their own modernity – at times their own relation to (various ideas of) modernism. Thus modernism as I understand it entails not only new understandings of key philosophical concepts (temporality, subjectivity, epistemology), nor merely a new repertoire of devices and techniques for representing such new understandings (free verse, stream of consciousness, spatial form), nor even a new cluster of technological developments (automobile, cinema, factory) which, with their attendant socioeconomic ramifications, might be seen as causes of those "superstructural" changes in the first place. Whether you take your version from Wilde or Shaw, Woolf or Lawrence, Fitzgerald or Hemingway, modernism – or, more loosely, being modern – involves codes of sophistication, codes which imply how we might respond emotionally both to the fact of human suffering and to the aesthetic forms that representations of such suffering must assume.

As a result of my effort to look at the intersection of a generic or modal term (satire) with a period term (modernism), my opening two chapters will serve as a kind of double introduction to the themes of the later ones. Chapter 1, "Satire and its discontents" describes the dynamics of satire, along with related genre terms, the grotesque and the sentimental; despite my conceptual emphasis, I try to address the relevance of these terms specifically for the modernist era of literary history. Satire, I argue, is a contradictory phenomenon in which its purported moralism or conservatism is conjoined with sadistic or anarchic desires, so that satire often in the end describes its own collapse or undoing. Complementary to this analysis of satire is an analysis of the affective excess, often called sentimentality, that modernist satire aims to avoid, denounce, or expose; and while the accusation of sentimentality is such that every expression of emotion risks incurring it, the threat of that accusation nonetheless exerts enormous pressure on modernist literature.

Chapter 2, "Modernism's story of feeling," further historicizes the emergence of modernist satire. This chapter provides a narrative of the modernist engagement with affect with attention to key figures from the earlier, more canonical decades of the modernist era who represent different stances regarding feeling. It culminates in a discussion of the 1930s (an era for which I use the term "late modernism" in order to mark its belated relation to modernism as traditionally described), the decade in which the bulk of the novels I study were written and published. I have selected these novels not from any single national tradition, but from the literary culture that cut across Great Britain, the United States, and Ireland, as I aim to provide a sampling of late modernist work that is wide-ranging yet coherent. Some of the novels that I discuss are immediately recognizable as satires, while others are valuable to this study because of their place on the outskirts of that generic territory.

In-depth readings of those novels begin in Chapter 3, which looks at the single figure most closely identified with English satire in the early-to-middle twentieth century, Evelyn Waugh. Waugh's *Vile Bodies* (1930) proves particularly fruitful for understanding the confluence of modernism and satire because it explores tensions identified in the introductory chapters between humanist and antihumanist strains of modernism, and between reformative and anarchic impulses of satire. Challenging traditional readings of the novel as a targeted attack on the young, rich, and idle, I read it as an elaborate exposure of the processes by which satire both expresses and spawns moral outrage. In Chapter 4 I turn to Waugh's *A Handful of Dust* (1934), in which the author's treatment of death attacks Victorian sentimentality but also questions the satiric attitudes toward suffering that the novel presents as modern. This impasse explains the puzzling shift of the novel's ending: as this drawing-room comedy flees the drawing room for the jungle, it modulates into the mode Freud called the uncanny – that side of the grotesque characterized by fantasy, anxiety, and repetition compulsion.

In Chapter 5 I investigate the relationship among satire, sentimentality, and gender in the fiction of the 1930s through a reading of Stella Gibbons's *Cold Comfort Farm* (1932). Gibbons's novel is useful here because it upends the traditional association of satire with masculinity and sentimentality with femininity. Critiquing the emotional excesses of both earlier high modernism and (putatively) female sentimentalism, it offers instead as an emotional protocol what Georg Simmel called a blasé attitude, a mode of social relation that turns out to be surprisingly consistent with a feminist, reformist politics.

Chapters 6 and 7 treat American writers of the grotesque, Nathanael West and Djuna Barnes. West's fiction, especially *The Day of the Locust* (1939), explores a persistent conflict between using suffering as a source of comic pleasure and a discomfort with such "worldliness and wit." Caught between the sentimental claims of a suffering public and an antisentimental impulse to transform such claims into pleasurable rhetoric, West's novels end up stalemated. His own best critic, West ultimately reveals his uncanny representation of the self as a fear of the consequences of satire. Chapter 7 then examines Barnes's *Nightwood* (1936), in which what I call "anti-procreative" thematics – sterility, impotence, abortion, infanticide – imply a frustration of inheritance. For Barnes, the modern *is* the satiric in its rejection of generational continuity. But if the novel is satiric in its attitude toward tradition, it also inscribes the uncanny as a space of authenticity marking satire's limit, and so demonstrates the hidden proximity of the two modes.

In Chapter 8, finally, Beckett's *Molloy* (1951) pushes the chronological framework of the study past the thirties and past the Second World War – and, moreover, expands it to include an Irish writer and an (initially) Francophone text. Beckett examines the nature of fascistic authority in a world that (at least vaguely) resembles wartime Europe, and his satire of modern authoritarianism and compulsion turns out also to be yet another satire of satire's own stringency, one in which the pressures of modern life are registered in the affective modulations both of the characters and of the act of reading.

Taken together, these readings provide a survey of late modernist satire in which recurrent themes emerge but peculiarities of individual authors and texts are, I hope, appreciated. By no means do they exhaust the catalogue of late modern satirists. Henry Green, Ivy Compton-Burnett,

Dawn Powell, Flannery O'Connor, and Flann O'Brien could all merit chapters in a longer study – yet they mark the emergence of a sensibility that is still very much at work in our culture at large, in which ironic detachment and sentimental excess seem always to be in contest. For as late modernist authors struggled to find forms in which to portray the ways that people experience, manage, and represent suffering, they provided new structures and models for feeling and expression. They recognized implicitly that if we are to praise literature for an ennobling moral quality of extending sympathy, then we must also recognize its power to play to our cruelty and stimulate our sadism.

It is therefore not by lauding writers for emotional magnanimity or chiding them for political insensitivity that we recognize the force of their achievements. Lionel Trilling, writing soon after the historical moment I examine in this book, complained that although "We have the books that praise us for taking progressive attitudes" we lack those "that raise questions in our minds not only about conditions but about ourselves, that lead us to refine our motives and ask what might lie behind our good impulses."[5] Trilling, whose own examination of our moral engagement with literature will provide an important critical touchstone for me, was expressing a skepticism about claims for the virtues of literature that, to my mind, is as necessary in today's critical climate as in his own. Late modernist satire, for all the pleasure it might give, raises still too frequently unasked questions about what might lie behind our good impulses.

In its long, slow growth from dissertation proposal to book, this study has benefitted from the generous attention of friends, teachers, and colleagues. Maria DiBattista has provided guidance and insight in every stage of this book's writing, and she has encouraged me throughout to hold fast to my convictions. Michael Wood has read my work with patience and acuity, and helped me to find the interesting ideas hiding behind my sometimes obvious ones. Doug Mao and Justus Nieland have read multiple chapters of this work and, sharing their intelligence and expertise, pointed me toward new directions for my argument. Discussion with graduate school classmates and teachers also informed this book; Sally Bachner, Michael Goldman, Martin Harries, Jonathan Lamb, Gage McWeeney, Lee Mitchell, Dan Novak, and Jeff Nunokawa deserve special thanks. My colleagues at Montclair State University have provided a congenial atmosphere for my professional life, and many have helped in different ways. Lee Behlman, Emily Isaacs, Lucy McDiarmid, and Art Simon generously read chapters and offered valued advice; Brian Cliff,

Naomi Liebler, Mary Papazian, and Tanya Pollard helped me to navigate the publishing world; my students, especially Norman DeFillipo, Anne DeMarzio, Terrence Ferguson, Katie Keeran, Peggy LeRoy, Sandy Reyes, Andrew Smethurst, and Curtis Zimmerman, prompted me to think anew about many of the texts I discuss. Chris Gaillard, Robert Caserio, and Michael Coyle also deserve thanks for their help at various stages. At Cambridge University Press, Ray Ryan, Gillian Dadd, Jo Breeze, and their staff have provided editorial guidance, and the comments of my two readers, Jesse Matz and Ed Comentale, helped to broaden and deepen the argument of the book.

Several institutions also supported the writing of this book. Princeton University granted me a Presidential Fellowship and a year of study at the University Center for Human Values; Montclair State provided a Global Education Grant, a Separately Budgeted Research Grant, and a year's sabbatical. The Interlibrary Loan staff at Montclair State's Sprague Library has obtained for me numerous books essential to my research. Chapter 4 appeared in somewhat different form in *Novel: A Forum on Fiction*; it is reprinted by permission of the publisher, Duke University Press. Chapter 6 appeared in *MFS: Modern Fiction Studies*, and is reprinted with the permission of the publisher, Johns Hopkins University Press. A small portion of the preface appeared in altered form as a book review in *Modernism/Modernity*; it is also reprinted with permission of Johns Hopkins University Press. A few short passages in Chapters 3 and 5 are drawn from an article in *Modernist Cultures*, and are reprinted with the permission of that journal.

My sister and brother, Judith Greenberg and David Greenberg, have read portions of this book and informed it with their own scholarly expertise. My children, Hank and Maggie, are younger than this book and still too young to be interested in the details of my argument, but their excitement about its publication gives me hope that some day not too far off they will open this book with scholarly interest, or at least amused curiosity. My wife, Megan Blumenreich, has been a wonderful, patient, sensible, devoted, and intelligent companion throughout the labor of writing this book. She has read and offered advice on all aspects of it; her love, care, and support have sustained me during its composition. Her devoted encouragement and gentle criticism have made the work immeasurably stronger.

My parents, Robert and Maida Greenberg, were the first to show me what intellectual inquiry entailed, and in their own thinking and scholarship I have seen what dedication and rigor can accomplish. The extent of their belief in my work, while bordering on the ludicrous, has been invaluable, and the depth of their interest continues to gratify me. To them I dedicate this book.

Abbreviations

CCF	Stella Gibbons, *Cold Comfort Farm* (1932; New York: Penguin, 2006).
DL	Nathanael West, *The Day of the Locust*, in *Nathanael West: Novels and other Writings*, ed. Sacvan Bercovitch (1939; New York: Library of America, 1997).
HD	Evelyn Waugh, *A Handful of Dust* (Boston: Little, Brown and Company, 1934).
M	Samuel Beckett, *Molloy*, in *Three Novels by Samuel Beckett: Molloy, Malone Dies, The Unnamable*, trans. Samuel Beckett and Patrick Bowles (1951; New York: Grove, 1955).
N	Djuna Barnes, *Nightwood* (New York: New Directions, 1937).
VB	Evelyn Waugh, *Vile Bodies* (Boston: Little, Brown and Company, 1930).

CHAPTER I

Satire and its discontents

Modernism changed the way we know and feel. Modernist literary works, and the intellectual and cultural currents from which they drew force, not only chronicled but also fostered changes in what Raymond Williams has called "structures of feeling."[1] Williams, recall, introduces this concept in an attempt to capture the inchoateness and complexity of an experience that is shared or social, even though it may be still emergent and therefore misrecognized as "private, idiosyncratic, and even isolating."[2] Just as "no generation speaks quite the same language as its predecessors," just as "manners, dress, building and other forms of social life" evolve gradually over time, so, Williams posits, an ever-changing but pervasive "set" of interlocking affective dispositions exists across a culture, forming a complex "structure" that can be discerned in "characteristic elements of impulse, restraint, and tone."[3] Like most talk of feeling, this is pretty fuzzy, but it furnishes a theoretical starting-point from which history can attend to the felt quality of experience and from which feelings, which common sense might take to be unchanging and universal, can be historicized.

As students of affect theory are aware, exactly such a historicization of feeling has recently been taken up by scholars in literary studies, who have argued that because modernity constitutes a new and in many ways unique social formation it cannot help but impinge on the ways that life is lived and feelings are felt. Sianne Ngai contends that a new set of minor, noncathartic, "ugly" feelings are characteristic of life under mature capitalism: "the nature of the sociopolitical itself has changed in a manner that both calls forth and calls upon a new set of feelings – one less powerful than the classical political passions."[4] Elizabeth Goodstein looks at boredom as an affect peculiar to the last century and half, when a modernity born out of processes such as "secularization, rationalization, and democratization" produced "experiential transformations" that "literally altered the quality of human being in time."[5] And Justus Nieland, examining modernism's representation of public performance, argues that feeling within modernism was reconfigured by seismic shifts in the character of an always mediated public sphere, shifts to which human beings as individuals and as collectivities were required, often abruptly, to adapt.[6] Without disavowing *all* continuity of human experience over time, then, we might recognize that during the era of modernism people were experiencing – were feeling – their world in new ways. As Ezra Pound put it in 1913: "if we still feel the same emotions as those which launched the thousand ships, it is quite certain that we come on these feelings differently, through different nuances, by different intellectual gradations."[7]

Feeling, then, has its own story *within* modernism, and one of the central points of this book is that an account of satire – specifically what I call late modernist satire – is indispensable to telling that story. This claim might seem surprising, since the great age of satire is generally held to be the eighteenth century, and satire's presence in modernism is often taken to be minor and peripheral.[8] Yet it is equally possible that the low profile of modernist satire derives from its very centrality: that satire is not spoken of simply because it goes without saying. Chris Baldick makes this point in claiming that, in modernist-era Great Britain at least, "Satire was invisible because omnipresent," inherent in the attacks on the "false idols" of Victorian culture that dominated new thinking about sex, religion, and politics.[9] Baldick quotes Cyril Connolly's 1938 diagnosis: "This is a satirical age and among the vast reading public the power of an artist to awaken ridicule has never been so great."[10] Yet what Connolly attributed to a plethora of good material might also be seen as an increased disposition and ability to *find* material, a change in a structure of feeling, the rise of a *modernist sensibility*. The raw material for satire may always have been there; what was new was a way of seeing the world that made this material available to ridicule.

Of course, particular modernist-era writers have long been recognized and studied as satirists, but these studies have generally been cordoned off from larger discussions of modernism or buried in the notoriously unfunny stacks of "humor studies." Only recently has the confluence of modernism and satire been looked at more closely, most notably in Tyrus Miller's *Late Modernism: Politics, Fiction, and the Arts Between the World Wars*.[11] James English and Michael North have at the same time reopened the topic of the comic novel, and Nieland has included a section on comedy in his discussion of "eccentric feeling" in modernism.[12] This book seeks to build on the work of these scholars and others by positing satire as a way of thinking, feeling, and writing central to modernism – to the very notion of what it meant for modernists to be modern.

In the analysis that follows, I use a variety of terms – satiric and sentimental, ironic and comic, grotesque and uncanny – which, like most genre terms, provide markers for the ways in which various kinds of literary works have engaged (or disengaged) their readers' feelings. Understanding the dynamics of satire and of the sentimentality it ostensibly refuses will then help to recast an account of modernism as one in which different affective possibilities are always contending and jostling, and in which modernism itself can be seen as an effort, or a variety of efforts, to grapple with the problem of how to feel.

THE DOUBLE MOVEMENT OF SATIRE

Most definitions of satire – too many to cite here[13] – have seen a moral aim as a necessary component of the mode.[14] The satirist is a "moral agent" according to George Meredith, is "an *ipso facto* moralist" according to Harry Levin, "takes a high moral line" according to Northrop Frye.[15] This moral element separates satire from pure comedy; the objects of satiric laughter are experienced not as trivial but as "harmful or destructive."[16] It also tends to make satire a conservative mode, the argument runs, since satire paints its target as deviating from a strong and stable set of communally held beliefs and at least implicitly urges reform. Such "conservatism," suggesting both a certainty of authorial meaning and a promotion of social consensus, resembles what Wayne Booth has called "stable irony"; irony is stable, according to Booth, if "once a reconstruction of meaning has been made, the reader is not then invited to undermine it with further demolitions and reconstructions."[17] This conservatism describes something different from a writer's overt political views; while in a case such as Evelyn Waugh's the writer's outspoken traditionalism appears to reinforce his satiric ridicule of all that departs from age-old standards, a novelist on the left like Nathanael West has just as frequently been read as conservative in the sense that, in his biographer's words, "his satire was designed to return man to himself, to his 'lawful callings'."[18] Thus, while satire is sometimes thought to trade in politics to the fault of being trivial – does anyone really care that the Treasurer of Lilliput was meant to represent Robert Walpole? – it is equally often felt to be redeemed by a metaphysical insight into that chimerical entity called human nature.[19]

Yet even if in satire the timely ultimately gives way to the timeless, political carping to moral vision, unadulterated moralism does not, according to the typologists, produce satire, but leads instead to sermon, invective, or polemic. To achieve its moral aims, satire has been understood to deploy techniques that involve wit, play, and fantasy. According to Alvin Kernan, satire has "two poles," "a rigid moral system" and "a graceful style"; Frye sees a "token fantasy" as well as "an implicit moral standard" as essential.[20] This playful or provocative dimension of satire, moreover, is not purely festive or comic, but involves mockery, malice, and derision.[21] The result is that satire can appear anarchic, subversive, and destructive. Kernan's "two poles" of satire create an unstable force field in which an ethical content clashes with a playful and often destructive form, in which subversive means are used to promote conservative ends.

It was, however, the peculiar achievement of modernist-era thinkers to attempt a theoretical resolution of this paradox by recognizing in the moral motive of satire a mere disguise for more primitive delight in the depiction of corrupt targets. A key figure here is Wyndham Lewis, who, in his 1934 treatise, *Men Without Art*, announces that "the greatest satire is non-moral."[22] "There is no prejudice so inveterate," he claims, "even in the educated mind, as that which sees in satire a work of edification. Indeed, for the satirist to acquire the right to hold up to contempt a fellow-mortal, he is supposed, first, to arm himself with the insignia of a sheriff or special constable."[23] But Lewis rejects these reformative and didactic claims of satire and seeks instead to recover ridicule for its own sake as healthy, primary, and pleasurable. Lewis describes a "perfect laughter" that, if it could be realized, "would be inhuman" – one that would not let moral compunction prevent it from taking delight in "the antics dependent upon pathologic maladjustments, injury, or disease."[24] This non-moral conception of satire, as Martin Puchner has pointed out, owes a debt to Nietzsche, who already in his *Genealogy of Morals* rejects what he calls an "ethics of pity" by invoking the origin of the modern European novel:

Consider, for instance, Don Quixote at the court of the Duchess. Today we read *Don Quixote* with a bitter taste in our mouths, almost with a feeling of torment, and would thus seem very strange and incomprehensible to its author and his contemporaries: they read it with the clearest conscience in the world as the most cheerful of books, they laughed themselves almost to death over it.[25]

Hence Nietzsche's famous slogan: "To see others suffer does one good. To make others suffer even more."[26]

If Nietzsche is Lewis's direct precursor in rediscovering the primal cruelty of literary satire, Freud is an equally important antecedent.

Freud, like Nietzsche, exposes the ruses of morality, the ways in which morality serves as cover for repressed motives and desires. In his 1905 study of jokes, Freud not only makes the fairly obvious observation that satire partakes of the structure of what he calls tendentious jokes;[27] more fundamentally, he posits that the sources of pleasure in such tendentious attacks are multiple and layered. In distinguishing between the "joking envelope" and the "thought it contains," Freud argues that the pleasure of a joke is – to use the word he made famous in discussing dreams – overdetermined.[28] On the one hand, "the pleasure in a joke is derived from play with words"[29] – from the indulgence of a childish, playful tendency to "jest" that in the adult has been suppressed by critical reason. On the other hand, however, the jest is supplemented with meaning that is "intended to protect that pleasure from being done away with by criticism."[30] The meaning of a joke protects the pleasure that the playful content produces. Yet when Freud arrives at his specific analysis of the *tendentious* joke he reverses his terms; in this special case, he contends, the authority to be circumvented is not just the inhibitory critical faculty but the repressive one.[31] Now it becomes the "envelope," or form, of a joke that serves as protection, offering an "incentive bonus" or "fore-pleasure" that relaxes moral inhibitions so that the transgressive content of the joke can be enjoyed.[32] The pleasurable *form* now protects the (tendentious) *meaning* from censorship. Thus it is that "the highest stage of jokes, tendentious jokes, often have to overcome two kinds of inhibition, those opposed to the joke itself and those opposed to its purpose."[33] Freud thus reconciles how contradictory impulses work in concert: the moral pretenses of satire do not simply contradict but in fact *make possible* its aggressive sources of pleasure.[34] In satire, moral outrage and sadistic pleasure *have the same stimulus*; whether a joke appears in good or bad taste depends only on the strength of internal and external inhibitions.

To this Nietzschean-Freudian move beyond good and evil, Lewis adds a Bergsonian concern with the materiality of the human. Already in his earlier (1927) account on comedy, Lewis riffs on Bergson's famous theory of the comic as "something mechanical encrusted on the living."[35] Writes Lewis: "The root of the Comic is to be sought in the sensations resulting from the observations of a *thing* behaving like a person."[36] Despite his predominant anti-Bergsonism, Lewis here retains Bergson's link between laughter and the recognition of the human as thing-like, and endorses the premise of a fundamental contradiction between matter and mind. Yet, as Justus Nieland notes, Lewis's formula is "a reversal of the humanist terms of Bergsonian laughter" that locates the comic in the human-like behavior of the thing, rather than the other way around.[37] While Bergson's account of comedy tells a story in which human flexibility or "spirit" is ultimately triumphant, Lewis drops this last step, concluding with the recognition of the human being as mechanical: "But 'men' are undoubtedly, to a greater or less extent, machines. And there are those amongst us who are revolted by this reflection, and there are those who are not."[38]

Rejecting the Bergsonian "internalist" interest in flux and subjectivity and interiority, Lewis favors instead an "external approach," the method of the eye, which he associates with scientific objectivity and Hulmean classicism. His surface-oriented satirist offers no recognition of human elasticity: "It will be his task ... like science, to bring human life more into contempt each day ... It will, by illustrating the discoveries of science, demonstrate the futility and absurdity of human life."[39] The ugly materiality of the human body for Lewis turns out to be only one more source of pleasure: "What you regard as hideous has the same claims on us even as your ravishing self. We are the reverse of squeamish ... This *matière* which composes itself into what you regard I daresay as abortions, is delightful to us, *for itself*. No artist yet has experienced any personal repulsion for a grotesque that sprang up beneath his hand."[40]

Thus, as Michael Seidel notes, for Lewis "the creative, meliorative, or restorative role of the satirist is part of a preserving fiction, a mere saving of appearances," and consequently the satirist is always "implicated in the debasing form of his action."[41] Like Swift's broomstick, he becomes dirty in the process of cleaning; he is a moral garbage collector who reveals his affinity with the filthy material he purports to purify. So described, the satirist is a perfect example of what William Ian Miller calls a "moral menial," a class of people that includes lawyers, politicians, and hangmen (not to mention Lewis's "sheriff or special constable"). Moral menials, according to Miller, "perform functions in the moral order similar to those played by garbagemen and butchers": "Moral menials deal with moral dirt, or they have to get morally dirty to do what the polity needs them to do. And despite the fact that we need to attract people to this kind of labor, we still hold them accountable for being so attracted."[42] The existence of such border guards reminds us "that the boundaries that separate vice from virtue, good from evil, pure from polluted, are permeable, and worse, necessarily permeable."[43] Walking this line, the satirist experiences the classic ambivalence between enjoying an illicit desire and experiencing guilt over that enjoyment – what Italo Calvino describes as "the mixture of attraction and repulsion that animates the feelings of every true satirist toward the object of his satire."[44]

Thus emerges what I will be calling the *double movement of satire*: on the one hand, the satirist speaks for a community, exaggerating and ridiculing his target in order to urge reform; on the other, he is a renegade who enjoys the subversion of traditional values, delights in his own aesthetic powers, even savors the cruelty he inflicts.

SATIRE, MODERNITY, AND THE GROTESQUE

Of these two notions of satire, "conservative" and "subversive," it is surely the first that Evelyn Waugh had in mind when, in a 1946 piece for *Life* magazine, he rejected the word as a description of his own works:

Satire is a matter of period. It flourishes in a stable society and presupposes homogeneous moral standards – the early Roman Empire and eighteenth-century Europe. It is aimed at inconsistency and hypocrisy. It exposes polite cruelty and folly by exaggerating them. It seeks to produce shame. All this has no place in the Century of the Common Man where vice no longer pays lip service to virtue. The artist's only service to the disintegrated society of today is to create little independent systems of order of his own. I foresee in the dark age opening that the scribes may play the part of the monks after the first barbarian victories. They were not satirists.[45]

In suspiciously similar language, Waugh's sometime nemesis, W. H. Auden, writing only six years later, dismissed the relevance of satire to the modern age. His analysis diverges from Waugh's only in that Auden's despair arises not from the scope of the century's democratic tendencies but from the scale of its brutality:

Satire flourishes in a homogeneous society where satirist and audience share the same views as to how normal people can be expected to behave, and in times of relative stability and contentment, for satire cannot deal with serious evil and suffering. In an age like our own, it cannot flourish except in intimate circles as an expression of private feuds: in public life the evils and sufferings are so serious that satire seems trivial and the only possible kind of attack is prophetic denunciation.[46]

Waugh and Auden alike voice nostalgia for a bygone age when satire was possible, and both men understand their own age as qualitatively different from past history. Their statements thus share not only an implied theory of *satire*, but also assumptions about *modernity*: both agree that the extent of modern corruption, no matter what its source, has led to the endangerment, if not the outright extinction, of a once-great genre. Auden's "prophetic denunciation" and Waugh's monastic withdrawal similarly interpret modernity as an era of unprecedented rupture, and posit a thorough redefinition of the role that literature can take in the heterogeneous social formation of modern democracy.

A third contemporary, Theodor Adorno (born the same year as Waugh, three years before Auden), also claimed, in 1951, that modernity makes satire impossible. For Adorno too, the loss of satire stands for the loss of much more:

> The impossibility of satire today should not be blamed, as sentimentality is apt to do, on the relativism of values, the absence of binding norms. Rather, agreement itself, the formal *a priori* of irony, has given way to universal agreement of content. As such it presents the only fitting target for irony and at the same time pulls the ground from under its feet. Irony's medium, the difference between ideology and reality, has disappeared. The former resigns itself to confirmation of reality by its mere duplication. Irony used to say: such it claims to be, but such it is; today, however, the world, even in its most radical lie, falls back on the argument that things are like this, a simple finding which coincides, for it, with the good.[47]

Those familiar with Adorno's vision of an administered culture will recognize his central complaint: when culture cannot stand outside of ideology, what results is a thoroughgoing conformity and a Panglossian refusal to imagine a better world. Adorno's argument is thus a mirror image of Waugh's. He maintains that modernity has produced not a "disintegrated society" but an overly integrated one, too monolithic for any critic to surmount: "There is not a crevice in the cliff of the established order into which the ironist might hook a fingernail."[48] According to Adorno, in fact, the belief Waugh expresses is "sentimental" – presumably because of the benign, if not affectionate, view it takes of obedience to inherited norms. (More on sentimentality, however, in just a bit.)

With some distance from these midcentury assessments, we can say, I hope, that the century just past, despite its indisputable evils, was neither as shamelessly libertine as Waugh complained nor as stupidly conformist as Adorno feared; and we do not diminish its horrors by noting that it has mercifully allowed modes of expression other than Auden's "prophetic denunciation." All these assessments may feel slightly off the mark, then, not only because they rely on an overly narrow definition of satire but also because they give us pictures of modernity that too greatly betray their authors' preoccupations – pictures of a present that, in the massiveness of its corruption, utterly overwhelms the possibility of any critical engagement at all. Yet in complete opposition to this view, I suggest not only that modernism and satire are not incompatible, but that they are very nearly *the same thing*. For modernism's complex relation to the past can actually seem to align it with satire; if, as Seidel argues, satire undermines and disrupts the inheritance of traditional literary forms, then satire itself can be viewed as a force or agent of modernity.[49] Satire and modernism are similarly susceptible to the (incompatible) accusations of both rearguard conservatism and decadent libertinism. On whichever side we place any of the major writers and thinkers of the time, what is clear is that satire, like modernism itself, requires a *rift* between the new and the old; it can only exist in the space opened between them.[50]

The modernity of satire, then, lies less in a particular moral, religious, or philosophical set of *values* that critical interpretation might recover from a novel or poem or film or play than in a kind of temperament or outlook, a satiric *sensibility* – a characteristic of the implied author and reader who savor the transgressive pleasures that satire affords, who may deride the chaos of modernity but also need it, even help to create it. Hence what I call (modifying a term from Richard Rorty) *ironic redescription* proves a central operation of modernist satire. "Anything can be made to look good or bad by being redescribed," notes Rorty, and what else is satire but a way of redescribing things in order to make them look bad?[51]

In making things look bad, satiric redescriptions frequently produce the grotesque. This term, which we have already seen Lewis invoke in his defense of satire, is at least as imprecise as "satire";[52] Mary Russo points out that the term can refer either to "discernible grotesque figures or style" or to "the rather vague and mysterious . . . category of 'experience.'"[53] The grotesque can describe either objective *content* – often, but not necessarily, deformed, misshapen, or hybrid bodies – or subjective *experience* – the emotional instability that grotesque content tends to produce in a reader. This emotional instability, moreover, is itself fundamentally ambivalent, mixing contradictory affective conditions. In a passage essential for theorists of the grotesque, John Ruskin saw the mode as "composed of two elements, one ludicrous, the other fearful": "As one or the other of these elements prevails, the grotesque falls into two branches, sportive grotesque and terrible grotesque; but . . . we cannot legitimately consider it under these two aspects, because there are hardly any examples which do not in some degree combine both elements."[54] The "ludicrous" element of the grotesque, its comic, playful, or "sportive" side, has obvious affinities with satire, irony, caricature, and cartoon, which stay on the surface of the object and exaggerate or deform their targets with the aim of ridicule. The "fearful" element has a different set of generic affiliations (the Gothic, the fantastic, horror, and, most crucially, the Freudian uncanny) that hint at a troubled interiority and move from laughter to anxiety. As Ruskin notes, these two elements do not disentangle easily. The laughter provoked by the grotesque is always uneasy, nervous laughter, never wholly free from disquiet.

There is yet another dichotomy to the grotesque as a critical concept, a dichotomy in the history of theorizing about it. While analyses of the grotesque have attempted to understand the grotesque in Jungian, Heideggerian, feminist, race-theory, deconstructive,[55] and, above all, Freudian[56] frameworks, the two most influential theories of the mode, those of Mikhail Bakhtin and Wolfgang Kayser, are both over a half-century old; they offer, moreover, radically divergent interpretations. Bakhtin's theory opposes the grotesque body to the classical. The grotesque body for him is "the epitome of incompleteness," "a principle of growth," "ever unfinished, ever creating."[57] This material body stresses functions like ingesting and excreting and serves as one of Bakhtin's major symbols of the concept of carnival, which brings about the festive suspension or inversion of social hierarchies. In the Bakhtinian grotesque, decay is a stage of renewal, individual death part of a collective life.

Kayser's theory, in contrast, is based primarily in Romanticism rather than the Renaissance and emphasizes the "ominous, nocturnal and abysmal features" of the grotesque "that frighten and puzzle us and make us feel as if the ground beneath our feet were about to give way."[58] Drawing on much of the same material as Freud does in "The Uncanny," Kayser sees the grotesque in loosely existential terms, as an invocation of, and play with, a fundamental human alienation from the world. Like Freud, Kayser emphasizes subjective experience over objective content, and his focus is the individual not the collective; he stresses Ruskin's fearful element rather than the ludicrous. For Kayser, the grotesque expresses not a fundamental unity of all things organic, but a fundamental division between self and world.

Bakhtin himself suggests a historical narrative that allows for at least a tentative reconciliation with Kayser. Whereas Bakhtin's medieval and Renaissance grotesque thrived during an era when collective folk culture was vibrant, the rise of the bourgeois subject reduced the grotesque to a nocturnal, subterranean, isolated phenomenon. As a result, the oversized, celebratory laughter of Rabelais "was cut down to cold humor, irony, sarcasm," and grotesque imagery "acquired a private, 'chamber' character."[59]

He concludes: "Kayser's definition can be applied only to certain manifestations of modernist form of the grotesque."[60] But of course the modernist grotesque is my interest here, and therefore Kayser's existential thematics are most germane to my reading of late modernism. Such affective conditions indeed link the grotesque to the "alienated" self that Fredric Jameson (among many others) takes to be one of the defining features of modernist art and literature.[61] Hence the grotesque often appears in modernism as a mark of psychosexual degeneration – Mann's Aschenbach, for example, or Leopold Bloom in "Circe" – and it might be seen as part of the era's widespread interest in primitivism, regression, decadence, and other allied categories. Thus even if modernism is too vast a field to make any blanket statements about its relation to such categories – whether it celebrates, disavows, analyzes, fetishizes, or exorcizes unreason or barbarism – we might nevertheless see the grotesque as deployed by modernism as part of a new emphasis on the redemptive value of negativity: what Kenneth Burke, writing about Djuna Barnes, called "a kind of transcendence downward" in which "corruption and distinction become interchangeable terms."[62] In this sense, this entire book might be seen as a short subchapter in a long history of the divorce of beauty from truth.

The grotesque as I use it then is neither wholly synonymous with nor wholly discrete from satire. It is more like a limit-case, in which satiric laughter or indignation becomes difficult to sustain and slides into a more uncanny affective state. The grotesque is both the target and the method of satire; satire, in its "conservative" impulse, may decry and ridicule grotesque content, but it also, in its "subversive" impulse – in representing its targets *as* grotesque – creates or promotes the very grotesquerie it purports to eradicate. The satiric mode both relies on grotesque imagery and evokes a grotesque reaction. The grotesque in turn can be seen as either a *problem*, a sign of a decadent and disordered world, or a *solution*, an aesthetic mode capable of representing the disorder of the world and presenting a reader or viewer with an authentic emotional experience. But to understand what exactly an authentic emotional experience might be, we will first need to explore the inauthentic – or, as it is often called, the sentimental.

RETHINKING MODERNIST ANTISENTIMENTALITY

A full account of modernist satire must recognize the prominence in modernism of the reaction against sentimentality, a reaction found in writers as disparate as D. H. Lawrence (who calls sentimentality "the garment of our vice") and James Baldwin (who calls it "the signal of secret and violent inhumanity, the mask of cruelty").[63] With the rise of feminist theory and the revision of the canon in the 1970s and 1980s, of course, the modernist reaction against the sentimental fell out of critical favor, and much scholarship sought to rehabilitate that aesthetic category, restoring attention to disparaged or forgotten works. An exemplary study here is Suzanne Clark's *Sentimental Modernism*, which reads the modernist rejection of sentimentality as a sign of an "adversarial relationship to domestic culture" on the part of "beleaguered avant-garde intellectuals," an animus that produced "a contemptuous treatment of women" and the mass-cultural artifacts they often consumed and produced.[64] Drawing on Andreas Huyssen's identification of mass culture as the feminine "other" of a masculine "high" modernism, and Jane Tompkins's recovery of nineteenth-century American women's texts, Clark's feminist critique of a patriarchal bias against the domestic neatly meshes with a Marxist sociological account of the historical enshrining of the literary as an autonomous cultural sphere.[65] This argument, for the most part, has passed into conventional critical wisdom, so that even Michael Bell, a critic largely sympathetic to the projects of the canonical male modernists, concedes that in modernism "the vehemence of the hostility to sentiment, often tinged with snobbery and implicitly gendered, tended to throw the baby of feeling out with the bathwater of sentimentality."[66] And who would argue that the modernists took extreme positions in their rejection of emotion? To allay any doubt on the issue, we only need to recall that remark of T. S. Eliot's which would delight generations of psychobiographers: "Poetry is not a turning loose of emotion but an escape from emotion."[67]

Despite the merit of such analyses, however, I do not intend to add one more brush stroke to a portrait of a misogynistic, fascistic male modernism, withdrawn into its library, unable to talk about its feelings. For one thing, this portrait reduces modernism, in Lawrence Rainey's words, to "little more than a reactionary, even paranoid fear of popular culture,"[68] a reduction that has been largely discredited by renewed attention to the productive traffic between different strata of culture in the era. But, even more fundamentally, making an aesthetic case for the sentimental under the banner of populism does not necessarily lead to a more progressive politics than an "elitist" rejection of it. For it is a central tenet of modernist antisentimentality that feeling can be coercive, the most subtle method of enforcing the stifling conditions of an oppressive modern world. Hence Milan Kundera's insight that the sentimental can be tyrannical: "When the heart speaks, the mind finds it indecent to object. In the realm of kitsch, the dictatorship of the heart reigns supreme."[69]

That said, neither am I interested in protecting modernism, or anyone's variety of it, from often deserved political attacks. I freely concede that some of my favorite writers held views or made jokes that were fascist, racist, sexist, homophobic, or simply obnoxious. Evelyn Waugh's benighted Africans are plainly racist caricatures; Stella Gibbons giggles at her own anti-Semitic stereotypes; Nathanael West makes fun of dwarves. The critic James English has argued, in response to overly formalistic analyses of comedy, that the mapping of the politics of a joke, is, like the analysis of any cultural event, a complex process; whether comedy works to enforce or resist cultural norms will vary according to context and audience. The comic, as English puts it, is multiaccented.[70] The joke-work of modernist satire, as my readings aim to show, is particularly likely to be volatile, more prone even than most literature to ramify in divergent directions, to assume contradictory political valences.

But, while defending modernism or particular modernists as champions of dissent is no more my interest than exposing the ideological sins of once-canonized giants, recognizing that early twentieth-century antisentimentality had behind it more than the reinforcement of a privileged social position does make possible a fuller understanding of the modernist sensibility. Something not too distant from this claim seems implicit in Charles Altieri's argument that many of the major modernist poets and painters aimed "to set the feelings against the emotions"[71] – an argument in which he distinguishes inchoate *feelings* ("the basic building blocks for other affective states") from more defined *emotions* (which "involve the construction of attitudes that typically generate some kind of action or identification").[72] Poetic attention to feeling in opposition to emotion becomes in Altieri's account a way of resisting "dominant cultural attitudes" that gain authority and force through emotional appeal, and hence a way of valuing an affective "subtlety and fluidity" outside of or prior to the recruitment of feeling for some ideological stance.[73] Similarly, Sianne Ngai has critiqued the "politics of compulsory sympathy" embedded in sentimental fiction,[74] while Martha Nussbaum has recognized the coercive power of feeling in her argument that emotions are "social constructs" that are "taught … through stories" but that can also be "dismantled."[75]

If the sentimental, then, represents what is seen as most coercive about emotion – its mobilization of feeling for the purpose of assimilating affective life to "dominant cultural attitudes" – then satire is a major, perhaps an essential, component of the modernist resistance to such coercion. Satire – with its sibling concept, the grotesque – often seeks to undermine precisely those dominant, conventional, or clichéd forms of representation that are based on stirring a reader's compassion. Such an undermining is likely what T. S. Eliot had in mind in 1917 when he declared: "We only need the coming of a Satirist – no man of genius is rarer – to prove that the heroic couplet has lost none of its edge since Dryden and Pope laid it down."[76] It is equally the impetus behind Thomas Mann's assertion that in modernism the grotesque had become "the genuine anti-bourgeois style" and its generic instability "the striking feature of modern art," and Flannery O'Connor's invocation of grotesque affect as a counterweight to sentimentality.[77] This conception of sentimentality as the handmaiden of a coercive, even tyrannical, ideology, wielding its power through the construction of a bourgeois public taste, completely reverses the political charge of modernist hostility toward sentimentality, and puts the modern satirist on the side of skepticism, rebellion, and creativity.[78]

Of course, satire is not the only way in which modernists sought to solve the problem of the sentimental, and questions of affect prove central to many non-satiric novels in the modernist canon. In Ford Madox Ford's *The Good Soldier*, for example, John Dowell attributes Edward Ashburnham's sexual infidelities not to libertinism but to sentimentalism, while in Virginia Woolf's *Mrs. Dalloway*, Peter Walsh uses the same term to dismiss Clarissa's taste in literature and "attitude to life."[79] And while a novel such as E. M. Forster's *Howards End* repeatedly stresses feeling as a guarantee of truth, it still conjectures that "the private emotions" may have "their gutter press" and can be stirred up for malign purposes.[80] In these novels and in many others, the sentimental seems less an epithet than an enigma, a marker of the peculiar ways that our affections and longings attach themselves to unlikely or unworthy objects.

As its central presence in these works might suggest, then, the sentimental proves stubbornly hard to define. The term, Eve Sedgwick notes, has a "strange career," which extends "from the later eighteenth century when it was a term of high ethical and aesthetic praise, to the twentieth when it can be used to connote, beyond pathetic weakness, an actual principle of evil."[81] Jay Dickson offers an authoritative summary of this career, in which a sensitivity to human feeling in the face of an increasingly industrialized and rationalized world comes to be seen instead as vulgar, vicarious, and exploitive falseness, disparagingly associated with the masses and with the feminine.[82] This transition makes *any* artistic venture a potential cause for ridicule; as Suzanne Clark points out, all commitment – political, erotic, emotional – is put at risk for foolishness.[83] Dickson poses the question: "at what point does earned sentiment – the hallmark of the artist – become excessive, and potentially risible, sentimentality?"[84] On what principle does one discriminate between legitimate and illegitimate, appropriate and excessive feeling? It cannot really be done, no more than one can (to recall Freud) distinguish a joke in good taste from a joke in bad taste. As Dickson notes, then, sentimentality "adheres to the same definition as that proposed for obscenity by the Supreme Justice Potter Stewart's quip about pornography: you know it when you see it."[85] But we can hardly rest here, because even this test only reinstates the criterion of feeling it seeks to identify and expunge.

Often the rap against sentimentality is that the feeling is, in Dickson's terms, "unearned," that a certain labor of participation in suffering is necessary for tears to be genuine. That criticism is clearly evident in the line from George Meredith that Stephen Dedalus famously quotes in *Ulysses* ("The sentimentalist is he who would enjoy without incurring the immense debtorship for a thing done"[86]) or in Flannery O'Connor's claim that "sentimentality is an excess, a distortion of sentiment usually in the direction of an overemphasis on innocence." For O'Connor, the sentimental, by taking a short cut to innocence, evades a "slow participation" in the death of Christ; it offers redemption without pain and thereby effects "an early arrival at a mock state of innocence, which strongly suggests its opposite."[87] The sentimental in her formulation is a denial of sin, of evil, and ultimately of the theological necessity of suffering; the denial, moreover, appears now not only as an aesthetic flaw but as a kind of corruption itself. O'Connor's explicitly theological framework thus makes clear what is hidden in Meredith's or Joyce's secular critique: the degree to which the sentimental lies at the crossroads of morality and aesthetics. By "skipping over" the "concrete reality" of suffering, sentimentality allows the emotional satisfactions of compassion without the emotional work of earning them. It is an emotional laziness or cowardice in which the reader or writer, by avoiding a kind of *aesthetic* labor, fails *morally*. He convinces himself that he is innocent when he is guilty. Yet this criterion of labor, helpful as it may be in understanding what we mean by sentimental, makes the process of identifying the sentimental no less circular than before, since the adequacy of a reader or writer's labor or participation in suffering relies (once again) on the criterion of feeling.

FEELINGS OF SUSPICION

Given that the logic of sentimentality is circular – you know it when you feel it, but that feeling must not be a sentimental one – the question how to tell sentiment from sentimentality becomes impossible to answer except in the particular case. The crucial questions to be addressed, then, might be reframed – not as what is sentimental, but as what lay behind modernist antisentimentality, and how satire emerged as its opposite or antidote. One place to begin such an inquiry is with Paul Ricoeur's claim that Marx, Nietzsche, and Freud bequeathed to modernist literature an "underlying legacy of hermeneutic suspicion."[88] In the late nineteenth century, class, morality, and sexuality came to be seen as objects demanding interpretation, considerably less transparent than common sense might take them to be. Such suspicion affected the modernist understanding of not only the outer world but also the emotions, as theoretical concepts such as false consciousness, *ressentiment*, and repression allowed even the most strongly felt feelings to be interpreted as self-deception or ideological mirage. This insight, as Michael Bell notes, impeded the ability of emotion to guarantee value: "The growing recognition that emotional life may run underground, and may even present overt manifestations directly contrary to true meaning, added a whole new dimension to its unreliability."[89]

But the notion that feelings can even *be* unreliable is a curious and perhaps counterintuitive one. Lionel Trilling took up this problem in his 1971 lectures, *Sincerity and Authenticity*. In describing the quality that he calls "sincerity" – defined as "a congruence between avowal and actual feeling" – as a significant criterion in "the moral life of Europe," Trilling takes as his paradigm the Polonian imperative, "To thine own self be true," and argues that such truth to oneself is absent from previous ideas of virtue.[90] But beginning in the nineteenth century comes a second shift: "a judgement [is] placed on sincerity that it is not authentic"; sincerity is displaced as a criterion for moral and literary value by the elusive quality Trilling calls "authenticity."[91] This "polemical concept" (whose problematic implications Trilling confronts) is also a *negative* one, defined predominantly as a rejection of some prevailing source of value: society for Rousseau, money for Marx, technology for Ruskin, nature for Marinetti.[92] Most crucially, an artist cannot achieve authenticity simply through loyalty to his or her feelings, since those feelings, culturally shaped and silently serving unacknowledged interests, are often precisely what make him or her inauthentic. Authenticity, rather, demands from the reader or artist a kind of psychic labor, "a more strenuous moral experience than 'sincerity' does";[93] this strenuousness recalls the critique of sentimentality as unearned or facile redemption. Thus sentimentality (a term Trilling does not himself use), while characterized by falseness, would not be, in Trilling's framework, *insincere*, but rather *inauthentic*. It is not a deliberate or conscious feigning of feeling but rather an *unfeigned* experience of *false* feeling – a feeling whose falseness derives from its production within a psychosocial or ideological frame that is itself under indictment. Indeed, in its most insidious form, sentimentality appears to be virtually synonymous with sincerity.[94]

Trilling's account overlaps in important ways with Fredric Jameson's recent discussion of the problem, where, following Adorno, he suggests that "we should think of the quintessential modern gesture as one of taboo rather than discovery."[95] By this logic, "modernism is seen as originating in an ever-keener distaste for what is conventional and out-moded, rather than as an exploratory appetite for the unexplored and undiscovered."[96] Much like Trilling's authenticity, Jameson's "taboo" works negatively:

The taboo is very explicitly a taboo on previous kinds of representational form and content: not the oldness of the older emotions as such, but the conventions of their expression; not the disappearance of this or that kind of human relation-ship, but rather the intolerable commonplaces with which it had become so intimately associated as to have been indistinguishable.[97]

In both Jameson's own language and in the process he describes, however, the taboo on a form of *expression* easily slips into a taboo on certain kinds of *feeling* themselves: "The outmoded and conventionalized literary expression, now identified as sentimentality, can also be seen to designate the obsolescence of a certain emotion in and of itself."[98] This slippage makes it difficult, often impossible, to say whether the "fault" of sentimentality is ethical–psychic (feeling things wrongly) or aesthetic–technical (expressing feelings artlessly).

Both Trilling and Jameson, then, suggest that modernist aesthetics turned on an ever-heightening suspicion of feeling – a suspicion of both feeling itself (conceived psychologically in some pre-linguistic, pre-representational sense) and of feeling expressed (realized in some linguistic, narrative, or other aesthetic form). In poetic practice this suspicion often manifests itself as a resistance to the pull of feeling, or an advocacy of emotional detachment. We might think here of Wallace Stevens's "The Snow Man" (1921) with its stripping away of human emotional investments in the natural world, its rejection of the pathetic fallacy in favor of an emotionally barren encounter with a stark winter landscape. Or the similarly hibernal "Lapis Lazuli" of William Butler Yeats (1936), which finds in a carved-stone image of Chinese monks a "tragic gaiety" that, rejecting a publicly minded, feminine hysteria in the face of looming war, chooses instead to gaze out upon the tragic scene from a lofty height with equanimity and quiet joy. Even W. H. Auden's "Musée des Beaux Arts" (1940), in situating suffering within a lively panorama of human and animal activity, endorses the wisdom of those Old Masters for whom indifference to pain may not be laudable but must at least be acknowledged. All three poems ground their aesthetics in a disavowal of what Nietzsche called the modern "overestimation and predilection for pity," or what, I am arguing, became identified in modernist shorthand as sentimentality.[99] Like Nietzsche glancing back at Cervantes at the opening of the seventeenth century, these poets look outside their own cultural or historical moments (or, in Stevens's case, outside culture itself) for better models of how to respond to or represent suffering.

In theoretical or philosophical expressions of modernist poetics, a similar affective stringency has gone by the name of "impersonality," a term which has found its most canonical articulations in Joyce's *A Portrait of the Artist as a Young Man* and the essays of T. S. Eliot. For Joyce's Stephen Dedalus, recall, "the personality of the artist," in moving from a personal lyric form – "the simplest verbal gesture of an instant of emotion" – to an impersonal dramatic one, "refines itself out of existence, impersonalises itself."[100] For him, the properly "dramatic" or "esthetic" emotion" is "static" rather than "kinetic" because it stimulates neither arousal nor revulsion as do didactic or pornographic arts; in the aesthetic emotion, "The mind is arrested and raised above desire and loathing."[101] Eliot also advocates the "depersonalization" of the poet in the creation of art, seeking to separate the "personal emotions" of the poet (which have little place in *his* definition of lyric) from "the emotion in his poetry."[102] Hence the famous definition of the objective correlative, which finds a verbal form wholly adequate to an affective condition.[103]

How, and whether, these prescriptions were realized, by Joyce, Eliot, or others, have long been topics for debate. Nonetheless, one potential consequence of critical attention to Joyce's "aesthetic emotion" or Eliot's "emotional adequacy" has been the view that the artist's task must be the sorting-through and *refinement* of feeling, the eradication of false feeling to get to the true. The modernist artist in this conception comes to resemble his Romantic forebear, a representative man with a more comprehensive soul who can distinguish gradations and qualities of feeling in a way that the larger public cannot – the twist being that the modernist must possess an even more finely tuned aesthetic sense, since Romantic excess, grandiosity, and anthropomorphizing of nature are now among the false feelings he must guard against. And, to be sure, in even the most ruthless satire there often emerges an occasional gesture where poignancy is salvaged; the balance is merely shifted so that increasing quantities of cruelty or suffering are required to justify (to "earn") the rare moment of tenderness. In a way, this is a version of the old claim that the satirist is really a closet sentimentalist, that the cruelty of satire is but another way to arrive at those very affective indulgences that are purportedly jettisoned. It also allows a recuperation of modernism within what I am loosely calling a humanist tradition – one in which ethical identification and imaginative sympathy remain fundamental to the construction of characters, stories, and meanings. And, to be sure, it would be a mistake to identify modernism too narrowly with irony itself, since, as Maria DiBattista observes, modernism frequently retains "a boundary beyond which irony may not pass," a retention that signals modernism's "inner debt to Romanticism and the cult of the heart."[104] One useful way to think about late modernism, indeed, is that it suspects an earlier modernism of not making good on its promises to banish the sentimental.

But while for certain authors, no doubt, such seeking of a golden affective mean – between irony and pity, or cruelty and compassion, or the reality principle and the pleasure principle – may suffice, finding a middle ground is not always possible. For it is precisely the difficulty of the distinction between sentiment and sentimentality that is at issue. Once feeling is understood as potentially sentimental, all appeals to feeling run the same risk. Rather than recovering some precarious balance where sentiment is present but not excessive, then, I want to suggest that this concern with feeling is rather a sign that modernism is inevitably caught between its *humanist* tendency and an *antihumanist* one that seeks to reject ethical identification completely. As Ella Zohar Ophir notes, in modernist literature – as opposed to the visual arts – the new value of abstraction less often proves to be anti-representational than it does anti-empathetic.[105] Its target is less mimesis than cathexis. Modernism exhibits many different ways of negotiating this dilemma, of assessing both the advantages and the liabilities of cutting free (or attempting to cut free) from the humanist, ethical concerns that have historically been central to the novel. To examine how modernism handles this negotiation, I offer in the following chapter a short survey of the decades of early and high modernism before the 1930s, a survey that suggests by way of representative figures how late modernist satire gradually emerges as a cultural dominant.

CHAPTER 2

Modernism's story of feeling

Seen through an ever-more-powerful critical microscope, the object once known as modernism is dissolving under our gaze. For some time now new (or renewed) attention to writers who for reasons of race, gender, politics, technique, or talent had been neglected by scholars has radically expanded, undermining a small canon of authors (Joyce, Eliot, Woolf, etc.) and works taken to exemplify Anglo-American high modernism; cultural history has further demanded that maps of modernism make room for popular forms ranging from newspapers to film to jazz. At the same time, the same canonical works have been subjected to new critical approaches in order to reveal their implication in wider social discourses.[1] As a result, an increasing amount of energy has gone into dismantling a high modernism that, we are gradually coming to understand, nobody actually practiced.

At the risk of simplification, however, I follow Pericles Lewis in his contention that the term modernism retains enough coherence to constitute a valuable critical tool.[2] In favoring Lewis's description over Lawrence Rainey's characterization of modernism as merely "a constellation of agents and practices," or that of critics such as Peter Nicholls who signal the heterogeneity of the era's culture through the plural *modernisms*,[3] I by no means disdain critical attention to the history of modernist patronage, publication and marketing, nor do I deny that the variety of modernist literature was for years ignored in a myopic reverence for a few great names. I mean, rather, that the work of theorizing modernism does not, for me, conclude with the abandonment of theory; and that I find Lewis's threefold crisis of representation, of liberalism, and of reason to provide a formulation of modernism that is neither too stringent nor too vague. At the same time, however, my own discussion does not center on the categories of technique, politics, and philosophy that have historically dominated discussions of modernism. Instead, I focus on problems of affect, and provide an account of feeling within modernism.

In this chapter, I divide this account of modernist feeling into four parts. First, I examine the affective protocols associated with an early modernist aestheticism, through attention to the writings of Oscar Wilde and to Max Beerbohm's novel *Zuleika Dobson* (1911). From there I turn to a reaction against that aestheticism, as found in the polemics of Ezra Pound and in *Tarr* (1918), the first novel of his sometime collaborator Wyndham Lewis. In both of these moments, I discern anticipations of the satire of the 1930s: Wilde and Beerbohm cultivate an indifference to ethical concerns, while Pound and Lewis exemplify satiric aggression. Next, I examine two novels of the so-called high modernist moment, Joyce's *Ulysses* (1922) and Aldous Huxley's *Antic Hay* (1923), both of which reveal the emergence of satire as an increasingly prevalent cultural mode. Finally, I briefly describe the late modernism of the 1930s as it has been theorized by other scholars and as I see it manifested in the writers I study in this book's later chapters. While such an account may imply a rigid chronology, my point is the opposite; history doesn't move in a line, and the satiric practices of the 1930s are clearly anticipated in earlier works of modernism. Yet because those earlier works have generally been studied as examples of a modernism fully realized, viewing them as antecedents to a later historical moment may shift our focus and help us to see aspects of these works that criticism has overlooked.

FORMS OF INDIFFERENCE: WILDE AND BEERBOHM

Fredric Jameson suggests that modernism can be said to have not one but two originary "moments," moments I will for brevity's sake call Symbolism and Futurism. The first, which Jameson associates with organic metaphorics, he uses to describe not only Symbolist poetry but also Impressionist painting, Art Nouveau, late Victorian aestheticism, and philosophical vitalism; the second, linked to technological motifs, can be found in Futurism, cubism, Vorticism, and the "purer formalisms" of movements such as architecture's International Style.[4] It is in the earlier, Symbolist moment that we might note a first shift in the theorization of affect, a move away from a Romantic or Victorian investment in feeling as a guarantee of value. This is the shift that Lionel Trilling identifies from sincerity to authenticity, and a key figure for Trilling is Oscar Wilde, who maintains a "principled antagonism to sincerity."[5] Wilde marks the moment where sincerity becomes sentimental and the importance of being earnest becomes laughable. Declaring that "all bad poetry springs from genuine feeling,"[6] he separates questions of *feeling* ("genuine feeling") from those of *expression* ("bad poetry"), and questions of ethics from those of aesthetics. In this new hierarchy, the aesthetic now takes priority: "There is no such thing as a moral or an immoral book. Books are well written, or badly written. That is all."[7] This dichotomy then further extends to the separation of content and form:

And just as out of the sordid and sentimental amours of the silly wife of a small country doctor in the squalid village of Yonville-l'Abbaye, near Rouen, Gustave Flaubert was able to create a classic, and make a masterpiece of style, so, from subjects of little or no importance ... the true critics can ... produce work that will be flawless in beauty and instinct with intellectual subtlety.[8]

As genuine feeling leads to bad poetry, so bad feeling (Emma's "sordid and sentimental amours") can produce genuine poetry ("a masterpiece of style"). Style is elevated over subject matter, form over content, aesthetics over ethics, expression over feeling. What ensues, finally, is Wilde's celebration of artifice over nature, and of lying over truth.

As Trilling observes, Wilde's polemical rejection of Victorian duty, earnestness, and sincerity entails the endorsement of a "doctrine of masks" which "proposes the intellectual value of the ironic posture."[9] Upholding the value of irony, Wilde professes antagonism toward Victorian morality, and to aesthetic practices that rely on it. Sounding much like Nietzsche decrying our compunction at laughing at Don Quixote, Wilde sees "the mere existence of the conscience" as "a sign of our imperfect development," and views a morality based on "self-denial" and "self-sacrifice" as "part of that old worship of pain which is so terrible a factor in the history of the world."[10] The result is a thorough skepticism whether our moral impulses serve any good beyond human vanity. The celebration of artifice thus entails a pronounced suspicion of the moral sentiments and suggests in their place a new emphasis on certain feelings – cruelty, indifference, aloofness – characteristic of satire.

It is at this historical moment, moreover, that indifference is recognized both as a precondition for laughter and as an affective state symptomatic of new social conditions. Wildean aloofness is at once akin to the freedom from emotion that Henri Bergson sees as necessary to the comic and to "the blasé attitude" that Georg Simmel sees as emblematic of modern metropolitan life. A fuller account of Simmel, Bergson, and the blasé will be offered in Chapter 5; for now it is enough to emphasize that Wilde's stance creates space for what Freud saw as the "benevolence" or "neutrality" necessary for successful joke-work.[11] If strong affect, as Freud contends, interferes with the pleasure that tendentious jokes afford, then low affect allows a receptivity to such pleasures.

But while Wilde has long been taken as the exemplar of aestheticist indifference, this "moment" in the development of modernist satire is perhaps best represented by that enigmatic work of his friend and protégé, Max Beerbohm's *Zuleika Dobson*. As a celebration of pure style, and as a narratorial display of a blasé indifference to the ethical stakes of his characters' fates, the novel is far more successful than Wilde's own moralistic *The Picture of Dorian Gray*. Robert F. Kiernan describes the ornate, self-conscious manner of *Zuleika Dobson* as "the play of high style against a higher awareness of that style's absurdity," and he places the book within a tradition of the "camp novel," taking the absence of clear targets as grounds for denying it the label of satire.[12] Here Kiernan is merely following the lead of the seventy-four-year-old Max himself, who, in a prefatory note to the 1946 edition, blithely disavows any political, social, or ethical commitment behind his narratorial equanimity, and exhorts the reader to look at the novel not as a "satire" but as "just a fantasy."[13] Indeed, with only a few exceptions, critics of the novel have found its frivolity incompatible with the darkness that is seen to characterize satire (untroubled, apparently, by its conclusion in a mass suicide). For Beerbohm, then, even the indirect "commentary" or polemicism of satire is still subject to being recuperated as a socially minded or utilitarian earnestness in disguise. But in *Zuleika Dobson*, he insists, all art is quite useless.

Yet if Beerbohm's own stated position, readable in his self-celebratory style and irony-laden characterizations, suggests a withdrawal of authorial affective commitment, he hardly shies from the *representation* of intense feeling. The subject of the novel, after all, is love. It is the tale of the arrival at all-male Oxford of the bewitchingly beautiful eponymous conjuror, with whom every one of Oxford's undersexed undergraduates falls self-abasingly in love. Yet because Zuleika herself can only love a man who refrains from the abasement that love demands, all desire in the novel must remain forever unrequited. Thus, while the reader's level of emotion and the narrator's are kept to a minimum, the characters experience their own feelings at a feverish intensity that can hardly be comic to them. Feelings in *Zuleika Dobson* are as irrefutable as facts. Despite her often sadistic treatment of the men who adore her, Zuleika herself is a slave to her own feeling and can only act in accord with its tyrannical demands. Her opposite number, a dandy called the Duke of Dorset, is equally in thrall to his own heart, and as a result his experience of passionate love shatters his adherence to a personal code of style. "A theory, as the Duke saw, is one thing, an emotion another,"[14] Beerbohm writes, and the entire novel stages a conflict between the Duke's "theory" – his adherence to his

dandiacal style – and his "emotion," which everywhere is treated as something that comes upon the characters from without. Through the act of
feeling, the Duke abandons the *theoretic* world for the *experiential*; a true
Lacanian subject, he discovers himself exactly at the moment of self-loss:
"he had no soul till it passed out of his keeping."[15] Beerbohm's most
whimsical and memorable illustration of this external property of feeling
is rendered through the supernatural changes of color that Zuleika's pearl
earrings and the Duke's pearl studs undergo, changes which signal the
characters' emotional states before they themselves are conscious of them.[16]

Here *Zuleika Dobson* seems curiously to resemble a contemporaneous
text like Forster's *Howards End*, whose narratorial earnestness and commitment to the truth of feeling would otherwise seem to lie at some
distance from Beerbohm's ironical maneuvers. But Forster tends to value
this force of feeling, whereas for Beerbohm its compulsory quality is all
the more reason that feeling should be resisted. For while emotion, in
opposition to theory, is irrefutable in *Zuleika Dobson*, it is also social.
Descending from aestheticism to life, from theory to emotion, involves
for the Duke a loss of social and aesthetic distinction. Loving Zuleika
makes the Duke merely "one of a number," rather than one "aloft and
apart."[17] Previously aloof from public circulations of feeling – "Never had
he given an ear to that cackle which is called Public Opinion" – the Duke,
having fallen, now sees the epidemic of love for Zuleika as equivalent
to "the noise made on the verge of the Boer War," a mob psychology
or groupthink that threatens to devastate Oxford. The narrator agrees: "If
man were not a gregarious animal, the world might have achieved, by this
time, some real progress toward civilization. Segregate him, and he is no
fool. But let him loose among his fellows, and he is lost – he becomes just
a unit in unreason."[18] In spite of Beerbohm's disavowals, the novel can
indeed be taken as a satire on "the herd instinct." The story is a parable
about how publicly circulating feeling can overcome a private style.

Yet Beerbohm's own style, unlike the Duke's, furnishes proof against
feeling's dangerous seductions; numerous readers comment on the novel's
"dehumanized characters" and the low ethical stakes of the action.[19] The
multiplicity of Beerbohm's playful stylistic devices – the sprinkling of
archaic, Francophone and neologistic diction, the slapstick gags under-
cutting scenes of high drama, the ludic intervention of the supernatural,
the parodic devices of melodrama – all work to deflect attention from
the empathic claims of the characters' emotional lives onto the artifice
of the novel itself. Beerbohm's success in banishing earnestness is nowhere
more evident than in the novel's treatment of death. While the casual

execution of a minor suitor, dispatched with blasé manners, anticipates Evelyn Waugh's technique ("And last of all leapt Mr. Trent-Garby, who, catching his foot in the ruined flower-box, fell headlong, and was, I regret to say, killed"), more characteristic of Beerbohm is the mass suicide with which the novel climaxes:

And over all this confusion and concussion of men and man-made things crashed the vaster discords of the heavens; and the waters of the heavens fell ever denser and denser, as though to the aid for waters that could not in themselves envelop so many hundreds of struggling human forms.[20]

Here sympathy for the characters is denied through the virtuosity of the writer's performance – the alliteration and assonance, the biblical echoes and cadences, the fanciful imputation of motive to nature – a performance that seems at first to rise to the importance of its subject and then to surpass it utterly. In so mitigating emotion through linguistic exhibition, Beerbohm, like the conjuror Zuleika herself, dazzles with virtuosity; he is "the omnisubjugant."[21] Zuleika Dobson, *c'est Max*. The deaths of so many of England's fine young men, an eerie anticipation of the war that will soon ravage the Continent, remains an exercise in style.

FORMS OF AGGRESSION: POUND AND LEWIS

If Wilde and Beerbohm will here have to stand in for a general "moment" in the story of modernist feeling, then what Jameson sees as modernism's second originary moment, Futurism, will have to be represented by the reaction against Symbolism and aestheticism as articulated in the Vorticist aesthetics of Ezra Pound and Wyndham Lewis. Granted, lumping Vorticism and Futurism together may appear problematic given the overt proclamations of enmity between English and Italian factions, but I deploy the term Futurism in the broad sense that Pound himself uses when he writes, in 1914, that "we are all Futurists,"[22] and I follow Marjorie Perloff in uniting the warring parties underneath a single avant-gardiste banner. For, despite the doctrinal heterogeneity within this Futurist moment, Pound and Lewis share with Marinetti a contempt for decadence, *art pour l'art*, and the cult of beauty. Their break with the Symbolists is clear enough: the revolutionary posture of the later generation rejects as ineffectual the reclusive aestheticism of the earlier one; its swaggering bravado disdains its predecessors as effeminate; its diatribes against prettiness recast Paterian impressionism as one more kind of fakery; its trademark genre, the manifesto, supplants the Wildean epigram.

Nonetheless, the saturation of Futurist rhetoric with disgust for Symbolism suggests an anxiety born of proximity.[23] Pound shares with Wilde a rejection of moralizing about art – "Good art however 'immoral' it is, is wholly a thing of virtue. Purely and simply ... good art can NOT be immoral."[24] Like Wilde, he firmly separates the ethical and the aesthetic, and takes all talk of morality in art as benighted Grundyism. Pound also emphasizes the necessity of technique, form, and control, so that however much he might reject the *particular* style of the Symbolists, the emphasis on style itself (and consequent adoration of Flaubert) remains firmly in place. And if Wilde's stance of moral indifference in "The Critic as Artist" owes something to Nietzsche's critique of a hypertrophied conscience in the (mis)development of the species, then so too does Marinetti's provocative, if pompous, declaration that art "can be nothing but violence, cruelty, and injustice."[25] Behind both originary modernist moments lies the same rejection of Victorian sentimentality.

That Futurism shared an antisentimental stance with its immediate precursor suggests a literary history that works via *differentiation*: each movement's need to distinguish itself from its predecessor dictates that the predecessor's rejection of sentimentality be rewritten as merely an illusory break, a continuation of sentimentality by other means. As Marinettian Futurism redefines *fin-de-siècle* aestheticism as a sentimental cult of beauty, so Lewis and Pound's *Blast* manifesto denounces Marinetti's automobilism as a "sensational and sentimental" rehash of Wilde.[26] The narrative of early modernism begins to look like an effort of each new splinter movement to surpass the previous in the completeness of its antisentimentality.[27]

But, as important as the ideological content of the antisentimental stance is the change in tone that separates these two moments. Pound, Lewis, Marinetti, even Lawrence – their *attitudes* are anything but blasé. And here lies their most pronounced contrast with Wilde and Beerbohm. There is among the Futurists an abundance of polemic that publicizes and justifies the revolutionary stance of their own art. These Futurist polemics share an argumentative, exhortative, antiacademic style, prone to sudden exclamations, slangy coinages, and derisive insults. As Perloff notes, "the aggressive, polemical tone, the unusual typography ... the extensive use of onomatopoeia, pun, and extravagant metaphor, and the 'destruction of syntax' and *parole in libertà*" are features that cut across particular schools or movements within the Futurist moment.[28]

It would be too hasty to conflate Futurist polemic or manifesto with satire itself, but two crucial qualities must here be noted that are relevant to the mechanisms of satire: (1) the ostensibly reformative or revolutionary motive of changing a corrupt modernity, and (2) an enthusiasm for that change whose violence often takes precedence over its professed ends. For Pound and Lewis, the "aggressive, polemical tone" is tied to the paradoxical position of the satirist in modernity, decrying fads and fashions while shrilly insisting upon newness. The opposition *both* to a corrupt modernity *and* to all the faulty modernisms that help to constitute that modernity begins to look like opposition for its own sake. Indeed, this aggression is something the Futurist polemic shares with important portions of Pound's early poetry, whose most memorable lines are often those which – to borrow the phrase with which Pound himself praised Yeats – strip poetry of its perdamnable rhetoric. It is equally a hallmark of Lewis's novelistic style, which has from Pound through Kenner and Jameson regularly been lauded for its violence and energy.

This violence with which Pound and Lewis confront a corrupt modernity is itself a kind of affect. Thus, while Hugh Kenner notes Pound's lifelong emphasis on technical rather than psychic criteria for poetry (corresponding to what I have called in Wilde the priority of aesthetics over ethics), Michael Levenson argues in response that in Pound's poetics a residual "psychic" criterion remains.[29] In Pound's famous "A Retrospect" (1917), for example, *sentimentality* is expectedly disdained (Poetry should be "austere, direct, free from emotional slither"), yet *emotion* remains a source of value ("Only emotion endures").[30] And if there is a hint of a contradiction in valuing emotion but not emotional slither, it is resolved by the distinction between false and true emotion. And true emotion, for Pound, is found in nothing other than satire itself: "I prefer satire, which is due to emotion, to any sham of emotion."[31]

In "A Retrospect," Pound leaves implicit the assumption that the emotion underlying satiric ridicule is authentic because it is negative and critical, but he comes closer to spelling out this idea over a decade later in "The Serious Artist" (1929). In this later essay Pound's tastes seem to have changed little. Although he praises beauty because it "reminds one what is worth while,"[32] he is again anxious to qualify his enthusiasm in a way that distinguishes his own appreciation for beauty from the bogus gushing he finds in aestheticism: "I am not now speaking of shams. I mean beauty, not slither, not sentimentalizing about beauty."[33] Even the diction here (sham, slither) is kept intact from "A Retrospect." As in the earlier essay, too, satire retains its critical, anti-slitherious function. Therefore, whereas "the cult of beauty" corresponds for Pound to the medical function of *hygiene*, "the cult of ugliness" is valuable for performing the complementary function of *diagnosis*, locating what is corrupt in culture. And satire reappears as an adjunct to this diagnostic function: "satire, if we are to ride this medical metaphor to staggers, satire is surgery, insertions, and amputations."[34] In short, satire eradicates emotional slither so that real beauty can be discerned. Pound's medical metaphor, then, promotes a view of satire as a corrective force but at the same time a violent and invasive one.[35]

But while Pound's essays contain a valuable, if glancing, recognition of the importance of satire to Futurist poetics, Lewis's *Tarr* (1918) offers a richer case study. *Tarr* is satiric, first of all, through its mockery of modern sophistication, particularly its send-up of the "Bourgeois Bohemians," the bad artists and sentimental poseurs who populate Paris's Latin Quarter. The Englishman Hobson is mocked for the "sentimental indulgence" of his deliberately shabby tweeds; the painter Lowndes has "just enough money to be a Cubist"; Bertha, Tarr's fiancée, walks naked around her apartment, taking an "air bath" amid a plaster cast of Beethoven and a photograph of the Mona Lisa.[36] This ridicule of aesthetic pretensions and second-hand tastes suggests the conservative or moralistic tendency of satire I have discussed: *Tarr* manifests an urgent need to distinguish good art from bad, even good modernism from bad, at the same time that it also anticipates a tendency that emerges more fully in satire of the 1930s wherein modernism's oppositional and satiric energy begins to take itself as its own target.

Given Lewis's own repeated dismissals of bourgeois moral standards, this moralistic reading of *Tarr* may seem counterintuitive; yet such a reading was easily available to the novel's first critics. In his 1937 *Blasting and Bombardiering*, Lewis recounts *Tarr*'s critical reception: "'A painful commentary on modern morals,' said a provincial paper. 'But it has a powerful fascination,' it added. Whether the 'fascination' lay in the morals or the manner of presentment the writer does not say."[37] While Lewis pokes fun at the philistinism of the provincial reviewer and his outdated concern for moral content, the reviewer's clichéd language still recognizes *Tarr*'s fundamental outrage with modernity. Nor is it off the mark to note that this outrage takes on a moral coloring; even the current tendency to read Lewis as a cultural critic capable of diagnosing the ills of capitalism despite his right-wing leanings – one reader calls him "a one-man Frankfurt school of the right"[38] – retains a touch of this moralistic revulsion from the modern.

The moral outrage underlying *Tarr*'s satire of modern artists places it in contiguity with Lewis's polemics and manifestos, whose doctrinal objectives often seem entwined with the dramatic action of the novel. The title character's dialogues, which Kenner has described as "*Blast* manifestos dramatized,"[39] are frequently cited in discussions of his creator's artistic principles, and Tarr's conversations with Anastasya even feature those repeated exclamations of "Bless" and "Curse" without which no modernist manifesto would be complete.[40] Tarr's argument for the deadness and the externality of art is fully consistent with Lewis's later treatises, and he distinguishes his own principles from the frauds about him in terms reminiscent of Pound's: "The second [condition of art] is absence of *soul*, in the sentimental human sense ... No restless, quick flame-like ego is imagined for the *inside* of it. It has no inside."[41] Pater and his acolytes, derided as sentimental humanists, are the obvious targets here, and from this attack on flux and egoism it is only a small step to the "external method" of satire valorized in *Men Without Art*.

Tarr's attack on what Lewis calls "Humour" similarly anticipates Lewis's later position of the 1930s. The novel opens with a preface that, as Martin Puchner points out, itself takes the rhetorical form of a manifesto.[42] This preface dwells on "the maudlin and the self-defensive Grin" of the Englishman, which, Lewis asserts, "usually accompanies loose emotionality."[43] This critique of British humor becomes an explicit motif when Tarr renounces his Englishman's humor as emotional weakness, a "national institution" that "provides you with nothing but a first-rate means of evading reality."[44] Thus Tarr traces all his "mock matrimonial" problems with his sometime fiancée Bertha to humor, and resolves "to gaze on Bertha inhumanly and not humorously."[45] Tarr eventually names this failure to be inhuman as "sentimentality" and concludes: "He had humanized sex too much."[46] In short, the slither of Humor is opposed to the form-giving, inhuman gaze of the painter's eye, which Lewis later identifies with satire: "There is laughter and laughter. That of true satire is as it were *tragic* laughter. It is not a genial guffaw nor the titillations provoked by a harmless entertainer."[47] To the Grin, then, Lewis opposes the Grimace, which signifies not evasion but confrontation: "If you look very closely at my grin, you will perceive that it is a very logical and deliberate grimace."[48] Only the animality of the satiric grimace, in contrast to the evasive geniality of the humorous grin, provides the basis for emotional and artistic integrity.

Yet while *Tarr* advocates for the emotional coldness that Lewis would later characterize as satiric, it is less clear whether Lewis actually achieves inhuman, satiric distance from his representations. Tarr, to be sure, never succeeds in extricating himself from the "slop of sex."[49] Having temporarily escaped his sentimental attachment to Bertha, he finds himself embroiled in an equally sentimental relation with Kreisler; he realizes that, despite his efforts, "the curse of humour was in him."[50] And Lewis himself also fails to escape the curse of humor. As one critic after another has noted, Lewis creates in Kreisler a much more vivid and engrossing representation than he achieves with Tarr, his authorial mouthpiece. As Kenner puts it, Lewis is "surreptitiously backing a rival horse,"[51] siding with the chaotic energy of the pathetic yet vital Kreisler rather than the disinterested cool that Tarr attempts to achieve. The two characters in fact might be seen as embodying the two poles of satire I have described; while Tarr discourses didactically on the principles by which modernist art can properly respond to a bogus modernity, Kreisler actually lives the aggressive energy of satire, which leaves behind its didactic aims in its outraged opposition to just about everything. Whether in the hilarious Bonnington Club dance, the grotesque duel (where slapstick misfortune slips into macabre revulsion), or his own suicide, Kreisler's solution to a problem is always action, usually violent action. There is, then, substantial slippage between the codified affective regimens articulated in Lewis's polemics and the more unpredictable practice of novel-writing: the impulsiveness of Kreisler overwhelms the intellection of Tarr.

Indeed, in *Tarr*, experience is always leaving theory disappointed. Tarr avers that art is "ourselves disentangled from death and accident,"[52] but in the novel accident usually gets the last laugh. Characters are constantly discovering their own narratives of self-definition to be contradicted by events, and they strain to form new narratives that will offer at least the illusion of control over life. As Paul Peppis writes: "Since persons can control neither their raging desires nor the actions of others, social activity becomes as chaotic as Kreisler's fanatic dances. Every scene, every interpretation, every plan of action invariably goes horribly wrong."[53] Tarr approaches Bertha with newfound indifference, only to discover her "ironical unsurprised eye" mocking him and turning his hard-won indifference into "truculen[ce]."[54] Kreisler, after seeing Anastasya with Soltyk, resolves to insult her in order to reclaim some control over events, even though he knows such an insult will fail to win her from his rival. Bertha, having spontaneously kissed the brutish Kreisler, constructs an account in which he appeared to her in need of help, thus "effacing, in some sense, the extreme involuntariness of the . . . incident."[55] In *Tarr*, one cannot author oneself outside of a hermetic world of art, because the contingencies of life are just too great.

One of the novel's most significant instances of experience defying theory is Kreisler's rape of Bertha, a scene that, as Ann Ardis points out, has largely been ignored by critics. Ardis maintains that this critical neglect speaks to a reluctance to confront the ethical questions involved in reading the rape, and argues that Pound and Lewis demand of their nascent modernist readership a willingness to overcome the "ideological response to violent content (i.e., a rape)" inherent in realist fiction.[56] It is certainly the case that Lewis posits a trained readership that breaks with realist traditions of ethical engagement; yet it is equally that case that rejecting the narrative conventions of realism is not the same as dispensing with ethical engagement altogether. Indeed, one could easily argue just the opposite: that for a narrator deliberately to cultivate sympathy according to a realist (or sentimental) narrative model would – especially given *Tarr*'s own indictment of sentimental patterns of feeling – interfere with not only aesthetic but also ethical judgment. To use Pound's phrase, realist conventions would produce only a "sham of emotion." The question thus becomes not *whether* Lewis engages a reader's ethical faculties in representing the rape, but rather *how* – the answer being that narratorial neutrality becomes for Lewis the most effective method of shaping readerly affect without giving way to fakery.

Yet to endorse narratorial neutrality as a means of indirectly implying moral judgment raises its own problems, as Ardis notes, nowhere more explicitly than in Lewis's own comparison of the rape to a joke:

As she stood there she looked like some one on whom a practical joke had been played, of the primitive and physical order, such as drenching, in some amusing manner, with dirty water. She had been decoyed into swallowing something disgusting. Her attitude was reminiscent of the way people are seen to stand bent awkwardly forward, neck craned out, slowly wiping the dirt off their clothes, or spitting out the remains of their polluted drink, cursing the joker.[57]

Although Lewis in *Tarr* does not confine himself to the external method he later advocates,[58] in this moment the aftermath of the rape is represented in painterly or sculptural terms. Feelings are only implied through the outward signs of posture and gesture; passions can be read only because they are stamped on lifeless things. From Bertha's physical appearance, however, the narrator associates to a very different sort of event, a practical joke – a humiliation of significantly lower moral consequence. And while the narrator's descriptions of practical jokes retain the sexually laden imagery of "drenching" and "swallowing," the shift from rape to joke entails an uncomfortable aestheticization of the victim's body.

Because comparison of the rape-victim to the joke-victim is made in purely visual terms, its moral dubiousness can, at first, only be inferred. Yet Lewis's narrator enunciates the difference between the two soon enough, pronouncing the "desperate practical joke" to be "too deep for laughter."[59] Lacking the laughter that for Bergson restores humanity, Kreisler's sexual assault both is and is not a joke: "At its consummation there had been no chorus of intelligible laughter."[60] Lewis's treatment does not deny the possibility of a reader's moral outrage, yet neither does it nurture that outrage. Tarr has vowed to view Bertha "inhumanly," and he later regrets having humanized sex too much. But in this scene the Bergsonian "anaesthesia of the heart" necessary to joke-work takes on darker connotations, equated now with Kreisler's cold-hearted sexual violence.

SATIRE EMERGENT: JOYCE AND HUXLEY

Having looked at two originary moments of modernism, I want to turn briefly to the moment of high modernism after the First World War, circa 1922. The hypercanonical novel here is *Ulysses*, and its place in the modernist story of feeling doubtless merits a study unto itself. Jay Dickson has in fact provided an in-depth account of the novel's engagement with the sentimental tradition, finding echoes of it in, for example, Stephen's pained encounter with his underfed sister, Dilly, or in Bloom's sympathy for the extended labor of the pregnant Mina Purefoy. But Dickson's analysis of the sentimental in *Ulysses* must be complemented by the recognition that even as Joyce negotiates the claims of feeling with an eye to the sentimental or humanistic tradition, he also indulges his satiric side quite lavishly. To be sure, the novel is generally viewed as "comic" rather than "satiric," and Joyce's view of his characters is typically regarded as forgiving of human failings. Yet this reading has not always dominated Joyce criticism. An early critic, *Imagiste* Richard Aldington, condemned the novel as "more bitter, more sordid, more ferociously satirical than anything Mr. Joyce has yet written ... a tremendous libel on humanity."[61] Soon after, Carl van Doren and Mark van Doren described the novel as "savagely satiric," and even Kenner's 1956 *Dublin's Joyce* reads *Ulysses* primarily as a satire.[62]

But even if a contemporary reader is prone to regard Bloom as a figure of compassion first and of ridicule second, the satiric spirit is nonetheless present in *Ulysses*: it is given the name Buck Mulligan. The Falstaffian figure of Mulligan, presiding over the novel's opening, exhibits traits of both the indifferent Wildean dandy and the aggressive Lewisian materialist – sometimes aloof and witty, sometimes combative and cruel, invariably performing a social role. Robert Bell goes so far as to take Mulligan as the guiding spirit of the novel, characterizing him as a Shakespearean clown in contrast to Stephen's humorless Malvolio or Jacques.[63]

As a materialist and a violator of boundaries, Mulligan embodies the Bakhtinian grotesque body; referring everything to one bodily function or another, he reduces ideals to the level of the material lower stratum. Stephen's mother's death, for example, becomes an anatomy lesson: "And what is death, he asked, your mother's or yours or my own?" He invokes his perspective as a medical student – a profession that has a long association with the role of the satirist – who (as Pound would have it) performs surgery, insertions and amputations: "I see them pop off every day in the Mater and Richmond and cut up into tripes in the dissecting-room. It's a beastly thing and nothing else . . . To me it's all a mockery and beastly. Her cerebral lobes are not functioning."[64]

Religious beliefs and rituals are similarly reduced to the corporeal. Mulligan's "Ballad of Joking Jesus" reverses the process of transubstantiation, reducing spirit to body:

> If anyone thinks that I amn't divine
> He'll get no free drinks when I'm making the wine
> But have to drink water and wish it were plain
> That I make when the wine becomes water again.[65]

This delight in the excretory re-surfaces when Buck interrupts Stephen's Shakespeare seminar:

> –The tramper Synge is looking for you, he said, to murder you. He heard you pissed on his halldoor in Glasthule. He's out in pampooties to murder you.
> –Me! Stephen exclaimed. That was your contribution to literature.
> Buck Mulligan gleefully bent back, laughing to the dark eavesdropping ceiling.[66]

Urination on Synge's door is very much Buck's contribution to literature, an avant-garde clowning turned performance art that in a later day and age might have won him a grant from the National Endowment for the Arts. The gesture here debunks not Stephen's self-indulgent grief or superstitious religious rituals, but his literary pretentions.

Buck's reductive materialism is often accompanied by outright aggression. From the beginning of the novel he is continually placing Stephen under intellectual siege, offering the reader what Bell calls "a valid satiric critique of Stephen."[67] "He fears the lancet of my art as I fear that of his,"

Stephen thinks; and later, when Buck appears in the National Library, "Hast thou found me, O mine enemy?"[68] Mulligan questions Stephen's aesthetic principles (or pretensions) and engages him in a bawdy and jesting but fundamentally threatening intellectual swordplay. In this sense, as Maureen Waters observes, "Although he is often comic, Mulligan's purpose is to negate or destroy."[69]

To these qualities of materialism and aggression, reminiscent of the Lewisian satirist, a third crucial characteristic must be added: histrionicism. For Mulligan, satire or wit is a *social* mode, a way of displaying (mostly to other men) his own intellectual and sexual prowess. As critics frequently note, he is a Wildean figure in his dandyish dress, his aura of ambiguous sexuality, and his willingness to play the jester at the court of the British Empire; Stephen considers him one of a "Brood of mockers."[70] Buck is not only histrionic but necessarily histrionic, and when he doesn't have an audience he summons one out of the air: "For this, O dearly beloved, is the genuine Christine: body and soul and blood and ouns. Slow music, please. Shut your eyes, gents. One moment. A little trouble about those white corpuscles. Silence all."[71] Mulligan is not merely acting here: he is pretending to be a stagemaster who pretends to be a priest, pretending to have an audience that he can transform into a congregation, all for the benefit of his real audience, Stephen, and the even realer audience beyond him, Joyce's readership. It is in fact impossible to take any of Buck's lines without some kind of irony; he always seems to be speaking someone else's words, and never fully seriously. While all the characters in *Ulysses* assume social roles, Buck is qualitatively different from the novel's principals, Stephen, Bloom, and Molly, in that *he has no stream of consciousness* that we overhear; he exists only as a performance. As a thought experiment we might imagine what it would mean to be granted access to Buck's solitary consciousness as we are with Stephen, Bloom, and Molly. It is hardly overstatement to suggest that it would destroy the representation.

Mulligan's histrionic clowning modifies the aggression and negativity of his debunking satire with a happily irreverent freedom from authority. When the Dublin literati, including Stephen, earnestly discuss the greatest of literary authorities, Buck has little use for such obeisance:

Buck Mulligan thought, puzzled.
–Shakespeare? He said. I seem to know the name. A flying sunny smile rayed in
   his loose features.
–To be sure, he said, remembering brightly. That chap that writes like Synge.[72]

(Yeats notoriously overpraised Synge as writing like Shakespeare.) No one possibly believes Buck to be this ignorant, nor does he expect anyone to. This feigned ignorance, rather, really is Buck's own theory of Shakespeare, just as pissing on Synge's door really is his contribution to literature. This is a sophisticated philistinism that engages the eggheaded intellectual contest in the reading room by pretending not to engage at all. His play-acting excuses him from the argument while trivializing it at the same time.

To be sure, the fraternal rivalry between Stephen and Mulligan is ultimately displaced by Stephen's more humane relation with the father-figure, Bloom. Even Bell, who argues that Mulligan's spirit of joking infects the novel's narrative style, must grant the ultimate predominance of Bloom, who "becomes the novel's center of value," offering a "comic" view opposed to Buck's "satiric" one.[73] The reasons behind this movement away from Mulligan's satire toward the more sympathetic mode of comedy may be peculiar to Joyce's psychology or aesthetics, yet the triumph of Bloom – talking earnestly about injustice and love – also suggests that the presence of satire within the moment of high modernism is, to use Raymond Williams's distinction, "emergent" rather than "dominant." (One might similarly find a visible, if emergent, strain of satire in that other monument of 1922, *The Waste Land*.) Thus, for Joyce, notes Waters, "satire is merely one facet in the larger comedy; the writers who came after him, or were younger contemporaries, were less optimistic."[74] Waters's survey of Irish writing points out the wider trend I mean to underscore: that in the late modernism of the 1930s satire becomes a cultural dominant at long last.

One of these "less optimistic" writers, not Irish but English, was Aldous Huxley, who enjoyed in the 1920s and 1930s critical prestige nearly equal to Joyce's; he was commonly described, Jerome Meckier notes, as both the voice of his generation and its intellectual and sexual liberator.[75] The Irish satirist Flann O'Brien pays (deliberately verbose) homage to both men equally in the opening pages of his 1939 *At Swim-Two-Birds*: "Each of [my books] was generally recognized as indispensable to all who aspire to an appreciation of the nature of contemporary literature and my small collection contained works ranging from those of Mr. Joyce to the widely-read books of Mr. A. Huxley, the eminent English writer."[76] I focus here on *Antic Hay*, his 1923 novel, not only because of its contemporaneity with *Ulysses* and *The Waste Land*, but also because it constitutes a compendium of the motifs and concerns of modernist satire, which will be taken up in different ways by the 1930s authors I discuss in my later chapters.

The modernity Huxley depicts is one of utter belatedness, lacking all possibility of meaning or redemptive value. The protagonist, Gumbril, Jr., observes of one character, "Other people's ideas, other people's knowledge – they were his food. He devoured them and they were at once his own." Yet he soon realizes that this secondariness is only an extreme version of his own: "He too was an assimilator."[77] This is what Tyrus Miller has a called a "condition of generalized mimetism," a world where all is copy or sham.[78] Gumbril therefore struggles to find values in which he can believe; his skepticism discredits religion, science, education, art, political reform, and even, for the most part, love. This problem of belatedness is, moreover, self-reflexive in that it poses a problem for the novelist as well as the character: what options remain for the artist after the heightened self-consciousness of modernism has discredited older values and modes of expression? Thus Gumbril tells his friend, the painter-poet Lypiatt, that "you can't say 'dream'" in a poem, "Not in this year of grace, nineteen twenty-two"; it is "altogether *too* late in the day," adds the aesthete Mercaptan.[79] The force of the word has been nullified by Freudian talk of latent and manifest content, and modern codes of "literary tact"[80] condemn such high-flown language as implicitly sentimental.

The problem of belatedness that permeates *Antic Hay* arises specifically as a result of capitalist modernity, manifested in a catalogue of technological developments that saturate the public sphere: "Cinemas, newspapers, magazines, gramophones, football matches, wireless telephones."[81] Even Gumbril's tailor can recognize these amusements not as the liberating gifts of a new utopian age, but as a further constriction of the modern subject: "take them or leave them if you want to amuse yourself. The ordinary man can't leave them. He takes; and what's that but slavery?"[82] In this world (anticipating Waugh's *Vile Bodies*) servants read newspapers that feed them grotesque accounts of violent crimes to satisfy their baser instincts, while sentimental tales reassure them of their good hearts: "For them, Her Majesty the Queen spoke kindly words to crippled female orphans; the jockeys tumbled at their jumps; Cupid was busy in Society, and the murderers who had disemboweled their mistresses were still at large."[83]

A post-war milieu in which nineteenth-century belief in progress has been discredited by mass death, Huxley's modernity is one in which the utopian enthusiasms of an earlier modernist moment have begun to wane, and modernism itself has been commodified. Gumbril's fantasies of wealth include "drawings by Picasso and Lewis," the terms "modern" and "Futurist" are used to describe curtains, and a businessman informs

Gumbril that "there is no better training for commerce than a literary education."[84] As in *Tarr*, modernism itself is subject to satire, and the novel presents an array of ludicrous figures espousing or embodying various strains of modernist dogma (including the sexually rapacious Coleman, a Mulligan-like clown, who is ceaselessly performing, parodying Christian liturgy and interrupting intellectual conversations with bad puns).

Of all the artists in the novel, Lypiatt alone might seem to offer a positive model, since he mounts the most sustained protest against modern imitation and the modernist accommodation to it. Lypiatt, like the Futurists, rejects the art-for-art's-sake credo as sterile and seeks to reintegrate life and art. Favoring an art "for God's sake," he scorns both Bloomsbury talk of significant form and the Wildean insistence that subject matter is incidental to the success of the artwork:

Life only comes out of life, out of passion and feeling; it can't come out of theories. That's the stupidity of all this chatter about art for art's sake and the esthetic emotions and purely formal values and all that. It's only the formal relations that matter; one subject is just as good as another – that's the theory.[85]

Such a protest places Lypiatt close to Huxley himself, who sees morality as central to art and rejects the idea that art can be grounded in form alone.[86]

But Huxley is self-critical enough that he makes Lypiatt a bad artist. Myra Viveash realizes that Lypiatt's own paintings "are so bad" precisely because they have "no life in them,"[87] and she notes that his talents are best suited for Cinzano advertisements. But Huxley intimates that Lypiatt's artistic failure is due to his own personal, emotional failure – his tendency toward sentimentality. Lypiatt "sees himself as a misunderstood and embittered Prometheus," and after receiving a bad review imagines himself as Christ crucified: "There, he was making literature of it again. Even now."[88] *Antic Hay* indicts the excesses of the sentimentalist as well as the sterility of the aestheticist. Huxley may scorn Wilde's aestheticism, but Lypiatt illustrates beautifully the Wildean principle that all bad poetry comes from genuine feeling.

The structures of feeling within modernity are thus a major theme of *Antic Hay*. Gumbril's foray into capitalism requires that he learn to exploit "the social instinct, the instinct of the herd," through advertising.[89] In Huxley's analysis, capitalism turns out to be based not on the rational operations of markets but on the manipulation of feeling, on exploiting the capacity of the public to feel good about consuming a product and to feel bad about failing to do so: "We must pull the strings of snobbery and shame; it's essential to bear mockingly on those who do not wear our trousers."[90] Yet if susceptibility to emotional manipulation is to be feared, the hardened blasé attitude of Huxley's urbane sophisticates proves equally perilous. Myra, emotionally deadened from having lost her true love in the war, best demonstrates this indifference; she is always bored and her search for stimulation proves fruitless. Her ennui comes to resemble a dull anxiety, a fear of introspection and repose – what Gumbril elsewhere calls "Restlessness, distraction, refusal to think, anything for an unquiet life."[91] In contrast to this need for stimulation, Gumbril does discover a few things that he can value: Mozart's twelfth sonata, the girl Emily whom he loves but mistreats and loses, and those "quiet places in the mind"[92] that offer a retreat from the chaos of modernity (and hint at the mystical direction of Huxley's later work). But while *Antic Hay* summons moments of poignancy amid its pervasive disgust for modern life, these moments are few and far between.

The indifference that Myra and most of the modern sophisticates experience is also shown to have a moral cost. One evening, while Gumbril and his friends are out, he overhears the story of an unemployed working-class man who has lost the horse that provided him with his only means to make a living. While Gumbril's friends smirk about their disdain for the poor, Gumbril finds himself "consumed with indignation and pity ... like a prophet in Nineveh."[93] Yet his companions remain indifferent. Gumbril's thoughts, meanwhile, give way to a contemplation of the enormous scale of suffering in the world as he considers the fates of wounded veterans, homeless elderly, asthmatic servants, desperate suicides. Anticipating Nathanael West's fiction, the extent of suffering here is so vast that it leads to despair rather than action.[94]

In a different way, the pathetic but risible Lypiatt later makes his own protest against a satiric norm: "Every man is ludicrous if you look at him from outside, without taking into account what's going on in is heart and mind. You could turn *Hamlet* into an epigrammatic farce ... You could make the wittiest Guy de Maupassant story out of the life of Christ."[95] Lypiatt brings to the fore one final theme of modernist satire – the idea that any ideal can be debunked by a sufficiently satiric view: "Everyone's a walking farce and a walking tragedy at the same time."[96] Anything can be made to look good or bad by being redescribed. Choices of language, genre, tone and expression shape affective possibilities. Yet such a realization also reopens the possibility of compassion and dissolves the basis on which a choice can be made, for the satiric and the farcical can also be rewritten. In this way, Huxley's satire proves important for the story of modernist feeling not only because it suggests a lack of redemptive

possibilities in modern life, nor only because it spoofs so many preten-
tious intellectuals and bad artists, but also because it begins to question
the cruelty and aloofness that makes satire possible in the first place.

LATE MODERNISM

The story of modernist feeling from the close of the nineteenth century
through the 1920s thus presents no single dominant position, but rather a
series of tonal possibilities and thematic concerns that make possible the
satire of late modernism. The notion of late modernism itself deserves a
few words, since it has only relatively recently emerged as an era worthy of
discrete nomenclature. The reasons for this emergence are numerous: the
expansion of modernist studies beyond the old canon has licensed critical
attention to the twentieth century's middle decades; the exhaustion of
efforts to schematize modernism and postmodernism has invited study of
transitional or anomalous works; the mere march of time has threatened
literary studies with the embarrassment of having to posit a "post-post-
modernism" unless new periodization can be imagined. Thus the rupture
between modernism and postmodernism has opened up to become a
period unto itself, and critics are coming to heed Tyrus Miller's exhort-
ation that the cultural activity of the era cannot be adequately understood
through the concept of transition alone.[97]

Like modernism and postmodernism, the idea of late modernism is
often caught between a narrow chronological sense and a formal and
nonhistorical one, and I try here to avoid both traps. For the sake of
coherence, my focus is on novels of the 1930s, but I make no claim that
late modernism ends abruptly with the Second World War, and
I recognize continuity with earlier works of modernism and later works
of postmodernism. Nor do I claim that the works under study are
exhaustive of the possibilities realized in the 1930s; rather, I identify
something like a cultural dominant, a set of family resemblances in a
group of novels produced in a short space of time. Taken together,
I suggest, the commonalities of the novels I examine appear significant
enough to constitute more than a historical accident, and charting those
commonalities is itself a form of history.

In much literary history, of course, the 1930s have been seen not as an
outgrowth of modernism, but its eclipse. The crisis of the Great Depression, the promises and threats of Communism and fascism, and the
looming possibility of another world war all shifted attention from
aesthetics to politics. Samuel Hynes's *The Auden Generation*, still one of

the most important studies of the decade, discerns in the poetry, fiction, and essays of English writers of the 1930s a steadily increasing pressure to take political action.[98] Confronting politics in a way the writers of the 1920s had not felt compelled to, the Auden group developed a mode Hynes calls parable in order to address these new concerns. Yet, despite certain similarities, the public, civic mode of the Auden generation (or, in the US, the publicly political mode of a new generation of social realists) is by and large not the one adopted by the writers in this study. While the political atmosphere of the decade is visible in some of the works I discuss, and available through critical recovery in others, these writers' politics, when they do appear, are often mitigated by irony, and their extra-fictional commitments represented satirically, if at all.

Alan Wilde, one of the first critics to call the 1930s a period of late modernism, agrees with Hynes that "external events forced on the thirties writers a series of troubling contradictions, centering in particular on the rival claims of artistic vocation and political commitment."[99] He argues that a new emphasis on clarity, transparency and rigor – exemplified by Isherwood's, "I am a camera," or Orwell's comparison of good prose to a clear window – suggests a moral and linguistic severity, a need to see and represent the world clearly.[100] Yet Wilde maintains that even as such new ideals resolve certain tensions between art and politics they also complicate notions of character and self, and he thus turns his focus to subjectivity as a way of marking off phases of modernism. For Wilde the "chief paradox of the decade" becomes the problem of the "subversion of depth through ... attention to surface."[101] Placing the 1930s writers somewhere between the depth-model of modernism and the surface-model of postmodernism, Wilde finds in the turn to surfaces "something like a new sensibility," one which "defines in the most basic way both the moral program of late modernism and the aesthetic retrenchments of its writers."[102] Despite "the assumption of a self" in later modernism, then, there is an agnosticism about the workings of that self: "it is at the last the radically external view that is ascendant ... we can do no more than register the unaccountable and unpredictable vagaries ... of character in all its contradictions."[103]

The category of subjectivity is also important to a major book-length treatment of late modernism, Tyrus Miller's *Late Modernism*. Miller's study, which centers on Barnes, Lewis, and Beckett, shares many of my concerns, including a focus on the role of laughter and satire and the representation of human behavior as shot through with automatism. Miller argues that in the era of late modernism "the vision of a general depersonalization and deauthentication of life in modern society" puts "subjectivity at risk of dissolution," a risk to which satiric laughter and grotesque bodies can be read as responses or symptoms.[104] Miller brings together an apprehension of modernity as secondary and simulated, a view of the self as discontinuous and dispersed, and a literary approach that rejects traditional modernist attempts to preserve or recuperate the self through heroic artistic gestures.

I aim both to extend and to revise Miller's important theorization of late modernism. First, I attempt, through a more thorough unpacking of terms such as satire, grotesque, and uncanny, to add specificity to an understanding of those late modernist concerns with surface and depth, outside and inside, self and character that have been identified by Miller, Wilde, and others.[105] For if an earlier confidence in the ability to represent interiority gives way to a new awareness of human automatism and a reluctance to represent a coherent personality, such awareness and reluctance are deployed in a variety of ways. In some cases, human mechanism is exploited for comic or satiric laughter, whereas in others it constitutes a source of uncanny apprehension.

Second, I would argue that despite his acknowledgement of "an already belated relation to high modernism as ruin,"[106] what Miller describes is often less a late version of modernism than what Marjorie Perloff has called a "counter" or "other" modernism – a tradition that would include works of Pound, Stein, and Marinetti. In Perloff's words, this counter-modernism was "iconoclastically anti-psychological, anti-formalist, and anti-aestheticist" and "its Utopian energies . . . were directed, not toward the making of beautiful autotelic objects, but toward changing the world."[107] As Miller to some degree acknowledges, the ostensibly late-modernist rejection of what he calls "an aesthetics of formal mastery" was always part of the modernist landscape, which at the time doubtless appeared less neatly partitioned than it does to us after generations of critical work.[108] Given the visibility of Lewis, Marinetti, and Pound in pre-First World War London, a Joycean or Eliotic "mythic method" might be seen as a reaction against this iconoclastic, anarchic counter-modernism rather than as a provocation for it. (Michael Levenson's *Genealogy of Modernism* in fact argues for something very much like this account.[109]) Thus Miller's argument slips from a theorization of laughter, satire, and automatism as the central components of late modernism to a more familiar divide between a progressive avant-garde aimed at a poetics of dispersal and a conservative high modernism aimed at sanctifying art. Lawrence Rainey has argued that such a schematization tends to result in invidious and unsustainable comparisons between an elitist and repressive "modernism" and a more "self-aware and emancipatory" tradition embodied in "the historical avant-garde and postmodernism."[110] Satire thus tends to disappear from Miller's analyses of particular texts, in favor of reading his chosen writers as critics of the bad old high modernists: Beckett becomes the anti-Joyce, Barnes the anti-Eliot; Lewis the anti-everyone.

I hardly wish to deny Miller's achievement in identifying a late modernism with a satiric proclivity, and my criticisms should be taken as recognition of the force of his arguments. Yet I would maintain that, for the writers of the 1930s, Lewis, Marinetti, and Pound were as much a part of the landscape in which they found themselves as were Eliot, Woolf, and Joyce. I don't therefore see the late modernists as seeking to overturn the aesthetic project of an ossified "high modernism," for in certain ways they very much sought to extend it. My account of late modernism is consequently not focused on either Hynes's return to the political, or Miller's proto-postmodern poetics of dispersal, nor even Wilde's emphasis on restoring transparency to language in a kind of "moral clarity" of the left. Instead, I focus on understanding the affective ranges of satire, the uses and disadvantages of aloofness, indifference, aggression, cruelty, pleasure, anxiety, and revulsion as they play out through the late modernist novel.

To be sure, the belatedness of the late modernists, their having come after modernism, is central to such an understanding. Joyce, Woolf, and Eliot grew up in a Victorian culture whose residue is evident everywhere in their work, but the writers I discuss were all – with the exception of Djuna Barnes – born after the turn of the century and grew up in an emerging "modernist" culture that was already reinterpreting that older Victorian moment. For this later generation, modernism had already happened; as Henry Green noted, Joyce and Kafka were for his generation "cats who ha[d] licked the plate clean."[111] Michael Gorra argues that the later generation of modernists (at least in England) turns away from the idea of the modernist novel as "having fulfilled the promise of the nineteenth-century novel" in providing "a new sense of freedom."[112] Instead, these writers display a sense of "impotence before history," and a "belief that everything important had happened already"; for Gorra, even as late modernism continues "the modernist attack upon convention," it "can only negate the clichés of [its] culture rather than transcend them."[113] And although his periodization is slightly different, Jameson likewise discerns a belatedness in late modernism: "The situation of the first or classical modernists can never be repeated since they themselves already exist."[114]

At the same time, however, Jameson also seeks to link late modernism to its historical conditions: "Late modernism is a product of the Cold War, but in all kinds of complicated ways ... the Cold War spelled the end of a whole era of social transformation and indeed of Utopian desires and anticipations."[115] Late modernism, in short, turns modernist skepticism against modernism's own revolutionary and romantic tendencies.

Therefore, while I do not see these writers as seeking to overthrow modernism, I do see them as having learned modernism in its many varieties, and in a sense learned it too well. For the writers of the 1930s, modernism was not yet the stuff of textbooks, but it was available by a kind of shorthand, and thus highly susceptible to ironic redescription.[116] This late modernist skepticism toward earlier modernist enthusiasms extends to Lewis's own idiosyncratic version of modernism, and Lewis's aesthetics are consequently no surer guide to late modernist novelistic practices than are Wilde's or Eliot's or Woolf's. Thus Waugh describes in *Vile Bodies* how the once-incendiary style of *Blast* has been adapted for party invitations; Stella Gibbons caricatures D. H. Lawrence's sexualized landscapes; Nathanael West writes of a whorehouse madam who discusses Gertrude Stein to provide an atmosphere of culture; Robin Vote appears in Barnes's *Nightwood* as a figure from an Henri Rousseau landscape; Samuel Beckett transforms Yeats's heroine from the Countess Cathleen to the Countess Caca. Never mind that Waugh endorsed Lewis's theory of satire, that Gibbons's tone embodies Simmel's blasé attitude, that West's own stylizations can sound highly Steinian, that Barnes's novel partakes of the primitivism that she recognizes as a prefabricated form – for all these writers, modernism was no longer new. For the late modernists, sexual transgression had lost its shock, revolutionary manifestos had lost their urgency, and innovation had lost its originality.

Having learned modernism, then, the late modernists represented themselves as more sophisticated than the sophisticates, and their new norms of sophistication are visibly at work in their treatment of feeling. To offer only the briefest of examples, in *The Dream Life of Balso Snell*, Nathanael West's John Gilson finds it impossible to consider the idea of death "sincerely" because his thoughts inevitably take the shape of clichés:

No matter how I form my comment I attach to it the criticisms sentimental, satirical, formal. With these judgments there goes a series of literary associations which remove me still further from genuine feeling. The very act of recognizing Death, Love, Beauty – all the major subjects – has become, from literature and exercise, impossible.[117]

Gilson's immersion in literature, his modernist critical sensibility, prevents the articulation of feeling because all such articulations are recognized as banal. Life becomes a copy of art. Not only the sentimental, but also the satirical and the formal are seen as received literary tropes that prevent an experience original with the self. Thus while modernists rejected sentimentality through various strategies (Wildean aloofness, Lewisian classicism, Eliotic impersonality), the late modernists came to see that those very strategies which had been staked out by their predecessors, and which had pointed the way to satire, failed to resolve their concerns about how to represent feeling – indeed about how to feel. For them, modernism can itself appear as either unpersuasively sentimental (as in Gibbons's version of Lawrence), or unsustainably inhuman (as in Waugh's version of Marinetti). But, either way, modernism turns out to provide more problems than solutions.

Thus many of these works remain skeptical about the reliability of feelings and their expression. In a passage that Waugh used as an epigraph for *Vile Bodies*, Lewis Carroll's *Through the Looking Glass* suggests such a skepticism, although it disguises its insight as a riddle or a joke:

"If I wasn't real," Alice said – half-laughing through her tears, it all seemed so
    ridiculous – "I shouldn't be able to cry."
"I hope you don't think those are real tears?" Tweedledum interrupted in a tone
    of great contempt.[118]

However fictional Alice is, she is certainly no more fictional than Tweedledum, and, she would like to think, probably a little bit less so. Reading these lines from Carroll, we laugh, like Uncle Fester at the movies, at tears which, however false they may appear, stubbornly insist on their own reality. Whether tears are real tears, whether suffering is ridiculous, whether to laugh or cry – these questions preoccupy the fiction of the 1930s, suggesting that because affect itself is so mobile, so given to changing shape and guise, true feeling might never be distinguished from false.[119]

Out of this dilemma the late modernists did fashion their own solutions of a sort. For although the novels I discuss are (except for Gibbons's *Cold Comfort Farm*) generally stories of failure, decay, and abjection, and tend to be more negative and critical than affirmative or utopian, they are by no means monolithically so. Indeed, their very existence still indicates the novelistic achievement of finding a form in which to treat such pessimism or skepticism. This is by no means to say that out of the ashes of life comes the reborn phoenix of art – only that the novels examined here of necessity discover their own representational strategies in confronting problems of feeling. Indeed, these strategies are as interesting for their own failures and contradictions as for their successes in offering clear aesthetic prescriptions or models.

Late modernist satire thus presents a cluster of questions, themes, and strategies rather than a single neat doctrine. It often advances an antihumanist strain of satire and champions various stances – restraint, irony, aloofness, ridicule, aggression – in challenging the perceived inauthenticity of sentimental feeling or moral sentiment within both modernism and its precursors. These stances sometimes endorse or even celebrate the comic-satiric work of affective regulation, ethical detachment, or defiant cruelty. Yet late modernism's wariness of compassion (and its ruses) is also frequently balanced by a creeping wariness of satire's own strategies and consequences; and thus in many novels satire breaks down or gives way to a grotesque aesthetic based in aversive feelings of uncanny anxiety, fear, and revulsion – feelings which furnish a kind of emotional bedrock or Trillingesque authenticity. This self-undoing (of) satire becomes an appealing form for late modernists because it recognizes paradoxes and problems in the moral, aesthetic, and affective standards developed during historical modernity. Late modernist satire thus registers the impact of powerful social and psychological forces on that elusive dimension of human life – how we feel.

CHAPTER 3

The rule of outrage: Evelyn Waugh's Vile Bodies

Evelyn Waugh, even more than Wyndham Lewis, is probably the most enduring satirist among British modernists, though he rejected both labels for his own work.[1] Yet while Lewis's reputation has undergone a triumphant rehabilitation in recent decades, Waugh still suffers from the preconception that his work is minor. Symptomatically, Fredric Jameson's *Fables of Aggression*, a book in part responsible for Lewis's soaring reputation, initiated its restorative project in 1979 precisely at Waugh's expense: "At best, in Britain today, [Lewis] retains a kind of national celebrity and is read as a more scandalous and explosive Waugh."[2] In other words, Waugh is merely a *less* scandalous and explosive Lewis – a less scandalous and explosive version, moreover, of the "old," misread, unreconstructed Lewis, of Lewis the eccentric gadfly rather than of Lewis the radical innovator and analyst of modernity who emerges in Jameson's feverish study. Waugh's rejection of his contemporaries' emphasis on interiority and consciousness cannot wholly account for this omission, for this same rejection has been the very basis for the critical reinstallation of Lewis in the modernist canon. But Waugh has – despite some excellent critical efforts – yet to find a regular place in wider critical accounts of modernism.[3] Located between the high and the low, he fits awkwardly into a narrative of the "great divide"; chronologically, he was born after the "men of 1914" but never belonged to the "Auden generation"; conservative but not extremist, his politics (unlike those of Lewis or Marinetti) have rarely proved interesting to dialecticians.[4] Yet his sensibility exemplifies what I named the Uncle Fester Principle: the idea that modernism can be regarded as a kind of refusal of, or ambivalence toward, affective excess, particularly in the creation of or response to representations of suffering. It is therefore precisely as a satirist that Waugh is necessary to an account of modernism.

47

WAUGH'S "PURGATORIO"

Vile Bodies, Waugh's second novel, merits particular interest not just because it shows his satiric procedure at work, but also because it can be read as a work *about* satire – or at least about the mechanisms of morality, authority, cruelty, and affect that prove central to my understanding of the mode. Published in 1930, it is sometimes described as an English equivalent of *The Sun Also Rises*, a chronicle of the dissolute and spiritually empty lifestyle of a lost generation of young upper-class socialites, whom Waugh calls the "Younger Generation" or the "Bright Young Things." In keeping with the view of Waugh as a cultural conservative, the novel has been read as a satirical condemnation of this set and of the decaying English values that have led them down a moral dead end. Although Waugh had not yet converted to Catholicism when he wrote the book, it is still seen as a critique of modernity and its accompanying irreligious humanism.[5]

While one can hardly deny that Waugh views his characters with a certain disdain, it is important to recognize, as several critics have,[6] that in this novel, as in much of his early fiction, Waugh plays both sides of the fence – he betrays some sympathy for the Bright Young Set even as he subjects them to ridicule. Their vitality animates his novel; their energy is impossible to separate from his own. Moreover, wherever one locates the author's sympathies, the novel offers an elaborate *staging* of the very mechanism by which satire both expresses and engenders moral sentiments. In other words, if Lewis was correct in claiming that "satirists suffer much as a class from an uneasy conscience – are always asking themselves 'how far they may go',"[7] then the satirist's guilty conscience may signal a covert knowledge that he transgresses his own moral sanctions. Consequently, we might be able to read *Vile Bodies* not as, or not only as, a condemnation of the manners and morals of a particular social class, but also as the struggle of a young satiric novelist to explore the constraints of his trade. Waugh's satire proves to be a fruitful text for exploring the satirist's dual role as mouthpiece for and object of public outrage. For the transgressive comedy of *Vile Bodies* invites, even as it levels, charges of immorality and cruelty – charges that for the whole of the author's career would continue to dog the wag.

As observed in Chapter 1, satire has a long association with the idea of hygiene – cleaning the body and the body politic even as it trades in filth. What I call the double movement of satire derives from satire's existence on the borders of socially, politically, or morally muddy terrain. Because it is impossible to clean up without getting dirty, the satirist's moral justification for his attacks contains the possibility – at times, the inevitability – of its own undoing. It is this idea of bodily cleansing, and in particular of satire as purgation, with which I begin my discussion of *Vile Bodies.* For the novel opens with a scene of literal physical purgation; in the rough passage of a boat across the English Channel, almost all of the characters introduced are on the verge of vomiting, and an American evangelist explicitly interprets this physical illness as a moral trial: "If you're put out this way over just an hour's sea-sickness . . . what are you going to be like when you make the mighty big journey that's waiting for us all?" (*VB*, p. 17). No sooner have the passengers reached land, moreover, than another purgation ensues: the second chapter opens in a customs office, whose officers, charged with protecting the health of the nation, attempt to eradicate criminals, contraband, and other pollutants from abroad. They detain two members of the Bright Young Set, the flighty Agatha Runcible and the novel's hero, the aspiring writer Adam Fenwick-Symes.

Adam's troubles begin when he reveals to a customs officer that he is carrying books:

The man's casual air disappeared in a flash.
"Books, eh?" he said. "And what sort of books may I ask?"
"Look for yourself."
"Thank *you*, that's what I mean to do. *Books*, indeed."
Adam wearily unstrapped and unlocked his suitcase.
"Yes," said the Customs officer menacingly, as though his worst suspicions had
    been confirmed, "I should just about say you had got some books."
One by one he took the books out and piled them on the counter. A copy of
    Dante's *Purgatorio* excited his especial disgust.
"French, eh?" he said. "I guessed as much, and pretty dirty, too, I shouldn't
    wonder. Now just you wait while I look up these here books" – how he said
    it! – "in my list . . . If we can't stamp out literature in the country, we can at
    least stop its being brought in from the outside." (*VB*, pp. 22–23)

Although the joke here is largely at the expense of the official who mistakes Dante for pornography, and of the government behind him, Waugh's joke goes deeper than scoring points off a philistine function-ary.[8] There is – as will become increasingly evident – a grain of truth in the error of the customs agent. As anyone knows who has spent time in the "Erotica" section of a mega-bookstore, the line between literature and "literature" is a hazy one. Aesthetic interest can cover less noble motives.

Thus although Waugh is clearly attempting to reduce the censor's stance to the absurd, he keeps alive the notion that literature itself is dangerous. When the customs officer discovers Adam's "memoirs," the manuscript becomes a bomb and Adam an anarchist out of Conrad's *The Secret Agent*: "Gingerly, as though it might at any moment explode, he produced and laid on the counter a large pile of typescript" (*VB*, p. 23). This metaphor of bomb-throwing (to which I will return) then gives way to an excremental metaphor – the memoir is a "*pile* of typescript," "downright dirt" (*VB*, p. 25). The censor is ridding the body politic of its waste. The reference to Dante's *Purgatorio* thus offers an oblique echo of the purgative process being carried out in the customs office. Aesthetically Adam's book is indeed of excremental quality, but more significantly for now its very corporeality makes it suspect. Another banned book mentioned is "Aristotle, Works of (Illustrated)" (*VB*, p. 24), and the parenthetical "Illustrated" implies that any visual representation of the human body is necessarily indecent.[9] By the censor's logic, all books are dirty books, all bodies vile bodies.[10]

From the first pages, then, Waugh places Adam's motives for writing and reading under scrutiny. And as Adam's literary pretensions meet the skepticism of the customs officer, so the customs officer's moral pretensions meet the skepticism of the savvier satirical narrator. It is after all the censor, not Adam, who exhibits the prurient interest in books; the volume of Dante "excited his especial disgust." The customs officer thus resembles the "moral menial" described by William Ian Miller — someone who "perform[s] functions in the moral order similar to those played by garbagemen and butchers in the system of provisioning."[11] Because moral menials trade in moral dirt for the sake of the larger polity, they are necessarily vulnerable to the charge of being excited by their own disgust. Therefore although Adam is the writer of books, the customs officer in his own way performs a function akin to the satirist's in identifying threats to the established order. In his excitement over books, and in his capacity to question such excitement in others, he exhibits the two faces of satiric judgment. This same logic, moreover, is at work in the simultaneous interrogation of Agatha, who, much to the reader's delight, is "mistaken for a well-known jewel-smuggler" and "stripped to the skin by two terrific wardresses" (*VB*, p. 23). Agatha's body is exposed to the reader just as Adam, taken into the "inner office" of the customs bureau, is exposed to the government's cache of confiscated pornography. The novel is beginning to display the vile bodies of its title.

The complementary nature of moral outrage and sexual-sadistic excitement are hardly limited to these opening scenes of interrogation. When Agatha emerges, reapplying lipstick and rouge, she announces that she is going public with her shame: "The way they looked ... too, too shaming. Positively surgical ... As soon as I get to London I shall just ring up every Cabinet Minister and *all* the newspapers and give them all the most shy-making details" (*VB*, p. 24). The mobility of Agatha's affect here is striking: shame is converted first into indignation, then rapidly into exhibitionism. However "shaming" and "shy-making" her experience may have been, Agatha finds such pleasure in her own moral outrage and sexual humiliation that she seeks to publicize them as widely as possible ("every Cabinet Minister," "all the newspapers," "all the details"). Indeed, in the course of the chapter, numerous characters enjoy Agatha's moral outrage; behind this outrage they partake of the prurience, cruelty, and "surgical" invasiveness of the "two terrific wardresses." Agatha tells her friends about her degradation, the newspapers embellish the episode, and the demand for voyeuristic details rises. By that evening the story is that Agatha has "had all her clothes taken off by some sailors" (*VB*, p. 37). At the end of the chapter Adam observes "an indignant old woman" (*VB*, p. 38) reading the evening headline and pronouncing yet another moral judgment: "Disgraceful, I calls it ... Nasty prying minds. That's what they got" (*VB*, p. 39). Prying minds, of course, are what the indignant readers of such stories – and of novels such as *Vile Bodies* – themselves possess.

From an initial affront, then, moral outrage and voyeurism dissipate and multiply through the novel, never losing their complementary nature. Adam's editor, Sam Benfleet, knows exactly what kind of material his market demands: "It was one of his most exacting duties to 'ginger up' the more reticent of the manuscripts submitted and 'tone down' the more 'outspoken' until he had reduced them all to the acceptable moral standard of his day" (*VB*, p. 32). Meeting "the acceptable moral standard of the day" involves not only censorship but "gingering up"; the reading public demands some sex, only not so much that it can no longer deny its own prurience. (The proliferation of scare quotes itself signifies the public demand for euphemism and the sophisticate's derision of it.) Mrs. Ape, the American evangelist, dresses teenage girls as "angels" to attract an audience for her religious cause; eventually she leaves England to "ginger up the religious life of Oberammergau" (*VB*, p. 150). It is no accident that in this novel the once-and-future Prime Minister is named Mr. Outrage: the engine of moral indignation set in motion with Agatha's body search soon leads to the collapse of Prime Minister Brown's government and the return of the rule of Outrage in Britain.

In *Vile Bodies*, then, a novel in which the vileness of the body both attracts and repulses, in which bodies are repeatedly probed, searched, and purged, noble motives are relentlessly exposed or ironically redescribed as justifications for baser ones. And as outrage masks voyeurism, so shame covers for exhibitionism. Despite her "shy-making" humiliation, Agatha hardly seems shy at all. After going public with her story, she shows up at Archie Schwert's party half-naked in "Hawaiian costume" (*VB*, p. 66) ready for the society-page photographers. Such a hypocritical attitude toward publicity was of course every bit as familiar to Waugh's readers as it is today in the age of Diana Spencer and Paris Hilton: "Everyone looked negligent and said what a bore the papers were . . . but most of them, as a matter of fact, wanted dreadfully to be photographed and the others were frozen with unaffected terror that they might be taken unawares and then their mamas would know where they had been" (*VB*, p. 67). In this culture of celebrity permeated by tabloid journalism and hypertrophied exhibitionism, Waugh discerns the fundamental complementarity of private shame and public exposure.

This interrelation of voyeurism and exhibitionism, of outrage and shame, reaches a climax when Agatha, still in Hawaiian costume and finding herself at breakfast with Prime Minister Brown and his family at 10 Downing Street, covers her (still mild) embarrassment by reading aloud from the gossip pages. She finds herself reading about her own exploits the previous night, satisfying her voyeuristic tastes with an account of her own exhibitionist behavior. She now simultaneously produces and consumes public outrages – incidents which, interpreted by newspapers and other mechanisms of publicity, supply narratives, images, and feelings for public consumption. And it is only through the illuminating power of these mechanisms of publicity that Agatha discovers where and in whose company she is breakfasting:

Suddenly the light came flooding in on Miss Runcible's mind as once when, in her debutante days, she had gone behind the scenes at a charity matinee, and returning had stepped through the wrong door and found herself in a blaze of flood-lights onstage in the middle of the last act of Othello. "Oh my God!" she said, looking round the Brown breakfast table . . .

Then she turned round and trailing garlands of equatorial flowers fled out of the room and out of the house to the huge delight and profit of the crowd of reporters and Press photographers who were already massed round the historic front door. (*VB*, pp. 74–75)

Agatha's realization jolts her into a moment of shame; transformed from the agent of mockery to its target, she recognizes that she has been laughing at herself. In a delightful further irony, her flight from the floodlights (both the gazing eyes of the Brown family and the remembered spotlights of the play) takes her once again through the wrong door and out into a third blaze of light, the popping flashbulbs of the press. Her embarrassed and hasty exit exposes itself as a grand and dramatic entrance ("trailing garlands of equatorial flowers"). The escape from voyeurism proves to be an even greater subjection to it; life and performance are one.

Far from merely offering a bitter chronicle of a morally dissolute social set, then, *Vile Bodies* deftly anatomizes the social and psychological mechanisms of outrage and shame and the voyeurism and exhibitionism that they barely conceal. And so in those moments when the facade of morality falls away from these feelings, the result is plain cruelty. Agatha's friends are cheered by tales of her suffering, while Adam amuses his fiancée Nina with the story of the hapless Simon Balcairn being "horse-whipped" at the newspaper office (*VB*, pp. 121–22). Later, at the motor races, spectators make no effort to hide their sadism, cheerily discussing "the possibilities of bloodshed," and seeking out "the most dangerous corners" (*VB*, p. 230) as viewing places. (Nathanael West describes a similar phenomenon in *The Day of the Locust* with his portrait of Californians hoping for the violence of a plane crash to relieve their boredom.) Insurers look to make money off the risk of dismemberment, while religious fanatics proclaim bloodshed necessary for salvation. Even boys seeking autographs are "predatory" (*VB*, p. 225).

The novel thus constitutes a veritable catalog of instances in which morality is exposed as voyeurism, exhibitionism, and cruelty. As a satire, *Vile Bodies* ostensibly performs this exposure not only to elicit laughter, but also to call attention to the corruption of a modern culture that disguises its meanest motives with such claims. Yet if calling attention to such vice remains a perennial justification for satire, this justification can hardly escape its own demystifying logic. Indeed, the author's willingness to use death – Flossie Ducane's fatal drunken fall from a chandelier, Simon's suicide after his failure as a columnist, Agatha's death after her crash in the auto race – to elicit laughter fatally undoes any claim to moral authority. In short, *Vile Bodies* cannot help but expose its own morality to the same charges of hypocrisy that it levels. Waugh's critique reveals that the satirist is, in Michael Seidel's formulation, "implicated in the debasing form of his action."[12] It is thus not only the young writer Adam whose motives are questioned, but also the young writer of *Vile Bodies* himself. As the moral pretense of English public opinion stands exposed as naked bloodlust, so too does that of the satirist and his laughing reader.

Of course, this is not to suggest that the *only* impulse behind the reading and writing of Waugh's novels is cruelty. In fact, one function of Waugh's exposure of cruelty – his own and his characters' – often appears precisely to be obtaining some purchase on the reader's sympathy by "proving" the author's unsentimental attitude toward suffering. Thus many critics have remarked with admiration on Waugh's capacity to evoke sympathy in the midst of cruelty, pity in the midst of irony, by the subtlest modulations in tone. Because death and loss are presented in laconic, undemonstrative, or ironically amused language, Waugh can conjure sympathy without courting melodrama.[13] But (as will become clearer in Chapter 4), what is notable is that such emotion is arrived at only by subtraction. Affective minimalism is necessary precisely because Waugh has mounted a pervasive interrogation of various emotions, threatening ironically to redescribe all virtuous feelings as justifications for baser ones. Still, despite this emotional restraint, affect abounds in *Vile Bodies* – it just exists in the wrong places. On the personal scale, it appears almost absent as characters and narrator alike regard various cataclysms with wry amusement or blasé indifference. But, in the public sphere, outrage, excitement, and shame appear as excessive, attaching themselves to the nearest and frequently most trivial objects at hand.

ALL THE TERRORS OF THE PSEUDO

In *Vile Bodies*, then, the satirist is implicated in his own dismantling of the moral sentiments of his characters, and reveals, through his treatment of others, the processes by which his own implicit claims to moral authority can sanction a wide variety of transgression. I now want to turn to a parallel process in the novel – how the satirist's stance toward modernity's conflation of fiction and reality reveals a similar ambivalence in which a subversive delight in the chaotic comic possibilities of this conflation is balanced by a "conservative" anxiety over the loss of a moral and epistemological certainty that accompanies a confidence in a stable idea of reality. For the interpenetration of fiction and reality characterizes Waugh's entire vision of modernity. His satires, *Vile Bodies* chief among them, describe the processes by which, in an age of mechanical reproduction, forms of mass communication seem to place human beings more than ever before at a remove from the world they inhabit. This is the condition that Tyrus Miller has described as a "condition of generalized mimetism"[14] and which I argued in Chapter 2 is a central concern of the satires of Wyndham Lewis and Aldous Huxley. Contemporary literary theory of course knows these themes well, but even in the 1910s and 1920s writers were beginning to identify a new tear in the fabric of reality, as in D. H. Lawrence's scornful remarks: "Heaven knows what we mean by reality. Telephone, tinned meat, Charlie Chaplin, water-taps, and World-Salvation, presumably."[15]

A more ambitious analysis of this new (un)reality came in Walter Lippmann's 1922 *Public Opinion*, where the journalist-turned-political scientist described the object of his study as "the human response" not to public events themselves but to a "pseudo-environment" created through the representation of events in the mass media and inserted "between man and his environment."[16] "Those pictures [of the environment]," writes Lippmann, "which are acted upon by groups of people, or by individuals acting in the name of groups, are Public Opinion with capital letters."[17] According to Lippmann, Public Opinion – a collective human response to the pseudo-environment – has effects in the real world behind those representations. The existence of this collective opinion thus allows the public to affect events it has never directly experienced. This new kind of mass experience, he argues, requires a new kind of analysis: "The analyst of public opinion must begin then, by recognizing the triangular relationship between the scene of action, the human picture of that scene, and the human response to that picture working itself out upon the scene of action."[18]

As we saw briefly in Beerbohm and Huxley, this new understanding of how feeling circulates through a vast public that is given coherence through mass-mediated images and narratives provides satire with cause for anxiety and scorn about the loss of truth, certainty, and individuality. As Michael North and Justus Nieland have both argued, the public sphere during this time came to be seen not (in Habermasian fashion) as a neutral marketplace of ideas for rational debate and consensus-building but rather as an arena permeated by unconscious prejudices and uninformed opinion.[19] *Vile Bodies*, indeed, goes beyond *Zuleika Dobson* and *Antic Hay* in the extent to which it attempts to represent the opinions of an inchoate public rather than just those of individuals. Like Lippmann's *Public Opinion*, *Vile Bodies* offers an anxious analysis of the "triangular relationship" between actual events, public representations of them, and personal and collective responses to those representations; like Lippmann decrying the dangers of the pseudo-environment, Waugh too specifically warns against "all the terrors of the pseudo."[20] Of course, Waugh's novel, unlike Lippmann's treatise, also delights in the potential for absurdity that the terrors of the pseudo generate; the destabilizing, disruptive force of modernity always provides for Waugh the consolation of good material. And far more than his precursors Beerbohm and Huxley, Waugh is able fully to exploit the opportunities for comic misunderstanding that arise when the mechanisms of the pseudo-environment are laid bare.

In the 1920s and 1930s, the primary way in which the pseudo-environment was "inserted" between the public and its environment was through newspapers. Patrick Collier has detailed the ways in which, during these decades, newspapers were often blamed for the promotion of intellectual laziness, the cultivation of a taste for the sensational, the corruption of the English language, and the malfunctioning of an expanding democracy.[21] Consequently, an analysis of the interaction of the press, the stories it reports, and the reading public is among Lippmann's major concerns. The economic motives of the newspaper industry, Lippmann recognizes, demand the loyalty of a consuming readership, a public which in turn demands that "facts" be presented within a familiar narrative – as Lippmann says, within "a pattern of stereotypes":[22]

> News which does not offer this opportunity to introduce oneself into the struggle which it depicts cannot appeal to a wide audience. The audience must participate in the news, much as it participates in the drama, by personal identification. Just as everyone holds his breath when the heroine is in danger, as he helps Babe Ruth swing his bat, so in subtler form the reader enters into the news. In order that he shall enter he must find a familiar foothold in the story, and this is supplied to him by the use of stereotypes.[23]

Since news is so constrained by stereotypes (the word is Lippmann's coinage), Lippmann questions the belief that the press can safeguard the operation of democracy by keeping a public informed. On the contrary, "analysis of the nature of news and of the economic basis of journalism seems to show that the newspapers necessarily and inevitably reflect, and therefore . . . intensify, the defective organization of public opinion."[24] Yet while the defective organization of public opinion can be disturbing, it also creates room for some of Waugh's most pervasive jokes in both this novel and the later *Scoop*, where the fictional reports of incompetent war journalists in Africa ultimately have global political consequences. In both novels the desire of the newspaper writer to get the facts gives way to his desire to get the story, news is constrained by stereotypes, and invented objects take on almost Borgesian extratextual existence.

In *Vile Bodies*, the newspaper writer who takes center stage is not the war correspondent but the gossip columnist, and in his creation of a fictional pseudo-environment he becomes, through the power and range of his invention, a stand-in for the novelist. Both are inventors, observers of manners and morals, experts on the intimate. The first comparisons between the two figures are implicit, attributing to both figures an inside knowledge and an inventive power: regarding Outrage's travels in Paris we learn that "what [his bodyguards] did not know about his goings on was not worth knowing, at least from a novelist's point of view" (*VB*, p. 5); of Simon, the narrator remarks with weary identification, "It is so depressing to be in a profession in which literally all conversation is 'shop'" (*VB*, p. 114); later Simon creates "lie after monstrous lie" (*VB*, p. 144) in his final column. But the similarity between novelist and columnist becomes explicit only in the second half of the novel, once Adam himself takes over for the (now-dead) Simon as "Mr. Chatterbox." Forbidden from mentioning any of the personalities libeled in Simon's raving swansong column, Adam begins "a series of 'Noble Invalids,' which was, from the first, wildly successful" (*VB*, p. 153). He writes about "deaf peers and statesmen, then about the one-legged, blind and bald" (*VB*, p. 153), painting deliberately sentimental portraits of stoical sufferers that elicit approving letters from all over England. Inventing freely, Adam completely inverts the genre of the gossip column, playing on the moral self-satisfaction that accompanies sympathy rather than the moral outrage that accompanies voyeurism. He replaces the sensational and the pornographic with the sentimental in exactly the way that television news shows do when they balance tales of sex crimes with human-interest features about dogs and cats saving children from floods or fires. The facility with which Adam effects this inversion reinforces the connection between the moral claims of sentimental narratives and their voyeuristic underside.

Although this critique of the sentimental remains a constant throughout Waugh's early fiction, Adam drops the Noble Invalids series and instead begins creating characters out of the blue. This outright fictionalizing cements the identification of gossip writer and novelist and further demonstrates the comic possibilities in the last leg of Lippmann's triangle: "human response ... working itself out upon the scene of action." The comedy lies not simply in Adam's wanton fictionalizing but in the way his fictional characters begin to inhabit reality. When Lord Vanburgh, a rival columnist, picks up on Adam's creations, and spins new stories about their private lives, Adam, with the same territoriality that Cervantes showed in reclaiming Don Quixote from Avellaneda, contests Vanburgh's tales by creating newer ones to contradict them. His fictional characters become celebrities, and their outlandish habits (most notably the wearing of a bottle-green bowler hat) become current fashion.

But even this strategy taxes Adam's powers, and he finds his creativity running dry: "As a last resort, on those hopeless afternoons when invention failed and that black misanthropy settled on him which await alike on gossip writer and novelist, Adam sometimes found consolation in seizing upon some gentle and self-effacing citizen and transfiguring him with a blaze of notoriety" (*VB*, p. 161). The narrator not only underscores, yet again, the parallel between Adam the columnist and Waugh the novelist, but also explicitly recognizes the ignoble emotions that can inform fictional creation. If in other places it is sexual prurience or greed that contaminates the satirist's moral motives, here it is "black misanthropy." The "blaze" of notoriety, like the "blaze" of publicity that greets Agatha as she flees 10 Downing Street, offers heat as well as light.

To its chaotic mingling of reality and fiction the novel opposes Lottie Crump's hotel, a place with old-fashioned customs and decor, a haven from modern confusion where one "can still draw up, cool and uncontaminated, great, healing draughts from the well of Edwardian certainty" (*VB*, pp. 40–41). Yet such certainty, a vestige from a lost pre-war world, itself exists only within the pseudo – within a cheesy simulacrum of Edwardian England. More typical of Waugh's modernity is the estate of Nina's father, Doubting Hall ("Doubting 'All" (*VB*, p. 86)), where the senile Colonel Blount mistakes identities, misconstrues meanings, and utters total non sequiturs. Adam, on his first visit, is greeted by a man he does not yet know is the Colonel in an extravagant vaudevillian exchange:

"What do you want?"
"Is Mr. Blount in?"
"There's no Mr. Blount here. This is Colonel Blount's house."
"I'm sorry . . . I think the Colonel is expecting me to luncheon."
"Nonsense. I'm Colonel Blount," and he shut the door . . .
Adam rang again.
"Yes," said Colonel Blount, appearing instantly.
"I'd wonder if you'd let me telephone to the station for a taxi?"
"Not on the telephone . . . It's raining. Why don't you come in? Have you come
     about the vacuum cleaner?"
"No."
"Funny, I've been expecting a man all the morning to show me a vacuum cleaner.
     Come in, do. Won't you stay to luncheon?"
"I should love to." . . .
They shook hands . . . Colonel Blount picked up a telegram and read it.
"I'd quite forgotten," he said in some confusion. "I'm afraid you'll think me very
     discourteous, but it is, after all, quite impossible for me to ask you to
     luncheon. I have a guest coming on very intimate family business. You

understand, don't you? ... To tell you the truth, it's some young rascal who
wants to marry my daughter ..."
"Well, I want to marry your daughter, too," said Adam.
"What an extraordinary coincidence. Are you sure you do?"
"Perhaps the telegram may be about me. What does it say?"
"'Engaged to marry Adam Symes. Expect him luncheon. Nina.' Are you Adam
Symes?"
"Yes."
"My dear boy, why didn't you say so, instead of going on about a vacuum
cleaner? How are you?"
They shook hands again. (*VB*, pp. 89–91)

Such comic confusions of logic and identity, indeed, are hardly confined to
Doubting Hall; throughout the text we see instances of absurd coincidence,
mistaken identity, and the confusion of the fictional and the real.

Vile Bodies is in fact populated by an epidemic of nonexistent people
and false names, of which Adam's creations for his gossip column are only
the most prominent. When Adam first calls Nina, they both pretend that
it is not she who answers the phone:

"May I speak to Miss Blount, please?"
"I'll just see if she's in," said Miss Blount's voice ... She was always rather
snobbish about this fiction of having someone to answer the telephone.
(*VB*, p. 37)

When Sam Benfleet gives bad news to his writers, he invokes the name of
his cruel-hearted and penny-pinching boss, "Old Rampole," who turns
out to be, if not quite fictional, the nearest equivalent: he never reads a
single contract, and his "chief interest in the company was confined to a
little book of his own about bee-keeping, which they had published
twenty years ago and, though he did not know it, allowed long ago to
drop out of print" (*VB*, p. 36). The night they first have sex, Adam and
Nina sign false names in the hotel guest book (*VB*, p. 120). Colonel
Blount signs his name "Charlie Chaplin" on the check he gives Adam
(*VB*, p. 109). Adam, Nina, Ginger, and Agatha sign more false names
when they go out clubbing (*VB*, p. 172). Simon, Adam, and Nina all take
on the nom de plume "Mr. Chatterbox." And, in the final chapter, Adam
returns to Doubting Hall on its own absurd terms; without the slightest
physical disguise and to the astonishment of the help, he commits
adultery with Nina while nonchalantly assuming the identity of her
husband, Ginger.

But while the proliferation of the pseudo is the source of much laughter
in *Vile Bodies*, this fakery has a dark side, and the pseudo has its terrors.

Many commentators have observed the gradually darkening tone of the novel: the manic energy of the Younger Generation peters out, the delight in anarchy gives way to world-weariness, the amused voice of the satirist becomes moralistic and strident. But although several critics have argued that the novel is fundamentally inconsistent in tone, and have traced this inconsistency to Waugh's discovery of his wife's affair and the darkening of his own personal mood,[25] the weariness of the novel's second half retains significant continuity with the energy of the first. Just as the moral outrage of gossip readers leaves behind the negative image of the cruel bloodlust of the spectators at the motor races, so the relatively benign comedy of the Colonel's illogic has as its underside the uncanny exposure of the mind in a state of decomposition. Instead of the Colonel's daffiness, it is Agatha's delirium that takes center stage in the latter half of the book. When Adam visits her in the hospital, she notes that "people are disappearing" (*VB*, p. 266); it is not just that the young people's parties are breaking up, but that the proliferation of extraneous, invented, and imagined characters in the text now seems to be reversing itself. The final, lame semblance of a party in the hospital room leads to a worsening of Agatha's condition as she slides into hallucination:

> She was sitting bolt upright in bed, smiling deliriously, and bowing her bandaged head to imaginary visitors.
> "*Darling*," she said. "How *too* divine … how *are* you? … and how are *you*? … how angelic of you all to come … only you must be careful not to fall out at the corners … ooh, just missed it. There goes that nasty Italian car … I wish I knew which thing was which in this car … darling, do try and drive more straight, my sweet, you were nearly into me then … Faster …"
> (*VB*, p. 271)

Reason withdraws, as perception, memory, and fantasy are intermingled in a phantasmagoric collage. The recombination of conscious and unconscious material, of the real and the fantastic, creates that juxtaposition of the ludicrous and the fearsome that Ruskin saw as the essence of the grotesque. Of course, the withdrawal of reason in Agatha's mind is only an extreme case of the apparent withdrawal of reason in the modern world outside. But if the previous lunacies of Colonel Blount have weighted the balance toward the comic and the fanciful, here the madness takes on more unsettling tones. The "imaginary visitors" who assume such vibrant reality throughout the novel are now solely confined to Agatha's mind.[26] The pleasurable presence of fantasy in the world gives way to a chilling sense of a dangerous loss of control.

The interpenetration of fantasy and reality that permeates *Vile Bodies* clearly anticipates the metafictions of postmodernism, but Waugh links the phenomenon to Lewis Carroll, from whom he borrows his two epigraphs for the novel. The second epigraph presents the entanglement of fiction and reality as a problem bound up with questions of feeling:

> "If I wasn't real," Alice said – half-laughing through her tears, it all seemed so ridiculous – "I shouldn't be able to cry."
> "I hope you don't think those are real tears?" Tweedledum interrupted in a tone of great contempt. (*VB*, unnumbered p.)

The insistence on the fictionality of what appears to be a real world is in keeping with Waugh's later position, taken in denying the satirical nature of his work, that "the artist's only service to the disintegrated society of today is to create little independent systems of order of his own."[27] But despite Waugh's, and Tweedledum's, insistence on the line between fiction and reality, the reader is caught up in the pleasure and illogic of the paradoxes that the epigraph implies. As Robert Murray Davis comments, Waugh uses the epigraph "both to deny and affirm the reality of his characters' suffering."[28] Alice's combination of laughter at the ridiculous and tears over her own suffering thus epitomizes the mixed emotional response that Waugh's fictions often provoke. Is the epigraph an affirmation of the power of lunacy to leaven sadness? A cold denial of human suffering for the sake of a fictional construction? A claim that emotions evoked by unreal events should not themselves be considered genuine?[29] The text may sanction all of these interpretations to different degrees, but perhaps the most persuasive reading is that there will always be one more level of fictionality to our (pseudo-) environment than we are aware of. One may say that we should not cry over fictional events, but we do and we will, despite being told not to. Living in pseudo-environments among pseudo-events and pseudo-people, we will all inevitably experience pseudo-feelings.

EVERYONE IS A BOMB: ESPIONAGE, ANARCHY, MODERNISM

We have seen in *Vile Bodies* how moral feelings such as shame, outrage, and even sympathy are exposed as doing satire's dirty work, licensing the pleasures of cruelty, voyeurism, and self-display. Satire similarly enjoys, even as it decries, modernity's confusion of the fictional and the real, a confusion that calls into question not only the reality of our environment but also the authenticity of our emotional responses to it. In turning to the rather vague political subplot of *Vile Bodies*, I want to trace a third, parallel contradiction in the satirist's stance, a contradiction in his attitude toward anarchy and the latent political and social implications of modernism.

In *The Auden Generation*, his landmark study of English literature in the 1930s, Samuel Hynes remarks that "Waugh was the first English novelist to see his own time as a period *entre deux guerres*";[30] while previous writers examined the fallout of the First World War, *Vile Bodies* makes repeated, if subtle, references to both the past war and the "coming war" of which Father Rothschild speaks (*VB*, p. 184) and with which the novel ends. Hynes links the dissolution of the Bright Young Set not just to a general human condition or the particulars of Waugh's biography, but to the political crosscurrents of a turbulent historical moment. The novel actually suggests connections between the events of the front page and those of the gossip columns quite overtly, as when Simon laments that he can't write about Agatha because "they're featuring her as a front-page news story tomorrow over this Customs House business" (*VB*, p. 62). Amid the rounds of party going, political instability is subtly but persistently present in this England of "the near future": the government of Great Britain changes repeatedly; Adam has an economics textbook confiscated along with his ill-fated memoir; on the first page of the novel, a Jesuit from a family of international Jewish bankers is revealed to be carrying a false beard in his suitcase.

But what exactly is the nature of this relationship between a vague suggestion of political subterfuge and a reckless lifestyle of party going? Within the novel, the editorial page – that mechanism which, according to Lippmann, "reinforce[s]" public opinion by "giv[ing] the reader a clue by which he engages himself"[31] – provides an easy answer. Upon the collapse of Brown's government, "The *Evening Standard* had a leading article, which drew a fine analogy between Public and Domestic purity, between sobriety in the home and in the state" (*VB*, p. 100). Yet the narrator's ironic intonations render such fine analogies facile. The novel attempts another answer when Lord Metroland asks Father Rothschild whether the current political instability can explain "why my stepson should drink like a fish and go about everywhere with a negress" (*VB*, p. 185), and Rothschild can offer no definitive response, no overarching theory: "I think they're connected … But it's all very difficult" (*VB*, p. 185). In this case the connection is not too easy but too vexed. Hynes himself suggests that the behavior of the Bright Young People is a generation's self-definition, achieved through a "withdraw[al] from history, into parties, into a passive submission to accidental events,"[32] a reaction to political forces that seem too vast for them to master or oppose. But even this explanation, while more expansive than those the text explicitly offers, fails to address the question of why their retreat should so resemble the political activities from which they are withdrawing, why the distinction between the news pages and the gossip pages should dissolve so easily. Ultimately, the novel seems stubbornly to refrain from answering the question of whether the connection between large-scale political instability and small-scale social anarchy is causal or coincidental.

But if this lack of an articulated connection "between Public and Domestic purity" might limit the extent to which *Vile Bodies* can be read as offering any specific political insight into Europe on the verge of war, it also reinforces the reader's sense of an omnipresent and polymorphous threat of chaos and instability. It is worth noting that instability, whether social or political, is often represented in the novel by the foreign, and in particular by a sexualized racial other: Margot sends Chastity to South America to undertake her career as a prostitute; the object of Prime Minister Outrage's adulterous advances is a Japanese Baroness; Mrs. Ape's religious revival is compared to "a negro camp-meeting in Southern America" (*VB*, p. 143); Prime Minister Brown mistakes Agatha for "a dancing Hottentot woman" (*VB*, p. 74); and images of "savages," especially "Red Indians" recur frequently. Yet this imagery does not identify real sources of disorder or subversion so much as it tinges Waugh's London with a pervasive sense of having been already irreversibly contaminated by the foreign. Images of a pristine and pure England are invoked, but only to mock the idea of purity, as when Ginger garbles John of Gaunt's famous "sceptred isle" speech from *Richard II*. In *Vile Bodies*, a pristine England only exists in Shakespearean monologues.

The novel might even be said to aspire in its very structure to keep the foreign element on the fringe; it begins on the English Channel and ends on a battlefield in France, while otherwise remaining within the geographical boundaries of England. The seasickness of the ferry passengers, furthermore, mirrors Nina's sickness on the airplane as she leaves England for her honeymoon, another physical purgation marking passage in and out of the nation. The novel thus presents a contradiction between a desire to contain anarchic forces by locating them in specific foreign elements, and an acknowledgement (with Rothschild) of the virtual impossibility of articulating the connection between large-scale political and small-scale social turmoil. In this contradictory logic, the novel perfectly reproduces the thinking of the customs officer when he declares, "If we can't stamp out literature in the country, we can at least stop its being brought in from the outside" (*VB*, p. 23); an ideal of purity is invoked with the same gesture that dismisses it as an unrealizable fantasy.

The most visible internal threat to the body politic is the press itself. The specter of espionage, arising in the customs house when Adam is seen as a potential anarchist, reappears when Simon penetrates Margot's party disguised as a clergyman in a false beard. The leaders of the older generation – Rothschild, Outrage, and Metroland – expose him in a scene that parodies the genre of the spy novel:

> Suddenly Father Rothschild turned out the light.
> "There's someone coming down the passage," he said.
> "Quick, get behind the curtains." ...
> The three statesmen hid themselves ... They heard the door open. The light was turned on. A match was struck. Then came the slight tinkle of the telephone as someone lifted the receiver.
> "*Now*," said Father Rothschild, and stepped through the curtain.
> The bearded stranger who had excited his suspicions was standing at the table smoking one of Lord Metroland's cigars and holding the telephone ...
> "Stay exactly where you are," said Father Rothschild, "and take off that beard."
> (*VB*, p. 139)

Incongruously imposing the high drama of an act of international espionage on the apprehension of a petty newspaperman, the scene hints at an anxiety about the illicit and subversive potential of the gossip columnist himself. It epitomizes the way that the threat of political subversion is comically deflected and diffused into episodes of moral, social, and even ontological disorder (e.g., Adam's creation of fictional beings), while at the same time betraying the high stakes of the novel's anxiety about its own trade in gossip.

The repeated images of bombs, flashes, and explosions reveal a similar structure, gesturing toward the wars and revolutions on the Continent, but ultimately returning to the material of the gossip pages. In Lottie Crump's hotel, the former "King of Ruritania," a refugee of the First World War, laments the demise of his wife, who, after the assassination of many royal relatives, now "thinks everyone is a bomb" (*VB*, pp. 44–45). But despite the genuinely murderous consequences of the political bomb-throwing she has witnessed, other explosions in the novel seem dangerous only by way of the facile public–private analogy proffered by the editorial pages. In the customs office, Adam's memoir was treated as an explosive device; at Doubting Hall, he misunderstands the "shooting" of Wesleyans to mean the massacre of religious dissenters rather than the creation of a commercial film. The film, when it gets shown, itself disappears in a flash of light with "a sudden crackling sound," and "a long blue spark" (*VB*, p. 302), while at Archie Schwert's party "There were two men with a lot of explosive powder taking photographs in another room. Their flashes and bangs had rather a disquieting effect on the party" (*VB*, p. 66). The flashes and bangs are like the "blazes" that publicize Agatha and Ginger; publicity, like terrorism, is represented with a burst of light. In sum, the gossip columnist is taken for a spy, the memoirist a terrorist, the filmmaker an executioner, the press photographer a bomb-thrower. All these figures might be seen as stand-ins for the novelist-satirist, who, as we have seen, resembles the columnist in his creation of narratives and images for public consumption, and who now, like Simon in his false beard, proves subversive to the state.

However ambivalently *Vile Bodies* treats this association of political anarchy and aesthetic activity, the link was of course familiar in the climate of literary modernism, despite the later separation by critics of a politically revolutionary "avant-garde" from a formalistic "modernism." Waugh's own position toward radical aesthetic practices, moreover, was in 1930 considerably more ambiguous and uneasy than his later disparagement of Joyce and others might suggest. The pastiche composition of *Vile Bodies* itself has been seen as an outgrowth of modernist experiments, and Waugh saw his work as learning from the formal innovations of Firbank, who, Waugh wrote in 1929, discarded "the chain of cause and effect," and "from the fashionable chatter of his period, vapid and interminable ... plucked, like tiny brilliant feathers from the breast of a bird, the particles of his design."[33] Remaining "objective" where other modernists are "forced into a subjective attitude," Firbank's novels mark a specifically technological advance; they "may be compared to cinema films, in which the relation of caption and photograph is directly reversed; occasionally a brief, visual image flashes out to illumine and explain the flickering succession of spoken words."[34]

In addition to Firbank (who might represent the indifference I have argued is characteristic of modernism's aestheticist moment), the novel also engages with the more politically volatile Futurist moment. Waugh's own distaste for the aestheticist tendency to wallow in drowsy numbness, and his preference for literature that engages with the technological changes of its time, is put quite clearly in his 1930 essay on the 1890s:

The truth is that the poor decadents were, less than anyone, in touch with their own age. All the time that they imagined themselves lapsing into over-civilized and slightly drugged repose, that apostle of over-civilization, Mr. Edison, was hard at work devising the telephone bell which was to render the whole of the next generation permanently sleepless.[35]

For Waugh, the noise and energy of the machine, with the excess social activity they induce, are the true legacy of the 1890s, rather than the aristocratic retreat from daily life; he sides here with the Futurist embrace of change rather than aestheticist retreat from noise. Shortly after the publication of *Vile Bodies*, Waugh reviewed Lewis's pamphlet, "Satire and Fiction," which would later be incorporated into *Men Without Art*. He found Lewis's ideas on satire, and in particular on the "external method" of rendering of character (in opposition to the dominant modernist emphasis on interiority and subjectivity), to be particularly valuable for his own writing: "The whole of this part [Lewis's theory of satire] is immensely interesting, particularly the observations about the 'Outside and Inside' method of fiction. No novelist . . . can afford to neglect this essay."[36] George McCartney in fact has argued that Waugh relied on Lewis for a theoretical articulation of his opposition to the perceived irrationalism of Bergsonian vitalism.[37]

Yet even if Waugh the critic finds Lewis philosophically congenial, Waugh the author of *Vile Bodies* does not spare Lewis his ironic derision. The novel makes teasing reference to party invitations "that Johnnie Hoop used to adapt from *Blast* and Marinetti's *Futurist Manifesto*. These had two columns of close print; in one was a list of all the things Johnnie hated, and in the other all the things he thought he liked" (*VB*, p. 65). The avant-garde aesthetic has been reduced to an empty fad. (This is, as I have noted, a recurrent motif in late modernist satire, where earlier revolutionary modernisms are ironically redescribed as passing fashion or outworn cliché.) Such skepticism toward the antihumanist side of avant-garde aesthetics is consistent with Waugh's 1928 representation of Otto Silenus in *Decline and Fall*. An émigré architect, Silenus understands the challenge of modern aesthetics to be "the elimination of the human element from considerations of form."[38] He claims: "The only perfect building must be the factory, because that is built to house machines, not men . . . All ill comes from man."[39] In case the satiric accents are not strong enough, the narrator adds, "His only other completed work was the *décor* for a cinema film of great length and complexity of plot – a complexity rendered the more inextricable by the producer's austere elimination of all human characters, a fact which proved fatal to its commercial success."[40]

In *Vile Bodies*, however, it is the motor races that offer the most extended critique of anarchic or revolutionary modernism, and the main target is Marinetti's Futurism.[41] Not only is the most ruthless driver in the race an Italian named Marino, but Marinetti's whole aesthetic of machines and motion is parodied. Marinetti of course upheld the machine and specifically the automobile as the emblem of his new movement:

We say that the world's magnificence has been enriched by a new beauty; the beauty of speed. A racing car whose hood is adorned with great pipes, like serpents of explosive breath – a roaring car that seems to ride on grapeshot – is more beautiful than the *Victory of Samothrace*.[42]

The narrator of *Vile Bodies* opines that "motor cars offer a very happy illustration of the metaphysical distinction between 'being' and 'becoming'" (*VB*, p. 227), and while this passage has sometimes been taken as Waugh's endorsement of a machine aesthetic, the ironic tone of the next paragraph calls that endorsement into question:

Not so the *real* cars, that become masters of men; those vital creations of metal who exist solely for their own propulsion through space, for whom their drivers, clinging precariously at the steering wheel, are as important as his stenographer to a stock-broker. These are in perpetual flux; a vortex of combining and disintegrating units. (*VB*, pp. 227–28)

The cybernetic merging of human and machine is described as a mélange of Bergson ("vital," "flux"), Marinetti ("cars," "metal"), and Lewis and Pound ("vortex"), and the narrator seems as skeptical of the dehumanization of art as he is excited by it. Like the malfunctioning film projector, the race car does not embody the transcendent possibility of a new modern age, but only futility. When Adam and his friends visit the Speed King, the sight is hardly an aesthetic wonder:

The engine was running and the whole machine shook with fruitless exertion. Clouds of dark smoke came from it, and a shattering roar, which reverberated from concrete floor and corrugated iron roof into every corner of the building so that speech and thought became insupportable and all the senses were numbed. (*VB*, pp. 225–26)

Marinetti's vaunted motion and speed are reduced to "fruitless exertion" as the human element is extinguished by the mechanical. Once again we have imagery of smoke, followed by the "shattering roar," if not the exploding light, of some unseen combustion. The revolutionary potential of the machine aesthetic that overcomes human limitations is redescribed as purposeless and dehumanizing sensory overload.

To mock this most aggressively antihumanist strain of modernism that Lewis and Marinetti represent would seem less remarkable if it did not come so close to an indictment of Waugh's own satiric method,

which seems to draw on the very externalist, almost behaviorist, prescriptions that Lewis himself offered. In other words, the target of the
satire seems dangerously close to the very aspects of modernity that
satire itself embodies. For if satire diagnoses the mechanization of the
human, it also brings about, even celebrates, this mechanization.
Numerous readers of Waugh have noted that keeping his characters
weak, passive, and unheroic is central to his technique; they remain less
fully developed in their humanity than the implied author.[43] Waugh's
socialites are named to represent their status as objects rather than
subjects: the Bright Young *Things*. And Agatha's madness, as we have
seen, is unsettling, even uncanny, in its revelation of human character
as mechanistic.[44] Waugh's satiric attacks on antihumanist, Marinettian,
and Lewisian modernism thus implicate the novel's own dehumanizing,
satiric technique. The novelistic principles that can render the characters of *Vile Bodies* as insubstantial as the inventions of a gossip columnist themselves begin to look like a threatening tendency of modernity
itself.

The connection between small-scale domestic and large-scale political
instability thus remains suppressed, subsumed in a concern over a more
generalized anarchy that comes to be represented by modernism –
specifically, by an antihumanist version of modernism that celebrates
the increasing saturation of the world with technology. Yet if the political
themes of the novel remain underdeveloped, it is the character around
whom the hints of political subterfuge seem to cluster who might be
taken as a final surrogate for the satirist in this novel, the character who
perhaps even more perfectly than the gossip columnist embodies satire's
power. This surrogate is Father Rothschild. With his supernatural omniscience – he predicts the war at the end of the novel – and "his happy
knack to remember everything that could possibly be learned about
everyone who could possibly be of any importance" (*VB*, pp. 1–2),
Rothschild has a mind that would be the envy of any young gossip
columnist or memoirist. And he is also a figure of authority. When he
speaks at Margot's party, his words resonate with such a tone of know-
ingness that critics regularly take his diagnosis of "a fatal hunger for
permanence" as the author's own. A conspiracy-theorist's fantasy come to
life, he represents the fusion of two great institutions: with his Jewish
surname he embodies the wealth of European banks, while with his title
Father he carries the religious authority of the Catholic Church. Like the
satirist, he speaks from a position of superiority with the backing of
communal and institutional power.

Yet, at the same time, there is something suspicious, even duplicitous about Rothschild. He may seem wise, but his physical appearance is downright grotesque:

His tongue protruded very slightly and, had they not been so concerned with luggage and the weather, someone might have observed in him a peculiar resemblance to those plaster reproductions of the gargoyles of Notre Dame. (*VB*, p. 2)

Seidel observes that satirists, like the targets they deride, are often represented as ugly or deformed: "it is one of the more plaguing paradoxes about the satiric mode that the satirist, having taken on a kind of monstrosity as his subject, makes something of a monster of himself."[45] He points out that "the first represented satirist in Western literature, Thersites of the *Iliad*, is also the most deformed warrior in the Greek camp."[46] Thus *Vile Bodies*' most powerful enforcer of stability himself resembles a repulsive gargoyle – and a cheap imitation at that. If he preserves the security of the state by exposing Simon at Margot's party, he also carries a false beard of his own. And while Adam and Agatha are detained and harassed at customs, the physically repugnant and politically suspicious Rothschild remains utterly unmolested by the officials: "Father Rothschild fluttered a diplomatic *laissez-passer* and disappeared in the large car that had been sent to meet him" (*VB*, p. 21). Waugh was not yet a Catholic himself when he wrote this, but the scene suggests that the weighty moral authority of a religious institution such as the Roman Catholic Church might provide the anarchist-writer with the diplomatic *laissez-passer* to avoid satiric censure. Rothschild's freedom is the novelist's fantasy of being whisked past one's own intrapsychic customs bureau, of evading one's own censors, of not having to ask how far one may go. For *Vile Bodies* ultimately suggests that the more secure one's position of moral authority the greater one's license to engage in the anarchic bomb-throwing, the sadistic bloodlust, and the shameless voyeurism of satire.

CHAPTER 4

Laughter and fear in A Handful of Dust

In Evelyn Waugh's universe, life is nasty, British, and short. Amid the author's clear-eyed dissection of national patterns of feeling, characters are killed with invention and glee. In his first novel, *Decline and Fall*, a schoolboy, Lord Tangent, is shot by a stray bullet from a track official's misfired starting gun. In 1932's *Black Mischief*, the hero unwittingly consumes the stewed body of his lover during an African emperor's funeral rites. In *Vile Bodies*, as we have seen, a gossip columnist puts his head in an oven when he is banned from the best parties, a prostitute falls drunkenly to her death from a chandelier, and an exhibitionistic socialite dies following an accident suffered in an auto race she enters on a lark. By the time Waugh wrote *A Handful of Dust*, the seemingly casual acceptance of violent and untimely death had become the signal characteristic of his dark humor.

With an ambivalence characteristic of Waugh's critics, Conor Cruise O'Brien has called this apparent indifference to death a "schoolboy delight in cruelty,"[1] distancing himself morally and emotionally from Waugh's enjoyment while still praising the author's peculiar talents. O'Brien discerns, even as he reproduces, a discrepancy in the fiction between ethics and pleasure, one that maps precisely onto the double movement of satire.[2] And if Waugh's fiction exemplifies the paradoxes of satire, it is equally valuable for the questions it opens in understanding modernism. As seen in *Vile Bodies'* ambivalent treatment of an anarchic modern world, Waugh's attitudes toward both modernism and modernity are vexed. In George McCartney's words: "Waugh's response to the modern was marked by a certain fruitful ambivalence. In his official pose he was the curmudgeon who despised innovation, but the anarchic artist in him frequently delighted in its formal and thematic possibilities."[3] In short, although Waugh later in life repeatedly positioned himself as antimodernist, his early fiction came to embody a modern sensibility in its apparent rejection of the novel's traditional ethical obligations. Hence, in

Waugh, the satiric and the modern often look very much alike; while the author may claim to satirize a decadent modernity, the disruptive mechanism of his satire fosters the very modern decadence he decries.

While my reading of *Vile Bodies* aimed at revealing the paradoxes of modern satire, how its attack on authority and on false morality doubles back to undermine its own implicit normative claims, *A Handful of Dust*, I will argue, pushes these contradictions even further, so that the very tone characteristic of Waugh's satiric method itself begins to break down. The novel is the story of Tony Last, an English aristocrat thoroughly devoted to his family estate, Hetton, and to the unchanging routines that the decaying neo-Gothic country house embodies. It tells of the dissolution of Tony's family, his beliefs, in a sense his entire world. But the novel also tells the story of the dissolution of *satire*; in it Waugh both thematizes and enacts the breakdown of the comic-ironic sensibility that characterizes his early work. Understanding this breakdown can explain a longstanding and unresolved critical conundrum – the abrupt tonal shift of the novel's concluding chapters, which modulate away from the comic into the mode Freud called the uncanny. In *A Handful of Dust*, Waugh pushes his satire to such limits that it must take another form.

THE DEATH OF PEPPERMINT

Early in the novel, Waugh gives his readers an object lesson in the ethics of fiction. While Tony and his young son, John Andrew, walk to church, John tells his father a story he has heard from the stable manager Ben about a mule named Peppermint "who had drunk his company's rum ration" in the First World War and subsequently died (*HD*, p. 37). Tony finds the story "very sad," but John Andrew responds: "Well I thought it was sad too but it isn't. Ben said it made him laugh fit to bust his pants" (*HD*, pp. 37, 38). Important here is not merely the difference in protocols of feeling – Ben finds comedy where Tony finds pathos – but the implied hierarchy among them. If Waugh is joking about the simplicity of the boy's logic, he is also using John to comment critically on Tony's easy sympathy for a long-dead mule. John's acceptance of Ben as the authority in such aesthetic judgments, in other words, indicates not only Tony's parental neglect[4] – a failure to instill in his son the values of his social class – but also the outmoded nature of those very values. For the cruel reaction here trumps the sympathetic one. Ben's response makes Tony's seem naive and foolish; Tony's does not make Ben's seem inordinately cruel.

"One must have a heart of stone to read the death of Little Nell without laughing," quipped Oscar Wilde, and like the death of Nell for Wilde, the death of Peppermint for Waugh forces a choice between laughter and tears. Wilde presumably laughs at Dickens's literary treatment of the death of Nell, his manipulation of his readers' emotions, not the child's death per se. (Little Nell, being fictional, has no death per se; her death has no existence outside Dickens's representation of it.) By laughing, and boasting about his laughter, Wilde rejects the entire system of values embedded in Dickens's novel and the culture from which it springs. Thus Lionel Trilling claims that Wilde's target is not merely "insincerity" (claiming virtuous feelings one does not experience) but the Victorian value of sincerity itself – the obedience to the social code that demands these virtuous feelings. Compassionate feeling, having failed to guarantee aesthetic quality, becomes the object of Wilde's suspicion.

This suspicion of the authority of feeling – the indifference discussed in Chapter 2 – situates Wilde as an important precursor to Waugh and a key figure in an influential strain of modernism. Wilde has become, Eve Sedgwick notes, "the very embodiment of . . . modernist antisentimentality,"[5] and it is the specific flaw of sentimentality that, I have argued, modernist aesthetics after Wilde often sought to repudiate. The loss of faith in feeling as a guarantee of moral or aesthetic value thus generates a very powerful idea of what it is to be modern. If we turn from an idea of "modernism" as a school or movement to a sense of "modern" as a sensibility, then modernity becomes a synonym, or near-synonym, for words such as sophistication, urbanity, refinement, aloofness. The anti-sentimental stances of writers such as Wilde and Waugh, and the value placed on qualities such as wit or indifference, signal not merely cultural distinction but a deep skepticism of inherited ideas of what it means to know and feel.

Placed in this context, *A Handful of Dust* becomes a much more significant novel for understanding modernism than its somewhat ortho-dox formal surface might suggest. Ben's laughter at the death of Pepper-mint, for example, can now be understood as a refusal to let the kind of "genuine feelings" that Wilde scorns deprive the mule's rum binge of its inherent comedy – as a rejection of Tony's reflexive sentimentality. The act of expressing sympathy, even the act of feeling it, comes too easily to be accepted as meaningful. Thus Ben's laughter is only one of many instances in the novel that bring to the fore a case of suffering only to undercut, ironize, or move past the ostensible sympathy the situation appears to elicit. Take the very first words of the book:

"Was anyone hurt?"

"No one I am thankful to say," said Mrs. Beaver, "except two housemaids who lost their heads and jumped through a glass roof into the paved court. They were in no danger. The fire never properly reached the bedrooms I am afraid. Still they are bound to need doing up, everything black with smoke and drenched with water and luckily they had that old-fashioned sort of extinguisher that ruins *everything*." (*HD*, p. 3; Waugh's italics)

Before the reader even knows the topic of conversation, she hears an apparent expression of compassion that provokes a deceptively complex response. Mrs. Beaver voices sympathy for the victims of the fire but her concern is immediately revealed as insubstantial, since she cares only for those of her own class. The injured (or dead?) housemaids are an afterthought; Mrs. Beaver implicitly dismisses their fates as deserved, since their injuries resulted from foolish panic. The reader, moreover, makes a second correction in understanding Mrs. Beaver's initial sentence. When Mrs. Beaver says the maids "lost their heads," the reader, still unaware of the fire, can easily take this phrase literally. How indifferent is Mrs. Beaver to the maids' suffering? Cold-hearted enough to dismiss their decapitation? And even when we learn that they "lost their heads" in only a figurative sense, we never discover the women's ultimate fates. Did they survive? How badly were they injured? Was anyone hurt? Mrs. Beaver moves onto her true concern, the property damage that her business can financially exploit.

Mrs. Beaver's initial concern with human suffering is revealed as mere conversational reflex, or idle curiosity, soon forgotten. The novel, to be sure, does not cultivate our sadism toward the housemaids; if anything, Mrs. Beaver's cavalier treatment of them may arouse a little sympathy or readerly indignation. Yet the narrative is content to let the Beavers' conversation unfold and to leave the residual question of the housemaids unaddressed. Instead, we laugh at the virtual nakedness of Mrs. Beaver's greed, or the shabbiness of her effort to cloak this greed in false compassion. The novel's concern is less with who is hurt, or how badly, as with how some people respond when others are hurt. This book is not about the housemaids or about Peppermint the mule, but about various responses to their fates.

A Handful of Dust is full of such small evasions. Jenny Abdul-Akbar, the former wife of a Moroccan prince, bears "the most terrible scars" (*HD*, p. 121) from her husband's abuse but comes off as a comic figure, absurdly eager to confess the details her "frightful nightmare" (*HD*, p. 115) to near-strangers. The prostitute Milly is absolutely blasé when telling

Tony about the circumstances that led to the birth of her daughter: "I was only sixteen when I had her. I was the youngest of the family and our stepfather wouldn't leave any of us girls alone. That's why I have to work for a living" (*HD*, p. 181). When Brenda reads to Tony from the morning papers, her disengaged sensibility runs together nightmarish grotesqueries and social gossip:

Reggie's been making another speech . . . There's such an extraordinary picture of Babe and Jock . . . a woman in America has had twins by two different husbands. Would you have thought that possible? . . . Two more chaps in gas ovens . . . a little girl has been strangled in a cemetery with a bootlace . . . that play we went to about a farm is coming off. (*HD*, p. 18)

As we saw in Lippmann's analysis of public opinion and throughout *Vile Bodies*, the newspaper serves as a metonymn for modernity itself, flattening all distinctions between news, crime, scandal, sensation, politics, and entertainment. In Brenda's reading of the paper, as in Milly's and Jenny's recollection of their abuse, violence remains a mild disruption on the surface of the text, troubling the reader briefly but remaining infused with the comic-ironic tone that pervades the novel. If the novel does hold any sympathy for the suffering of Brenda, Milly, or the girl in the cemetery, it refuses to make a direct plea for compassion. Such a plea, presumably, would only give way to something resembling Tony's naive and sentimental affection for a mule poisoned by rum. Instead, the material of "frightful nightmare" (to use Jenny's phrase) is converted, through a kind of emotional alchemy, into social comedy.

Such moments, frequent as they are, may lead the reader to expect a kind of moral failure in Waugh's characters, but they hardly prepare her for the novel's most shocking instance of a troublesome response to pain – Brenda's reaction to her son's death. (John Andrew dies in a hunting accident.) Jock Grant-Menzies travels to London to tell her the news, and when Brenda hears that "John" has died she mistakenly assumes Jock to be speaking of her lover, John Beaver:

"What is it, Jock? Tell me quickly, I'm scared. It's nothing awful, is it?"
"I'm afraid it is. There's been a very serious accident."
"John?"
"Yes."
"Dead?"
He nodded.
She sat down on a hard little Empire chair against the wall, perfectly still with her
         hands folded in her lap, like a small well-brought-up child introduced into a

room full of grown-ups. She said, "Tell me what happened? Why do you
know about it first?"

"I've been down at Hetton since the week-end."

"Hetton?"

"Don't you remember? John was going hunting today."

She frowned, not at once taking in what he was saying. "John . . . John Andrew . . .
    I . . . Oh thank God . . ." Then she burst into tears. (*HD*, pp. 161–62;
    Waugh's ellipses)

That Brenda feels relief and thanks God that her son has died instead of
her loathsome lover clearly reveals her depravity and secures the reader's
moral judgment against her. Her response to the news – unlike her
reaction to the news report of the strangled girl – is so shocking that
whatever laughter it might provoke is overwhelmed by the shock or
revulsion a reader likely experiences.

But if Brenda's moral failure provides interpretive certainty in one
sense, it offers only confusion in another. For Brenda's reaction validates
Mrs. Rattery's earlier comment to Tony that the death might not upset
Brenda as much as he fears: "You can't ever tell what's going to hurt
people" (*HD*, p. 149). Echoing the novel's opening question – or
obliquely answering it – Mrs. Rattery's remark intimates not only that
Tony's naive faith in Brenda's decency will be disappointed, but also
that in Waugh's universe *all* human passions are too thickly disguised
for others to assess accurately. Waugh's external method – the technique, which he praised in Lewis, of rejecting the representation of
consciousness and describing observable behavior alone – does not so
much deny the interiority of the self as it suggests that self is unknowable, buried beneath sedimented layers of social custom and ritualized
expression.

Unlike the death of Little Nell, or of Lord Tangent in *Decline and Fall,*
or of the schoolgirl in the cemetery, John Andrew's is one fictional child's
death at which no one can laugh.[6] Yet the comedy manages to proceed.
Brenda's friends see the death as gossip for their circle, and Jenny
narcissistically blames herself: "O God . . . What have I done to deserve
it?" (*HD*, p. 157). The most ridiculous response is that of Brenda's
mother, who writes what Brenda calls "a sweet letter":

*. . . I shall not come down to Hetton for the funeral, but I shall be thinking of you
both all the time and my dear grandson. I shall think of you as I saw you all three,
together, at Christmas. Dear children, at a time like this only yourselves can be any
help to each other. Love is the only thing stronger than sorrow . . .* (*HD*, p. 170;
Waugh's italics, ellipses)

The grandmother's clichéd expressions of grief, contradicted by her refusal to be inconvenienced by travel, bear no more weight than Mrs. Beaver's professed concern for the victims of the fire. The platitudes return us from the discomfort of the death to a world where narrator and reader are both more comfortable: we again laugh at the moral inadequacy of the novel's characters.

While other characters come off more respectably, nearly all are implicated in the collective refusal to assign blame or take responsibility for John's death; the refrain of "nobody's fault" does not indicate any kind of stoic acceptance of the uselessness of blaming, but rather, by directing attention to the many small acts of irresponsibility that made the accident possible, suggests an unseemly readiness to write off the whole episode, as if in an unspoken pact among the guilty. In contrast, Tony, despite his own blank, apparently affectless behavior in the wake of the shock, soon proves unable to assume the indifference, to the death and to Brenda's affair, which comes so easily to Brenda and her friends. The middle of the novel, in fact, focuses on the very clash between his pain and the nonchalance of those around him. Thus, when Brenda's mother urges Tony to take Brenda back, the reader begins to feel what must be Tony's outrage:

I will tell you exactly how it happened, Tony. Brenda must have felt a tiny bit neglected – people often do at that stage of marriage. I have known countless cases – and it was naturally flattering to her to find a young man to beg and carry for her. That's all it was, nothing wrong. *And then the terrible shock of little John's accident unsettled her and she didn't know what she was saying or writing. You'll both laugh over this little fracas in years to come.* (*HD*, p. 175; Waugh's italics)

The suggestion that the death (safely euphemized as "little John's accident") and the break-up of the marriage ("this little fracas") might be the subject of laughter is outrageous – an outrageousness particularly remarkable in the work of a novelist who so often displays his own modernity by laughing at death and suffering. Waugh, who in *Vile Bodies* so deftly exposed the variable and ignoble motives tied up in moral indignation, now cultivates, on Tony's behalf, the reader's own outrage.

We have arrived at a paradox: Waugh, whose "schoolboy delight in cruelty" seems to owe so much to Wilde's stance of laughing at the death of Little Nell, directs his greatest indignation at the character who trivializes the death of John Andrew and laughs at the subsequent dissolution of his parents' marriage. Waugh's own attitude toward Wilde embodies this paradox. He repeatedly derided Wilde as a figure of fashion, and described him as "at heart radically sentimental,"[7] even though the anti-Dickensian Wilde seems most influential on Waugh precisely in his rejection of sentimental poses. Likewise, the modernity of Brenda and her friends, whose delightfully extreme nonchalance shares much with the postures of Waugh the satirist, itself now becomes subject to the author's ironic inflections. Terry Eagleton observes in both the characters and narrators of Waugh's fiction "an inability to be surprised and disoriented by experience," and Ian Littlewood has similarly noted a "sophistication" shared by characters and narrator, which he describes as "the refusal to be shocked, disoriented, embarrassed or involved."[8] Yet this very quality – which *Vile Bodies* illustrated so vividly in the flattened or misplaced affect of the Bright Young Things – becomes quite visibly the target of satiric condemnation in *A Handful of Dust*.[9]

Brenda and her clique are implicitly condemned because they transform life into a kind of art to be judged only on aesthetic, not moral, grounds:

[Brenda's] very choice of partner gave the affair an appropriate touch of fantasy; Beaver, the joke figure they had all known and despised, suddenly caught up to her among the luminous clouds of deity. If, after seven years looking neither right nor left, she had at last broken away with Jock Grant-Menzies or Robin Beasley … it would have been thrilling no doubt, but straightforward drawing-room comedy. The choice of Beaver raised the whole escapade into a realm of poetry for Polly and Daisy and Angela and all the gang of gossips. (*HD*, pp. 74–75)

Drawing-room comedy is the genre through which Brenda and her friends usually view their world, a genre populated by "joke figure[s]" such as Beaver. But the invocation of the "realm of poetry" and the "touch of fantasy," echoing Tony's private vocabulary of English Romance, suggests that Brenda's own world view is also built on fantasy. Brenda's Wildean equanimity may stand in contrast to Tony's more overtly outmoded devotion to a Victorian way of life, but both characters understand the world through a set of aesthetic forms at once grandiose and clichéd.[10] Ironic postures of indifference, so often characteristic of Waugh's own narrative tone, become Waugh's target every bit as much as sentimental affectations of feeling. If weeping at the death of Nell can allow us, too easily, to judge ourselves sensitive and humane, cold laughter can with equal ease allow us to congratulate ourselves on our hard-headed sophistication.

That such aggressively antisentimental postures, whether Wilde's or Brenda's, reveal themselves as susceptible to the charge of sentimentality suggests a larger contradiction within the idea of sentimentality that Sedgwick has discussed at length: the collapse of the distinction "between sentimentality and its denunciation."[11] Sedgwick notes that accusations of sentimentality tend to expose the accuser to similar charges, according to the logic of "it takes one to know one": "Only those who are themselves prone to these vicariating impulses . . . are equipped to detect them in the writing or being of others."[12] As a result, merely "to enter into the discourse of sentimentality . . . is almost inevitably to be caught up in a momentum of . . . scapegoating attribution"[13] – trying to expose the "real" sentimentalist. Yet that act of exposure is specifically what the paradoxes of the term "sentimental" imply *cannot* be done, since naming or denouncing a "real" or "closet" sentimentalist only adds one more link to a potentially endless chain. Waugh, I suggest, runs up against precisely this paradox. His own satiric sensibility, so acute in detecting the sentimental in others – including literary precursors such as Wilde – now cultivates readerly sympathy for Tony in a decidedly unsatiric, even sentimental, manner, and he indicts those characters whose accents of indifference most closely echo the authorial-narratorial voice itself.

A brief look at Waugh's personal biography might help to make the point. Waugh's biographers have noted that Tony's situation resembles Waugh's own after his first wife (also named Evelyn) left him for a lover. In a letter to Harold Acton, Waugh expresses frustration that friends and relatives are urging him not to make too much of the affair:

Everyone is talking so much nonsense on all sides of me about my affairs, that my wits reel. Evelyn's family & mine join in asking me to "forgive" her whatever that may mean . . . I did not know it was possible to be so miserable & live but I am told that this is a common experience.[14]

In a letter to Henry Yorke (Green), furthermore, Waugh voices a desire to find solace in the humorous reactions of others to his plight: "If you hear any amusing opinions about my divorce do tell me. Particularly from the older generation. The Gardner line is that I am very 'unforgiving'."[15] Finally, a few months later, Waugh again writes to Yorke:

I have decided that I have gone on for too long in that fog of sentimentality & I am going to stop hiding away from everyone. I was getting into a sort of Charlie Chaplinish Pagliacci attitude to myself as the man with a tragedy in his life and a tender smile for children.[16]

The parallels between the letters and the novel are significant. Like Tony, Waugh feels pressure to affect a blasé sophistication others seemed to possess quite naturally, and, like the narrator of his novel, he shifts attention from the experience of pain to the amusement derived from the responses of others. Yet the differences are equally instructive. Most obviously, the glaring asymmetry that there is no dead son in Waugh's life implies that the author needed a dramatic incident to precipitate the collapse of the Lasts' marriage. It suggests that Waugh loads the dice in favor of Tony, manipulating his reader's emotions in a manner worthy of Wilde's Dickens. More subtly, however, Tony never expresses the dissatisfaction with, and persecution by, the responses of others that Waugh articulates in his letters; these feelings are only implied, left for the reader to experience. Nor does Tony seek solace by mocking those who respond to his fate in "amusing" ways; this too is left to the reader. Finally, Tony never assumes enough self-consciousness to regard his own feeling of victimization as sentimental in the way that Waugh does (likening himself to Chaplin); in the novel, it is Brenda's piggish brother Reggie who suggests that Tony is merely "taking the line of the injured husband" (*HD*, p. 204). In short, the whole range of feelings that Waugh expresses in his letters – anger, self-pity, self-reproach – are in the novel either left implicit or put into the mouths of untrustworthy characters. This is wholly in keeping with Waugh's adherence to a Lewisian external method that refrains from rendering the interior lives of characters, but it also suggests that certain reactions are suppressed for the sake of the aesthetic or affective demands of the genre.

There is, moreover, an important exception to Waugh's external method in the novel, and it is the ultimate indication of the author's sympathy for Tony that he violates his aesthetic principles in order to render his hero's interior mental state.[17] When Tony is compelled to stage an affair legally to justify his divorce, the madness of his circumstances begins to terrify him:

For a month now he had lived in a world suddenly bereft of order; it was as though the whole reasonable and decent constitution of things, the sum of all he had experienced or learned to expect, were an inconsiderable, inconspicuous object mislaid somewhere on the dressing table; no outrageous circumstance in which he found himself, no new mad thing brought to his notice could add a jot to the all-encompassing chaos that shrieked about his ears. (*HD*, p. 189)[18]

The episode at Brighton, in which Tony is forced into increasingly ridiculous behavior, appears farcical to the reader, but to Tony it seems "phantasmagoric, and even gruesome" (*HD*, p. 189). This rift between the comic and the "phantasmagoric" or "gruesome," visible in the narrator's departure from principle in order to enter Tony's mind, points up the limitations of the "drawing-room comedy" genre epitomized by the mock-affair. Waugh must explicitly *tell* us that the events are phantasmagoric and gruesome because the protocols of his method demand that he represent these same events as comic.

However effective Waugh's satire may be as a critique of sentimental-ity, then, it also appears incapable of rendering certain emotional states. In drawing-room comedy, phantasmagoria will always appear as silly, never gruesome. The problem Waugh's satire faces thus may be the paradig-matic challenge of all literature. Roland Barthes has written:

A friend has just lost someone he loves, and I want to express my sympathy. I proceed to write him a letter. Yet the words I find do not satisfy me: they are "phrases": I make up "phrases" out of the most affectionate part of myself; I then realize that the message I want to send this friend, the message which is my sympathy itself, could after all be reduced to a simple word: *condolences*. Yet the very purpose of communication is opposed to this, for it would be a cold and consequently inverted message, since what I want to communicate is the very warmth of my sympathy. I conclude that in order to correct my message (that is, in order for it to be exact), I must not only vary it, but also that this variation must be original and apparently invented.

This fatal succession of constraints will be recognized as literature itself.[19]

For Barthes, the aim of literature is not to express the inexpressible, but rather, working with a received, public language, to "unexpress the expressible,"[20] to render an essentially banal emotion in an original language. Hence the indirectness of literature, hence the ironic represen-tation of grief. One could of course dismiss the problem altogether, and dispense with the effort to render grief; to do this might be to realize the theoretical possibilities suggested by Lewis in his insistence that "*perfect laughter*, if there could be such a thing, would be inhuman," or by other champions of modernist abstraction, such as José Ortega y Gasset, who urged the "progressive elimination of the human, all too human elements predominant in romantic and naturalistic production."[21] But Waugh, pulling back from the antihumanist position as he did in *Decline and Fall* and *Vile Bodies*, rejects this option and presses upon his reader the ethical dimension of his characters' struggles. What results is a satiric attack on ironic attitudes – a satire that ceases to look like a satire, a drawing-room comedy that flees the drawing room for the jungle.

PHANTASY WITH A PH

Tony's flight to South America in the novel's final chapters, and the fate he meets there, provide a drastic change from the rest of *A Handful of Dust*, not only in setting but also in tone, even genre. Quite possibly the first reader to worry about this shift was his friend Henry Yorke, who wrote to Waugh in 1934:

I feel the end is so fantastic that it throws the rest out of proportion. Aren't you mixing two things together? The first part of the book is convincing, a real picture of people one has met ... But then to let Tony be detained by some madman introduces an entirely fresh note and we are with phantasy with a ph at once.[22]

Yet if the generic and geographical shifts undermine the social realism of the novel, this perceived discrepancy has a clear explanation in the genesis of the book. Waugh initially composed and published the episode of Tony at "Chez Todd" – in which Tony is rescued but then held captive by an old man, Mr. Todd, who forces him to read aloud, over and over, the complete works of Dickens – as a free-standing story entitled "The Man Who Liked Dickens"; only later did he write the rest of the novel.[23] The "fantastic" short story, by this argument, possessed unity on its own, but clashed with the comic-satiric tone of the novel that was appended to it.

Waugh, however, while acknowledging the "fantastic" and artificial nature of the episode, insists to Yorke that it is necessary: "The Amazon stuff had to be there. The scheme was a Gothic man in the hands of savages – first Mrs. Beaver etc. then the real ones, finally the silver foxes at Hetton."[24] Yet Yorke objected to tonal, not thematic discord; Waugh never answers his complaint. Is it possible, then, to go beyond a merely genetic explanation of this tonal shift? Rather than seeing "mixing two things together" as a flaw resulting from the vagaries of the creative process, might we see the disjunction as symptomatic of the very questions that occupy the novel?

In calling the final episode "phantasy with a ph," Yorke situates the story within an aesthetic tradition that dwells on the "phantasmagoric" and the "gruesome" – to use the terms from Tony's interior monologue in Brighton. Freud famously called this tradition "the uncanny," and Wolfgang Kayser used the term "the grotesque." This latter term, recall, has generally been characterized by a duality or ambivalence that, in Ruskin's analysis, combines "two elements, one ludicrous, the other fearful."[25] In the ludicrous aspect of the grotesque lie its affinities to satire and caricature; in the fearful side – that side emphasized in Kayser's seminal study – its relation to Freud's uncanny. The conclusion of Waugh's novel, then, moves from one face of the grotesque to another, from laughter to fear. "I will show you fear in a handful of dust," wrote T. S. Eliot in the line that gave Waugh his title, and in this ending the phantasmagoric and the gruesome, the materials of what Jenny Abdul-Akbar calls "frightful nightmare," are no longer converted into comedy. Of course, the idea that reading Dickens interminably – a lifetime of reading the death of Little Nell – might be a Dantean punishment indicates that Waugh has not entirely abandoned the comic, and I will return to the comic undertones of these concluding chapters. But the reader's laughter, as Yorke's response attests, becomes increasingly uneasy.

Criticism of *A Handful of Dust* has avoided linking the novel's ending with Freud's uncanny, whether because Waugh's readers have obediently followed the author in their distaste for psychoanalysis, or because such concerns have not seemed germane to their efforts to locate in the novel a stable system of moral and religious beliefs. In a widely accepted reading, Richard Wasson has argued that it is a kind of poetic justice that Tony should live out his days endlessly reading the author so deeply associated with the Victorian values that have led him astray.[26] Without wholly rejecting Wasson's argument, I want to suggest that a psychoanalytic reading can help not only to discern thematic parallels between the two parts of the novel but also to account for why Waugh's novel breaks out of the confines of the drawing room, literally and figuratively. If, as I have argued, the satiric mode of the opening chapters of the novel stages a *failure* of feeling, relentlessly working to avoid excessive sentiment by allowing reader and narrator to laugh at the moral inadequacy of its characters, these final fantastic chapters reintroduce sentiment, only in an estranged, uncanny guise.

Like the genre terms I discussed in Chapter 1 (satire, sentimental, grotesque), the uncanny as a literary category has been the subject of significant theoretical work. For some years it functioned as a minor buzzword of deconstructive criticism, whose dead authors so often left ghostly traces.[27] But Freud used the term in a much less metaphorical sense; in defending his foray into aesthetics, he defined that field as "the theory of the qualities of feeling," and wrote of the uncanny: "It is undoubtedly related to what is frightening – to what arouses dread and horror . . . Yet we may expect that a special core of feeling is present which justifies the use of a special conceptual term."[28] Freud himself has some trouble further describing this variety of fear or anxiety, as his descriptions tend to slide into psychoanalytic explanation of the origins of the feeling. But in his literary discussion he reserves the term for those works – most extensively, E. T. A. Hoffmann's "The Sandman" – that elicit in readers this feeling of anxiety or dread. Ghost stories, tales of the supernatural, Gothic novels, horror movies, and the like are thus natural (although not necessary) loci of the uncanny.

A brief review of Freud's theory may be useful. For Freud, the experience of the uncanny derives from either the revival of repressed infantile complexes or the confirmation of surmounted primitive beliefs.[29] The category of "infantile complexes" includes such Freudian favorites as the castration complex and "womb-phantasies," while "primitive beliefs" – for example, in animism, magic, or evil spirits – entail a failure to demarcate psychical from material reality. This failure in turn stems from an over-valuation of the power of one's own thoughts, or a projection of those thoughts onto the external world.[30] In short, it is the regression to magical thinking, linked to the childhood of the individual or the species, which induces the feeling of the uncanny. But there is a second condition necessary for the production of the uncanny in fiction, a condition less psychological than narratological. The phenomenon that produces the uncanny must survive the process of "reality-testing," that is, scrutiny to determine whether it is real or illusory. An author can deliberately create supernatural fictional events that do not stand up to reality-testing (e.g., fairy tales), and therefore do not seem uncanny. By the same token, however, an author can manipulate the reader to believe *more fully* in the reality of supernatural phenomena than she would in real life by first establishing a reader's faith in the reality of the characters; as a result, fiction can, *more easily than life*, induce the feeling of the uncanny.[31] The uncanniness of Waugh's conclusion is thus enhanced by the author's having first created, in Yorke's words, "a real picture of people one has met."

What is it, then, in "Du Côté de Chez Todd" that induces the feeling of the uncanny? Where is the fear in *A Handful of Dust*? To begin, we might recognize in Tony's exile a variation on the modernist paradigm of the voyage as a return to beginnings. Like Conrad in *Heart of Darkness*, Waugh uses the barbarism of the wilderness to comment ironically on the savagery of "civilization."[32] A latter-day Marlow exploring the blank spaces on the map, Tony finds himself at the remotest reaches of European exploration: "The stream which watered [Mr. Todd's land] was not marked on any map" (*HD*, p. 285). For both authors, too, the journey to the ends of empire is a temporal regression; Marlow explicitly calls his voyage a trip back in time, and Tony returns to a world of animistic belief in which, Todd suggests, there exist magic potions for every purpose, including raising the dead (a favorite uncanny theme). Even in Waugh's composition of the novel, the tale "began at the end" with the short story about reading Dickens.[33] In all sorts of ways, the conclusion in the jungle turns out to be the origin of the narrative.

In typically modernist fashion, moreover, Tony's regression is psychological as well as anthropological. He travels back to a land of childhood as well as pre-civilization; geographical dislocation becomes the occasion for, or literalization of, a metaphorical exploration of the self. Deep in the

Amazon jungles, he finds himself seeking an idealized version of his childhood home, a lost city he imagines as "Gothic in character, all vanes and pinnacles, gargoyles, battlements, groining and tracery, pavilions and terraces, a transfigured Hetton" (*HD*, p. 222). Tony traverses the ocean seeking the Hetton that eluded him in England.

Chapter 5, "In Search of a City," serves as a transition into this world of childhood fantasy. Throughout the chapter, Tony's memories of England and fantasies of the City work their way into his conscious and semi-conscious thoughts as he daydreams or drifts off to sleep; ultimately, he is stricken with a hallucinatory fever, and they overwhelm his senses. Like Agatha Runcible in *Vile Bodies*, Tony envisions an absurd and often comic series of events, pasted together from scraps of memory, perception, and his own romantic imagination. These passages have the logic, or illogic, of Joyce's "Circe" episode, occurring on the border of reality and imagination, of rationality and absurdity, of consciousness and unconsciousness.[34] They effect the generic transition that Yorke commented on, a passage from a comic-satiric mode to "phantasy with a ph." They also signal a kind of psychic transition, as Tony, feverish, weak, and beset by visions, is reduced to childish whimpering:

All that day Tony lay alone, fitfully oblivious of the passage of time. He slept a little; once or twice he left his hammock and found himself weak and dizzy . . . He lit the lantern and began to collect wood for the fire, but the sticks kept slipping from his fingers and each time that he stooped he felt giddy, so that after a few fretful efforts he left them where they had fallen and returned to his hammock. And lying there, wrapped in his blanket, he began to cry. (*HD*, p. 277)

The emotion stifled by the social pressures of Tony's world, and by his own upper-class English manners, now emerges unchecked. When Tony's guide, Dr. Messinger, dies, the narrative surrenders its objective point of view in favor of simply recording Tony's hallucinations as if they were real:

At last he came into the open. The gates were open before him and trumpets were sounding along the walls, saluting his arrival; from bastion to bastion the message ran to the four points of the compass; petals of almond and apple blossom were in the air; they carpeted the way, as, after a summer storm, they lay in the orchards at Hetton. Gilded cupolas and spires of alabaster shone in the sunlight. (*HD*, p. 283)

The narrative mode has shifted considerably from the detached and straight-faced, if slightly amused, recording of social behavior; it now describes sense-impressions wholly internal to Tony's mind.

When the next chapter opens, however, the narrative has returned to an objective point of view, and instead of a golden city with gates and spires, we see Mr. Todd's hut, made, in Yeatsian fashion, "of mud and wattle" (*HD*, p. 284). There is no grand castle, but a little house in the woods. In *The Uses of Enchantment*, Bruno Bettelheim writes that in fairy tales "the house in the woods and the parental home are the same place, experienced quite differently because of a change in the psychological situation."[35] Positive and negative associations are split between the safe parental home and the dangerous house in the woods in order to organize the ambivalent feelings attached to domesticity and family. And lest we apply Bettelheim's symbolic code too freely, the text has already pointed us in this direction with its references to Hetton; the hut is indeed "a transfigured Hetton," although not transfigured as Tony imagined. It is a space at once home and not home, familiar and unfamiliar – precisely the terrain that Freud called the *unheimlich*. For, in Freud's theory, the uncanny is familiar but appears as unfamiliar because our knowledge of it has been repressed: "the prefix '*un*' is the token of repression."[36] Tony has traveled from the drawing-room comedy of England, through a jungle of confusion, and emerged into a clearing. This enclosed space is both the unconscious psychic space of childhood and the literary space of "phantasy with a ph."

Discerning the parallels between the stately country home of Hetton and the little house in the jungle makes clear that the two parts of the novel share thematic concerns beyond the rather obvious analogies Waugh himself described between savagery at home and abroad. And while the fear provoked by Tony's powerlessness at the hands of Todd can be understood on a merely psychological plane, a psychoanalytic reading accounts for a number of otherwise peculiar details. For example, Tony relies on Todd for his daily food; when Tony refuses to read to him, the old man deprives Tony of his supper. Todd provides medicine too, which Tony drinks down like a little boy: "'Nasty medicine,' [Tony] said, and began to cry" (*HD*, p. 288). Most strikingly, Todd first appears as menacing when he describes his neighbors: "The Pie-wie women are ugly but very devoted. I have had many. Most of the men and women living in this savannah are my children. That is why they obey – for that reason and because I have the gun" (*HD*, p. 288). The old man's surprising and unsettling sexual potency makes him the father of the whole community around him, and the gun, while offering a joke about the obedience of children, serves as a garish emblem of phallic power. Supplying food and medicine, fathering children, enforcing his will as the law, Todd's behavior makes perfect sense if his hut is understood as a dream-like, transfigured Hetton and Todd himself as a transfigured father. In the original short story, Mr. Todd was called "Mr. McMaster," and Tony turns out to be a prisoner at this master's house just as he for so many years was unable to leave his father's estate.[37]

But, in spite of the paternal role that Todd assumes, much of his behavior fails to fit such a model. Todd is illiterate, infantile, and needy; he demands to be read to like a stubborn child. In fact, it is Todd who explicitly compares Tony to *his* father: "You read beautifully ... It is almost as though my father were here again" (*HD*, p. 293). Like a child as well, Todd habitually strikes a pose of mock-innocence when he knows he is doing wrong. This childlike old man, moreover, constitutes "a unique audience" for Tony to read to, in an oddly disturbing passage:

The old man sat astride his hammock opposite Tony ... following the words, soundlessly, with his lips. Often when a new character was introduced he would say, "Repeat the name, I have forgotten him," or "Yes, yes, I remember her well. She dies poor woman." He would frequently interrupt with questions ... He laughed loudly at all the jokes and at some passages which did not seem humorous to Tony, asking him to repeat them two or three times; and later at the description of the sufferings of the outcasts in "Tom-all-alones" tears ran down his cheeks into his beard. His comments on the story were usually simple. "I think that Dedlock is a very proud man," or, "Mrs. Jellyby does not take enough care of her children." (*HD*, pp. 292–93)

The simplicity of Todd's concerns, his unsophisticated diction, his attempt to follow along silently, and, above all, the utter excess of his emotional (indeed sentimental) reactions belong more properly to a young child than to an old man. Thus, if Todd's earlier name, McMaster, suggests his role as paternal master, it also more deeply might suggest his role as son; like the "un" in *unheimlich*, the "Mc" ("son of") in McMaster is "the token of repression."

With the sentimental reactions of a child, but the sexual and punitive power of a father, Todd can be said to represent the son's usurpation of paternal authority, Tony's triumphant rival in an oedipal struggle. Tony's captivity, after all, evokes a complex of desires and fears bound up with succession and inheritance, impotence and generativity, usurpation and punishment, which have been latent throughout the novel. Tony's surname, Last, signals the extinction of his line, and John's death leaves him without an heir. The death and the divorce bring about the end of Tony's procreative life. The emergence of Mr. Todd in the novel's final episode is a defamiliarizing, a rendering un-homely, of the familial romance already operating among Tony, Brenda, and John Andrew. For, young as he may be, John Andrew is a sexual rival of his father, and Waugh's insights into childhood sexuality are wonderfully Freudian. When Brenda, to assuage her guilt, tries to engineer an affair between Tony and Jenny, it is the son who falls for the "Princess": "I think she's the most beautiful lady I've ever seen ... D'you think she'd like to watch me have my bath?" (*HD*, p. 118). Later, when Jenny says good-night, he is even more forward:

> They sat on John's small bed in the night-nursery. He threw the clothes back and crawled out, nestling against Jenny. "Back to bed," she said, "or I shall spank you."
> "Would you do it hard? I shouldn't mind."
> "Oh dear," said Brenda. (*HD*, p. 119)

To recognize the sexual rivalry between Tony and John is to see that it is more than mere coincidence – indeed more than the author's rigging up a joke at Brenda's expense – that John Beaver and John Andrew Last share a first name. For while John Andrew might be Tony's rival in an intrapsychic struggle, John Beaver is both a second and more literal sexual rival. We have another case of a psychoanalytic "splitting," where the potentially patricidal agent is symbolically divided into a good figure and an evil one, between an innocent victim, John A., and a loathsome perpetrator, John B. Brenda's mistaking one for the other, while manifestly displaying her own misplaced affections, may also voice a latent *textual* desire to kill off the evil rival while sparing the good one. Her mistaken conclusion that John Beaver has died summons an alternative situation with which the reader and author, in their implied sympathy for Tony, would probably be much happier.[38]

But the psychoanalytic *content* of Tony's situation is only one source of the uncanny anxiety that Waugh's phantasmagoria produces. For Freud's essay on the uncanny, as Neil Hertz observes, contains an important ambiguity. Hertz notes that Freud wrote "The Uncanny" while he was working out the theory of the repetition compulsion that would be described in *Beyond the Pleasure Principle*, and that Freud viewed the repetition compulsion as a fundamental source of the uncanny.[39] But, Hertz argues, Freud is not always clear whether it is the *content* of the repetition or the mere *fact* of repetition that arouses anxiety; often the former seems trivial in comparison to the latter: "Whatever it is that is repeated – an obsessive ritual, perhaps, or a bit of acting-out in relation to one's analyst – will ... feel most compellingly uncanny when it is seen as *merely* coloring, that is when it comes to seem most gratuitously rhetorical."⁴⁰ When involuntary repetition appears uncanny, the particular act that one finds oneself repeating might seem utterly benign – as benign, even, as reading a novel by Dickens.

For, in a peculiar way, the triviality, even the silliness of Tony's fate is exactly what makes the scene so disturbing, giving it a power over readers that even Marlow's confrontation with Kurtz no longer quite possesses. The repetition is, in Hertz's phrase, "gratuitously rhetorical," or purely formal. Indeed, Todd's demand for reading echoes *Beyond the Pleasure Principle*, where Freud cites the child's desire to hear a familiar story repeated as an example of the repetition compulsion *par excellence*:

> If a child has been told a nice story, he will insist on hearing it over and over rather than a new one, and he will remorselessly stipulate that the repetition shall be an identical one.⁴¹

When Mr. Todd articulates a desire for repetition he is every bit as "remorseless":

> You see, they are the only books I have ever heard. My father used to read them and then later the black man . . . and now you. I have heard them all several times by now but I never get tired. (*HD*, p. 292)

Mr. Todd quite literally *is* the compulsion to repeat; he forces Tony to read and reread to him, in what has seemed to most readers an endless repetition.⁴² As his German-derived name would indicate, then, Todd is an externalization of Tony's own death drive, the drive that gives rise to the repetition compulsion, which Freud describes as "the inertia inherent in organic life" the instincts that "tend toward the restoration of an earlier state of things."⁴³ The novel's title, in fact, while directly invoking *The Waste Land*, may also, via Eliot, allude to Genesis 3:19, where God announces the mortality of Adam in language that perfectly illustrates this tendency of life to revert to an inorganic state: "Dust thou art, and unto dust shalt thou return." As an externalized agent of Tony's own unconscious instinct, Todd/McMaster is Tony's master, the law that "overrides the pleasure principle,"⁴⁴ the law that Tony must obey even as he recognizes the absurdity of such obedience. And the final event that secures Tony's enthrallment to Todd is the loss of his watch. Tony, who knows that "time is different" in Todd's forest (*HD*, p. 288), has now been stranded in the province of the unconscious, which, as psychoanalytic theory has it, knows no sense of time.

In this estranged form, Todd's arbitrary exercise of authority very literally assumes the "daemonic character" that Freud attributes to the repetition compulsion.[45] Of course, before and after Freud, literary works have embodied elements of the unconscious as devils, vampires, evil spirits, or little old men in the jungle. As Hertz notes, the relation between "demonic" and "psychological" explanations of uncanny experience is one of manifest to latent. Within the rules of a given fictional world, there may indeed exist "real" demons or spirits, but their affective power still derives from their psychodynamic origin.[46] The idea of the unconscious as demonic thus reminds us of what Slavoj Žižek calls "the status of the unconscious as radically external."[47] To see ourselves as the puppets of unconscious forces is to realize the automatism of our own selves, the stubborn unconsciousness of the unconscious.[48]

Of course, recognizing the automatism of our behavior is also the source of laughter in Bergson's theory of the comic as "something mechanical encrusted on the living";[49] similarly, it is central to Lewis's externalist prescriptions for satire. The uncanny thus shares this fundamental perception with the comic, and the proximity of the two modes in Waugh's work is no accident. Yet there is a difference. Freud himself (discussing none other than Oscar Wilde) notes that the comic tends to work *against* the production of uncanny anxiety: "Even a 'real' ghost, as in Oscar Wilde's *Canterville Ghost*, loses all power of at least arousing *gruesome* feelings in us as soon as the author begins to amuse himself by being ironical about it and allows liberties to be taken with it."[50] Laughter serves as a corrective force, rescuing us from the gruesome, whereas the uncanny fails to restore us to ourselves.[51]

In the novel's uncanny conclusion, then, the reader not only confronts the violent oedipal psychodynamics underlying the novel's social comedy, but also glimpses the phantasmagoric underside of the novel's satiric disavowal of sentimentality. Sentiment, combated so aggressively in the novel's earlier episodes, returns – and literally with a vengeance. Waugh's use of Dickens thus offers a variation on Wilde's laughter at the death of Nell. This time around, the sentimentality of the Victorian author induces not laughter but horror; Dickens is not aesthetically laughable, as he was for Wilde, but aesthetically dreadful. The heart of darkness is revealed to be the sentimental pieties of Victorian culture. In its antisentimental operations Waugh's fiction thus helps to illustrate the paradoxes in the manner that modernist literature structures and models the ways in which we respond emotionally to the pain of others. The collapse of satire into the uncanny suggests that the efforts of so many modernists to escape the sentimental might give rise to an undertow in which the claims of feeling reassert themselves in negative form.

In an interesting footnote to Todd's encounter with Dickens, Waugh, in 1953, reviewed a study of Dickens in which he, not surprisingly, referred to Dickens as a "tear jerker." Yet he also recognized the novelist's "unique genius," and in Dickens's habit of mesmerism saw an apt metaphor for the author's peculiarly compelling power over his readers.[52] Strikingly, Waugh compared Dickens to Chaplin, the same figure of sentimentality to whom he had likened himself, disparagingly, two decades before:

> The happiest comparison perhaps is to Mr. Charles Chaplin, in particular to the film *City Lights*. There we have scenes of appalling sentimentality and unreality ... but we have a unique genius in full exuberance ... We all have our moods in which Dickens sickens us. In a lighter, looser and perhaps higher mood we fall victim to his "magnetism." Like Mme. de la Rue we unroll from our sensible ball and do what the Master orders.[53]

Without entirely dropping his ironic tone, Waugh concedes that however "unreal" the emotion that Dickens and Chaplin elicit, it retains its pull on even the most sophisticated of readers. Here the sentimental itself appears as uncanny: the tear-jerker captivates us just as the hypnotist does; the "Master" Dickens forces us to obey his will just as the Dickens-loving McMaster forces Tony. If satire points out to us the ludicrousness of our sentimental impulses by reducing human character to the laughably rigid operation of mechanized emotions, then the uncanny describes our susceptibility to feeling as a more disquieting subjection to demonic or unconscious forces.

A decade later, Waugh testified a third time to Dickens's uncanny power. In his autobiography, *A Little Learning*, he recounts how his father, another man who loved Dickens,[54] would read to his sons:

> For some eight years of my life for some three or four evenings a week ... he read to me, my brother and to whatever friends might be in the house, for an hour or more from his own old favourites – most of Shakespeare, most of Dickens, most of Tennyson ... Had it not been so well done, there might have been something ludicrous about the small, elderly, stout figure impersonating the heroines of forgotten comedies with such vivacity. In fact he held us enthralled.[55]

Although the experience is recounted as pleasurable – even bordering on the "ludicrous" so amenable to Waugh's satire – this Dickensian scene of domestic novel-reading curiously anticipates (or echoes) Tony's encounter with his own bizarre father-figure, Mr. Todd. Indeed, in *Ninety-Two Days*, the account of his South American travels that furnished material for *A Handful of Dust*, Waugh conceded that while reading Dickens in the jungle he recovered a pleasure in reading he had not experienced since childhood.[56] Like the novel, these autobiographical accounts suggest that the engagement with Dickens is a situation of supernatural enthrallment to a master with uncanny powers – uncanny because, as in childhood, the sentimental pull of the novel can still possess us.

CHAPTER 5

Cold Comfort Farm *and mental life*

Did Evelyn Waugh actually write the cult classic, *Cold Comfort Farm* under the female pen-name Stella Gibbons? According to Gibbons's nephew and biographer, Reggie Oliver, such was the conjecture of one contemporary reviewer who was skeptical that a woman journalist could have authored such a witty novel.[1] Although the reviewer's suggestion may today seem both sexist and bizarre, it recognizes, as Faye Hammill observes, "the similarities between Waugh's comic and parodic practice and Gibbons's" even as it misses the feminist force of the novel.[2] Even more significantly, perhaps, it makes explicit the assumption that satire is primarily a male mode of writing. Dubious as this assumption may sound, it is only a correlative of the widely accepted critical view that the sentimental is a female mode – a view endorsed by both boosters of sentimental fiction such as Jane Tompkins, and detractors, such as Ann Douglas.[3] Their debate, although begun as an aesthetic-political argument about nineteenth-century American fiction, clearly has relevance to both the valuation of twentieth-century consumer culture and the agenda of contemporary feminist scholarship. But, despite the differences, both sides share certain assumptions. As Philip Gould has noted, Tompkins's "revisionist critique" of Douglas ends up reproducing "Douglas's gendered premises for understanding nineteenth-century sentimentalism." Tompkins may reject Douglas's criteria for aesthetic value but she "does not interrogate the category of sentiment so much as revalue it as a feminine possession. [Her] revisionism is founded, in other words, on the same opposition between male and female writers that underlies Douglas's work."[4]

One way to complicate such a schematic position has been to attend to the suffering male as a site of sentimental cathexis, as in the works of Eve Sedgwick, Julie Ellison, and others – to show, in other words, that the structure of sentimental affect is by no means essentially feminine.[5] But another approach is to attend to the figure of the female satirist, to explore the way in which the very different affective dynamics of satire can structure women's writing as well as men's. While other female satirists of the 1930s might serve to develop this argument – Dorothy Parker or Dawn Powell in the United States, or Ivy Compton-Burnett in England – my case study here will be *Cold Comfort Farm*. For Gibbons's novel is both sharp enough in its satire that it could be mistaken for Waugh's, and compelling enough in its feminism that it has been claimed for a tradition of female middlebrow writing,[6] and this convergence itself argues against any easy alignment of antisentimental poses with elitism and misogyny – an alignment, it should be clear by now, that seems to me too readily assumed in contemporary criticism. The witty woman, as Regina Barreca notes, has long been regarded as dangerous and subversive of social norms;[7] reading Gibbons can unsettle, I suggest, both the patriarchal prejudices of the 1930s and the critical orthodoxies of literary study today. To get beyond the old oppositions, then, we should attend to the complexity of the ways in which Gibbons positions her protagonist and her novel within discourses of class, and the way that class in the novel moves along multiple axes – wealth, language, education, literacy, manners, and, most crucially here, affect.

SOME PERVERSIONS OF PASTORAL

Stella Gibbons was born a year before Waugh, and achieved literary success just a few years after him, with *Cold Comfort Farm* in 1932. In the novel, Flora Poste, having completed her education and lost her parents, decides to live with her rural cousins, the Starkadders, at Cold Comfort Farm in Sussex, where she assumes the Herculean task of "tidying up" their unruly lives. Despite some vague and ominous Gothic mysteries hanging over the decaying farm, Flora single-mindedly achieves her aims, as one by one the comically barbarous and filthy Starkadders are cleaned up and/or shipped out of Cold Comfort – a project for which Flora deploys a panoply of modern fads and technologies ranging from birth control and psychoanalysis to cheap consumer goods and the promise of celebrity. Thematically, the central conflict is the clash between Flora's modern, urban way of life and the traditional, rural one of the Starkadders; as Chris Baldick says, the novel "pits contemporary rationality against regressive primitivism and romanticism."[8] Onto this clash can be mapped numerous other thematic oppositions: future/past, intellect/emotion, culture/nature, sublimation/desire, cleanliness/dirt, normality/deviancy, and so on. Stereotypically, of course, these oppositions have been gendered, with masculine culture seen as imposing form upon the raw material of a feminine nature. Gibbons, however, as a female comedian, significantly complicates that formulation by presenting a heroine who unswervingly champions the benefits of modernity, culture, and rationality, and who in taming a wild nature through the strength of her own female agency undoes the linking of that nature with any purported feminine principle.

Frequently characterized as a satire, *Cold Comfort Farm* is by almost all accounts a funny book, although it generally lacks the pessimistic undertones that pervade Waugh's fiction and that are often associated with the satiric. Oliver's assessment is illustrative: "What is striking about the comedy of *Cold Comfort Farm* is that, while maintaining a keen satirical edge and making few concessions to sentimentality, its values are essentially humane."[9] Still, if Gibbons seems less cruel than Waugh, her novel can hardly support Emily Toth's idealistic claim that women's humor is neither exclusive nor mean-spirited, for it scores many of its laughs through the ridicule of Flora's uncultured country cousins.[10] Like *Vile Bodies, Cold Comfort Farm* is set in the "near future," that favorable setting for science fiction, where for the purposes of political propaganda, Futurist fantasy, or satiric emphasis, incipient cultural trends can be imaginatively exaggerated. Like Waugh's work too, it often appears to refuse not merely sentimental but empathetic engagement entirely. On the other hand, in many ways Gibbons reverses the terms of Waugh's project: she champions the urban modernity of the class that he calls the Bright Young Things (with one crucial exception, to be discussed below – Flora hates parties) and attacks the putatively traditional customs of the benighted countryside.

As caricatures, the Starkadders show almost exclusively the comic face of the grotesque which, to recall Ruskin's formulation, embraces both the ludicrous and the fearful; and if the reformative motive of satire works by ridiculing the deviant, *Cold Comfort Farm* seems a textbook case of authorial derision in the service of reform. (Again, I offer this definition only provisionally, since the double movement of satire ultimately breaks down the very distinction between normality and deviancy.) Still, Gibbons easily wins the reader over to her project of imposing on the deviant Starkadders the rudiments of Flora's Enlightenment Code, which is drawn in equal parts from Jane Austen and a fictional *philosophe* dubbed the Abbé Fausse-Maigre. Indeed, Flora's whipping her cousins into shape enacts quite ruthlessly the kind of disciplining and policing regimes that literary studies have come to associate with the social-discursive analyses of Michel Foucault. Every deviant, unruly, or dangerous practice, from incestuous sexuality to slovenly dress to regional habits of speech, is standardized, brought into line with Flora's own metropolitan, bourgeois norms.[11]

Symptomatically, the Starkadders, although they live only a train ride from Flora's London, are repeatedly introduced through metaphors of colonial encounter. When Flora first meets her Aunt Judith, for example, the elder relation regards Flora with stupefaction: "So, Flora mused, must Columbus have felt when the poor Indian fixed his solemn, unwavering gaze upon the great sailor's face. For the first time a Starkadder looked upon a civilized being" (*CCF*, p. 49). Later, when cousin Reuben accedes to Flora's social norms by offering a handshake, Gibbons updates Keats's encounter with Chapman's Homer: "This was the first sign of humanity she had encountered among the Starkadders, and she was moved by it. She felt like stout Cortez or Sir James Jeans on spotting yet another white dwarf" (*CCF*, p. 120). Of course, the Cortez and Columbus comparisons are jokes, jokes that gain their force from the (disrupted) assumption of a significant *difference* between Flora's English country cousins and actual "savages." But in both cases the joke gives away the quasi-imperialist nature of Flora's tidying-up. Flora may not be exactly a conquistador, but she is more than once compared to Florence Nightingale (*CCF*, pp. 20, 163) and behaves very much like (take your pick) a tourist, a social worker, a missionary, or an anthropologist, all of whom, it should be noted, perform relatively similar work in the Foucauldian order of things. (To the extent that Flora is herself satirized for these missionary tendencies, *Cold Comfort Farm* exhibits another typical dynamic of satire, in which the "sympathetic" characters more closely identified with the position of the satirist, such as *A Handful of Dust*'s Tony Last, are themselves subjected to satiric scrutiny.[12]) Hence even before she arrives at Cold Comfort, Flora amusedly imagines Sussex life to enact the sort of violent rituals she would most likely know through racist colonial stereotypes: "Perhaps the farm belongs to Judith now, and her man was carried off in a tribal raid from a neighbouring village" (*CCF*, p. 25).

This analogy between the rural and the colonial in *Cold Comfort Farm* extends well beyond these few moments of laughter, into the novel's representation of language. The natives of Sussex speak a foreign tongue, a language filled with obscure words of apparently Saxon origin (*scrantlet, snood, mirsky, wennet*) and possess a regional accent that surpasses in its eccentricity even the most impenetrable passages of *Wuthering Heights*. ("Mun I? . . . Mun I, Miss Judith? Oh, dunna send me. How can I look in her liddle flower-face, and me knowin' what I know? Oh, Miss Judith,

I beg of 'ee not to send me" (*CCF*, p. 36)). Flora's struggles to grasp this "local idiom" (*CCF*, p. 85) offer Gibbons a rich vein of comedy. Flora sometimes imposes on her cousins more modern manners of speech – asking to be called "Miss Poste" or "Miss Flora" rather than "Robert Poste's child" (*CCF*, p. 57) – while at other times she has to ask the meaning of various regionalisms, as she slowly "learn[s] how to translate the Starkadder argot" (*CCF*, p. 116). Eventually, however, she masters the dialect:

"If ye doan't mean you, who do ye mean?"
Flora abandoned diplomacy, and said, "You."
"Me?"
"Ay, you." She patiently dropped into Starkadder. (*CCF*, p. 118)

In language, then, as well as in other customs (dress, diet, hygiene, sexuality), the colonial metaphors serve to widen the distance between progressive city life and regressive country life into a gulf not between cousins, but between nations or races or even species. Indeed, an evolutionary divide emerges in Gibbons's imagined future almost as stark as that between H. G. Wells's Eloi and Morlocks.

Yet even if the Starkadders, as deviants to be disciplined, or savages to be civilized, suffer a healthy dose of ridicule, Gibbons's real target, as initial reviews realized, often appears to be less the rural per se than the rural novel.[13] Gibbons's experience as a reviewer of such novels is in fact frequently cited as a key source of her inspiration. From the first, the Starkadders are seen to conform to all the clichés of "novels dealing with agricultural life" (*CCF*, p. 26) – a tradition that includes Gibbons's largely forgotten and predominantly female contemporaries as well as more-remembered canonical predecessors ranging from the Brontë sisters to the Powys brothers.[14] Baldick points out that despite our general association of modernism with metropolitan locations and experimental techniques, the realist regional novel was still thriving in 1932. Like little imperialists, the regional novelists struggled to stake out their terrain: "The careers of many of these [rural] novelists illustrate a process by which steady popularity could be achieved by cornering the market in the fictional celebration of a particular unclaimed territory."[15] For these would-be Hardys, the literary marketplace of modernism amounted to a scramble for England.

The rural novel, infused with Gothicism, had become so well known a set of conventions that not only can Gibbons count on her readers getting her references but Flora herself can know in advance exactly how her cousins will conform to generic expectations. Seth and Reuben are named Seth and Reuben because "highly-sexed young men living on farms are always called Seth or Reuben" (*CCF*, p. 14); the Starkadder matriarch Aunt Ada Doom (remembered best for the tag line, "I saw something nasty in the woodshed") is pegged as "the Dominant Grandmother Theme" (*CCF*, p. 57); Meriam the hired girl is recognized as the creation of "women novelists" who "occasionally creat[e] a primitive woman, a creature who was as close to the earth as a bloomy greengage" (*CCF*, p. 69). Hackneyed plot devices such as the dark family secret and the curse lying on the place are also deployed parodically. Crucially, too, Flora is steadfast in *refusing to accept* these conventions and the "medieval superstition" (*CCF*, p. 126) that they imply. She responds, for example, to being told about the curse on the farm with unflappable rationality: "perhaps Cousin Amos could sell the farm and buy another one, without any curse on it, in Berkshire or Dorsetshire?" (*CCF*, p. 56). In thoroughly frustrating the reader's desire to know what nasty something Aunt Ada saw in the woodshed or what wrong was perpetrated against Flora's father, Gibbons shows herself to be similarly rejecting such premodern irrationalism.

Because Gibbons's primary target is a set of literary conventions rather than the lives of real farmers, she parodies not only the plots and characters of the rural novel but also, famously, its narrative description, which teems with metaphor and hyperbole and which anthropomorphizes and sexualizes the landscape:

The brittle air, on which the fans of the trees were etched like ageing skeletons, seemed thronged by the bright, invisible ghosts of a million dead summers. The cold beat in glassy waves against the eyelids of anybody who happened to be out in it. High up, a few chalky clouds doubtfully wavered in the pale sky that curved over against the rim of the Downs like a vast inverted *pot-de-chambre.* (*CCF*, p. 86)

Raymond Williams cites the first chapter of Lawrence's *The Rainbow* as the *locus classicus* of "the rural-sexual metaphor":[16]

They knew the intercourse between heaven and earth, sunshine drawn into the breast and bowels, the rain sucked up in the daytime, nakedness that comes under the wind in autumn, showing the birds' nests no longer worth hiding. Their life and interrelations were such; feeling the pulse and body of the soil, that opened to their furrow for the grain, and became smooth and supple after their ploughing, and clung to their feet with a weight that pulled like desire.[17]

Williams goes on to discuss the way Gibbons spoofs such purple prose:

Some of the more vulnerable examples came to the obvious parody of *Cold Comfort Farm*, but what has to be said about that odd work is not easy.

The excessive gestures of some of the regional novels led straight to this kind of satire, but what is also drawn on, in it, is a suburban uneasiness, a tension of attraction and repulsion, a brittle wit which is a kind of evasion by caricature.[18]

In hesitant and choppy language, Williams goes on to argue that what is evaded – both in Gibbons's novel and the works of the "women novelists" whom she parodies – is the "tension of an increasingly intricate and interlocking society," a tension already explored in the rural novels of Eliot and Hardy. In contrast to these Victorian greats, he claims, the post-1900 rural novel *fabricates* rural isolation precisely because such isolation no longer exists: "The degree of isolation which is actual in the nineteenth-century novels can easily become, in their apparent successors, factitious."[19] And because this isolation is only factitious, as Wendy Parkins notes in enlarging on Williams, modernity has to be understood not solely as the urban but as a dynamic whole that encompasses both country and city, and, crucially, the characters' mobility between the asynchronous temporalities of the two.[20]

Cold Comfort Farm's comedy therefore results not simply from the urbane urbanite's depiction of the rural, but rather from the confrontation of what Bakhtin called two chronotopes, or time-spaces, whose juxtaposition is characteristic of an unevenly developing capitalist modernity. In other words, there would be much less to laugh at without Flora to represent the modern, urban reader's mixture of amusement and revulsion toward the rural. Modifying Williams's claim that the novel is an "evasion by caricature" of the early consequences of globalization, we could say instead that Gibbons's novel rather identifies and plays out the desire within an "interlocking society" to restore and even to *heighten* the diminishing differences between urban and rural, in order to attenuate or repress the social relations between them.[21] Such a heightening in fact would deny not only the social but also the familial relations between country and city: Flora is expressly *not* interested in her inherited "rights" to the farm. She balks at accepting free room and board because "if she lived at Cold Comfort as a guest, it would be an unpardonable impertinence were she to interfere with the family's mode of living; but if she were paying her way, she could interfere as much as she pleased" (*CCF*, p. 63). The exchange of money keeps the relationship professional rather than familial.

At the same time, however, this desire for separation between the urban and rural is undercut by repeated reminders of their interlocking nature. Life on the farm is permeated with suggestions of the modern well before Flora's arrival – Seth stealthily looks at Parisian "art" postcards under the dinner table and turns out to be a cinema junkie, while Meriam's mother aspires for her grandsons to form a jazz band.[22] (This discovery of the familiar in the heart of darkness is a version of the same joke with which Waugh ends *A Handful of Dust*, where Tony's Brazilian adventure concludes with a confrontation with Dickens and domestic English culture.) Because of the latent kinship of city and country, Sussex life proves to be surprisingly recognizable to the young protagonist who has spent time among London's artier crowds. A tense conversation with Cousin Seth is a "conversation in which she had participated before (at parties in Bloomsbury as well as in drawing-rooms in Cheltenham)" (*CCF*, p. 82); sitting in silence with her cousins gives her "the feeling that she was acting in one of the less cheerful German highbrow films" (*CCF*, p. 89). In fact, Gibbons and Flora both prove ingenious in finding unexpected parallels between the two chronotopes, whether it is in comparing the preacher Amos's expression of silent fury at the intrusion of a tardy parishioner to that of maestro Sir Henry Wood when disturbed during a performance of Beethoven's "Eroica" (*CCF*, p. 97), or in likening a tableau of stunned Starkadders shadowed by firelight with a gallery of waxworks at Madame Tussaud's (*CCF*, p. 170). Here the novel uncovers a hidden similarity between rural and urban experience and produces laughter through the unlikelihood of the conjunction. Thus even as the novel's exaggeration of the difference between city and country works to repress or disavow Flora's similarity to the Starkadders, at the same time – moving in the opposite direction – it undermines that difference in order to expose the false idealizations of the regional novel.

One way to resolve this tension between competing forces in the novel is to posit a gap between author and character. Flora may seek to disavow her connection with her barbaric cousins, but Gibbons one-ups Flora by reminding her, and us, of that connection. She thereby reveals what by now might be a familiar structure of desire whereby it can only be recognized when exhibited in another. So while Flora apprehends her difference from the Starkadders, Gibbons reveals that such difference is, to use Williams's word, factitious, a fantasy of difference created precisely for enjoying vicariously whatever unruly pleasures the Starkadders are shown to enjoy. Hence George Orwell's cutting observation on the rural novel: "Experience shows that overcivilised people enjoy reading about rustics (key-phrase, 'close to the soil') because they imagine them to be more primitive and passionate than themselves."[23] The pleasure of reading about the rustic is vicarious, one that can be simultaneously enjoyed and disavowed.

GORGEOUS EMOTIONAL WALLOWINGS

The satiric force of Gibbons's novel then is directed less at the Starkadders of the world than at the novelists who create them. It takes as its primary target not the mundane realities of (modern) English rural life but the excesses of a neo-Gothic or neo-Romantic strain of writing that valorizes everything that Flora abhors – what she calls "gross romanticism" (*CCF*, p. 135). For this reason, the novel's fictional Foreword positions both the author and her reader against a highbrow obscurantist modernism that Gibbons's first-person authorial persona calls "Literature."[24] With an allusion to "Tintern Abbey," Gibbons dedicates her book to the fictional novelist Anthony Pookworthy:

Your books have been something more to me, in the last ten years, than books. They have been springs of refreshment, loafings for the soul, eyes in the dark. They have given me (in the midst of the vulgar and meaningless bustle of newspaper offices) joy. It is just possible that was not quite the kind of joy you intended to give, for which of us is infallible? But it was joy all right. (*CCF*, p. 6)

The twist on Wordsworth here is double: first, for Gibbons it is not *nature* which consoles the author amid the din of towns and cities but rather *nature writing*; and second, because the joy Gibbons experiences is not Wordsworth's "joy / of elevated thoughts" but instead the unintentionally provoked mirth (known all too well by college professors and second-string book reviewers like Gibbons) that is occasioned by exceptionally bad writing. Against Pookworthy's highbrow excess Gibbons positions not only herself but also her middle-class, often female readers, "all those thousands of persons not unlike myself, who work in the vulgar and meaningless bustle of offices, shops, and homes" (*CCF*, p. 6), readers for whose sake she has "adopted the method perfected by the late Herr Baedeker," and marked particularly lush passages with asterisks: "In such a manner did the good man deal with cathedrals, hotels, and paintings by men of genius. There seems no reason why it should not be applied to passages in novels" (*CCF*, pp. 6–7). Gibbons's reader, like her narrator, is a tourist in the land of Starkadder.

This middlebrow, commonsense taste manifests itself not only in the Foreword but throughout the novel. Gibbons makes cracks about Bloomsbury bohemianism and its penchant for swapping sexual partners, and sends up Freudianism via the (unfortunately anti-Semitic) depiction of Mr. Mybug, who finds sexual imagery everywhere, and whose intellectualism poorly conceals an unsavory and misogynistic sexual rapacity.

Modernist drama gets its lumps in a line about Eugene O'Neill plays, "the kind that goes on for hours and hours, until the R.S.P.C. Audiences batters the doors of the theatre in and insists on a tea interval" (*CCF*, p. 177), and in the form of an experimental play on the London stage:

a Neo-Expressionist attempt to give dramatic form to the mental reactions of a man employed as a waiter in a restaurant who dreams that he is the double of another man who is employed as a steward on a liner, and who, on awakening and realizing that he is still a waiter employed in a restaurant and not a steward employed on a liner, goes mad and shoots his reflection in a mirror and dies. It had seventeen scenes and only one character. (*CCF*, p. 146)

Avant-garde film, finally, is represented when Flora recalls a date with a "friend who was interested in the progress of the cinema as an art" (*CCF*, p. 93) and who takes her to a screening of "a film of Japanese life called Yĕs, made by a Norwegian film company in 1915" that consists entirely of "close-ups of water-lilies lying perfectly still on a scummy pond and four suicides, all done extremely slowly" (*CCF*, p. 93).[25] While the audience, dressed in outlandish bohemian style, sits rapt, Flora finds one "conventionally dressed" viewer who shares her tastes, a Hollywood producer whose "gaze had dwelt upon [Flora's] neat hair and well-cut coat with incredulous joy, as of one who should say: 'Dr. Livingstone, I presume?'" (*CCF*, p. 94). The metaphor of colonial encounter, seen earlier in Flora's interactions with the Starkadders, here applies equally well to her existence among barbaric bohemian cinephiles.

It might appear in these instances that Gibbons is simply turning her fire from the rural to the urban, from the unsophisticated to the ultrasophisticated, and these jokes are certainly reminiscent of Waugh's filmmaker-turned-architect Otto Silenus whose desire to transcend the human form leads him to create buildings without staircases. Yet these supposedly forward-looking urban modernists are in fact represented as precisely those "overcivilized people" who promulgate the value of the rural and the primitive and write the very novels that Gibbons spoofs. (It is in a London flat, after all, that a naked Rupert Birkin expounds the virtues of African art in Lawrence's *Women in Love*.) It is well beside the point that Gibbons's jokes might conflate the anti-Freudian Lawrence with the psychoanalytically minded Bloomsbury, and lump both of them with the vaguely Dadaist plays and films whose inanities she details with such glee. For such discriminations hardly matter in the bigger picture, a picture in which all varieties of modernist experimentalism, primitivism, or neo-romanticism are conflated with the behavior of the Starkadders themselves.

For this reason, most critics, following the Birmingham English Studies Group, discern a middlebrow stance not only in the Foreword but in the novel as a whole.[26] Yet, while the send-up of highbrow international modernism is undeniable, it would be far too simple to read *Cold Comfort Farm* as the revenge of an unpretentious middlebrow woman writer on a pervasively male high modernism. For, even as Gibbons spoofs modernism and upholds bourgeois socioeconomic hierarchies (Flora has to instruct the Starkadders in the proper use of their servants), she singles out for ridicule various "women novelists" (*CCF*, p. 67) – of whom the most significant are generally understood to be Sheila Kaye-Smith and Mary Webb – whom she classifies according to the kinds of literary clichés they peddle. Rather than siding with the middlebrow woman novelist against the highbrow male modernist, Gibbons is in fact triangulating – working both sides of Andreas Huyssen's great divide. What Joseph Litvak says of Flora's adored Jane Austen holds true equally for Gibbons herself: "Playing both sides against the middle – against itself – middle-class sophistication vulgarizes mere (i.e., aristocratic) sophistication and sophisticates mere (i.e., lower-class) vulgarity."[27] (In Gibbons's case, "aristocratic" and "lower-class" would denote aesthetic or cultural strata rather than strictly socioeconomic ones.) Even her Baedeker joke in the Foreword is double-edged, catching with one stroke the highbrow aspirations of modernist Pookworthys and with the other the middlebrow desire for an easy shortcut to aesthetic elevation, the need for what Ezra Pound wryly called a "Guide to Kulchur." In *Cold Comfort Farm*, then, putatively male high modernism and putatively female sentimental popular fiction become almost indistinguishable in their flights of stylistic and emotional excess.

These apparent complications make more sense, however, if we frame the conflict of the novel less as one of cultural strata (middlebrow versus highbrow) and more as a problem of affect. Gibbons and Flora both assume that blasé attitude diagnosed by Georg Simmel, and enacted, as we have seen, by Wilde, Beerbohm, and Waugh. Simmel's theorization of the blasé derives directly from the contrast of country and city life that Gibbons explores. In his 1903 essay, "The Metropolis and Mental Life," he claims that levels of affect differ in the metropolis and the provinces. In reaction to the intense stimulation of metropolitan life, he argues, the individual "creates a protective organ for itself" by "reacting [to stimuli] primarily in a rational manner."[28] As a result, "the essentially intellectualistic character of the mental life of the metropolis becomes intelligible as over against that of the small town."[29] An extreme form of this intellectualistic character is what he calls the blasé attitude, a radical intellectualization which levels distinctions and sees all things as quantifiable and interchangeable – in the same way that the abstract character of money replaces more concrete social relations. (Flora, recall, tries to keep her relationship with her cousins one of fee-for-service.) As Simmel puts it in *The Philosophy of Money*, "The blasé person ... has completely lost the feeling for value differences. He experiences all things as being of an equally dull and grey hue, as not worth getting excited about, particularly where the will is concerned."[30]

Flora, much like the Bright Young Things of *Vile Bodies* or Brenda Last's circle in *A Handful of Dust*, embodies this blasé attitude.[31] One of the first things we learn about her is that "The death of her parents did not cause her much grief" (*CCF*, p. 9). She has caused a minor scandal at school because of her inability to "care about lacrosse" (*CCF*, p. 12) or other athletic games; when asked what she does care about, Flora is "not quite sure" (*CCF*, p. 12). She can barely conceive of anything that excites emotional commitment. Most of the activities she finally comes up with are framed in the negative: "not being bothered to do things," "not being asked to express *opinions*," "laughing at the kind of joke other people didn't think at all funny" (*CCF*, p. 12). The negatives imply that responding to stimulus in even the most perfunctory way requires an excessive expenditure of energy, and that the only acceptable response to the emotional commitments of others is a private and minor sense of amusement. When it comes to marriage, too, Flora is pragmatic and unromantic, regarding it with a "compelling, ... almost Gallic, cynicism" (*CCF*, p. 14). Flora can't even be moved by parties; the one form of stimulus that seemed capable of exciting Waugh's Bright Young Things leaves her flat.

If Flora suffers from a deficit of affect, however, Cold Comfort Farm offers a surplus. Aunt Ada Doom, the matriarch of the farm (whose very name provides a rhythmic echo of the place's), revels in everything Flora abhors:

Persons of Aunt Ada's temperament were not fond of a tidy life. Storms were what they liked; plenty of rows, and doors being slammed, and jaws sticking out, and faces white with fury, and faces brooding in corners, and faces making unnecessary fuss at breakfast, and plenty of opportunities for gorgeous emotional wallowings. (*CCF*, p. 57)

Her daughter Judith, similarly, has "a habit of multiplying every emotion she felt by twice its own weight" (*CCF*, p. 203), while Cousin Harkaway is "given to bursts of fury about very little, when you came to sift matters" (*CCF*, p. 39) – here the narrative voice takes on the blasé outlook of Flora herself. Indeed, Flora realizes early on that "things seemed to go wrong in the country more frequently, somehow, than they did in Town" (*CCF*, p. 21). That the country, not the city, should be the site of emotional display accords fully with Simmel's assessment: "The mental life . . . of the small town . . . rests more on feelings and emotional relationships."[32] Yet we should also note some distance now from Simmel's formulation: while for Simmel (as for Lawrence in the passage cited above) the country offers affective rhythms associated with "the steady equilibrium of unbroken customs," it appears for Gibbons as wild and regressive.[33]

But if Flora can't abide excessive emotion, why does she head off to Sussex in the first place? The short answer is that even as she aims to *discipline* the Starkadders' unruly affect, Flora also seeks to *experience* the affect for her own pleasure. Here we see again the tension between Flora's disavowal of her kinship with the Starkadders and the consistent narratorial recognition of it – the tension that Orwell discerns in mocking the overcivilized for their pleasure in reading about the rustic. Such tension is, moreover, a version of the duplicity that I am arguing is characteristic of satire itself, excoriating vice and representing it in the same gesture. What the Starkadders offer Flora is pleasurable stimulation. Flora believes that living with relatives will be "more amusing" (*CCF*, p. 20) than working, which offers only the routinization of experience that Simmel and many other social theorists discerned as a signal aspect of modern urban life. Even the skeptical Mrs. Smiling concedes that life with the Sussex cousins "does sound *interesting* and appalling" – although ultimately not interesting enough to overcome Flora's blasé attitude: "You will soon grow tired of it, anyhow" (*CCF*, p. 26). When Flora boards the train for Howling(!), Sussex, she reassures her friends that she will "find it very amusing and not at all too much for me" (*CCF*, p. 30), and later finds the place "not without its promise of mystery and excitement" (*CCF*, p. 58). In the end, the place makes good on this promise; just before her departure she tells Reuben that her stay has "been the most enormous diversion" (*CCF*, p. 211).

Without doubt, there is, in addition to this pleasurable "diversion," a hint of revulsion or horror that plays around the edges of Flora's consciousness as she anticipates and actually experiences life on the farm. Her first words in Sussex are "How revolting!" (*CCF*, p. 46), and the "revolting," "appalling," "mysterious" aspect of Cold Comfort Farm suggests the "fearful" side of Ruskin's grotesque. Yet throughout the novel Flora fulfills her pledge to her friends by mastering such revulsion and taming her own affect, with the end result that the Sussex holiday provides just enough of an affective charge to divert her, but never so much as radically to disconcert her. No longer merely a descriptive term, used by Simmel to identify a reaction on the part of the modern subject to metropolitan life, the blasé is now a prescriptive one, an emotional protocol imposed with the aim of extending bourgeois norms.

In its imposition of modern codes of affect, then, Flora's quest to discipline the Starkadders departs from the paradigmatic nineteenth-century novelistic plot as formulated first by Georg Lukács and later by Walter Benjamin as a search for the meaning of life on the part of a hero who senses the fragmented nature of modern existence.[34] Such a formulation – what Lukács called "transcendental homelessness,"[35] and which, Elizabeth Goodstein argues, owes a direct debt to Simmel's attention to "the subjective effects of modernization" and his analysis of the ways in which the subject resists or adapts to the demands of modernity[36] – posits a gulf between an inner need and an (unattainable) outer meaning. As Lukács puts it, "The novel is the epic of an age in which the extensive totality of life is no longer directly given, in which the immanence of meaning in life has become a problem, yet which still thinks in terms of totality."[37] However, Flora's desire hardly hints at the heroic, Lukácsian scale of reconciling individual(ized) experience with the meaning of life. For she seeks nothing so grand as "the meaning of life" but only desires "amusement." And amusement – as opposed to pleasure, or joy, or ecstasy – designates merely a base-level pleasurable stimulus, the smallest possible elevation of affect above boredom itself. Thus where Lukács finds in the grand aspirations of the novelistic subject a heroic desire for meaning, Gibbons replaces the heroic *character* with a *type*, a type whose inmost desires are no more than itches, whims, and hankerings.

In this idea of a type, rather than a fully individuated character, we can see the frustration of what Simmel calls the Romantic urge for individual distinction, the desire of "individuals who had been liberated from their historical bonds ... to distinguish themselves from one another."[38] Thus while the Romantic strain of the novel – or even what I've earlier called the humanist-ethical strain – places a premium on what Simmel calls the individual's "qualitative uniqueness and irreplaceability" as "criteria of his value,"[39] Wyndham Lewis's anti-Romantic "classicism" scoffs at such an individuating desire and chooses instead to see all human beings as types. Indeed, the reduction of characters to types is exactly what Lewis calls the external method of satire.

Moreover, as soon as the novel's conflict is framed as a problem of the regulation of affect – of avoiding both boredom and emotional overload – then once again its many seemingly superficial references to the colonies prove telling. Mrs. Smiling's numerous suitors earn from Flora and Mrs. Smiling the Whitmanian nickname of "the Pioneers-O" for their far-flung travels to the outposts of empire: "All the Pioneers-O had short, brusque nicknames rather like the cries of strange animals, but this was quite natural, for they all came from places full of strange animals" (*CCF*, p. 10). Sure enough, whereas Mrs. Smiling's hobbies include "the imposing of reason and moderation into the bosoms of some fifteen gentlemen of birth and fortune who were madly in love with her" (*CCF*, p. 10), her suitors conversely are marked by affective regression, as Flora observes: "Curious how Love destroys every vestige of that politeness which the human race, in its years of evolution, has so painfully acquired" (*CCF*, p. 30). Thus the emotionally profligate Pioneers-O serve for Mrs. Smiling the same function that the effusive Starkadders serve for Flora: that of providing affective stimulus through the vicarious experience of regression.

In addition to the goal of amusement, however, Flora confesses to another motive behind her visit to Cold Comfort; she hopes to "collect ... material" for a novel she will someday write that she intends to be "as good as 'Persuasion', but with a modern setting" (*CCF*, p. 19). The novel for her is a kind of travel writing (again the Baedeker reference in the Foreword proves resonant), a gathering of exotic rural experience and packaging of it for the consumption of the metropolitan stay-at-home.[40] In like manner, the Pioneers-O return from the colonies with their own hoard of narrative treasures, real-life tales that still possess the ability to thrill; at a dinner in London, a suitor named Bikki "pleased [Flora and Mrs. Smiling] by corroborating all the awful rumours they had heard about [Kenya]" (*CCF*, p. 10). For the city-dweller, therefore, the colony (or the countryside) offers not only resources and labor to be exploited but also life experiences that are still capable of rousing affective response. Indeed, this stimulative potential of the colony goes a long way to explaining the modernist cultural interest in the colonial itself: it serves as a counterweight to the deadening effects of the European metropolitan present. If Picasso weren't bored with European art, he might never have picked up those African masks.[41]

In short, while both the countryside and the colony are marked by emotional tempest, Flora seeks both to impose and to project outer calm on Cold Comfort just as Mrs. Smiling seeks to impose it on her Pioneers-O. Flora imposes it through modern technologies. When instructed in the use of birth control, Meriam is told to use her "intelligence" to ensure that "nothing will happen to [her]" (*CCF*, p. 69), while the intractable Aunt Judith, oedipally fixated on her son Seth, is simply sent to a Viennese analyst who re-routes her emotions onto old European churches: "It was one of his disagreeable duties as a State psycho-analyst to remove the affections of his patients from the embarrassing objects upon which they were concentrated; and focus them, instead, upon himself. It was true that they did not remain focused there for long: as soon as he could, he switched them onto something harmless, like chess or gardening" (*CCF*, p. 201). Indeed, this therapeutic re-channeling of affect is what has *already* happened to Mrs. Smiling, whose only erotic commitment is her hobby of collecting brassieres (a sublimation of sexuality through shopping), and even to Flora herself, whose own "harmless" hobby is nothing less than the very project of disciplining the Starkadders that constitutes the novel.

But as important as Flora's imposition of equanimity on Cold Comfort Farm is her imposition of it on herself. Throughout the novel, Flora's interactions with her cousins, and her social exchanges more generally, are characterized by disinterestedness in her pursuit of predetermined aims, a kind of professional neutrality that emerges in the repeated comparisons of social relations to games of strategy. Thus although Flora "detested rows and scenes," of the kind favored by the Starkadders, she gains a reduced pleasure from more bloodless intellectual games and contests: "[She] enjoyed quietly pitting her cool will against opposition. It amused her; and when she was defeated, she withdrew in good order and lost interest in the campaign" (*CCF*, p. 129). A conversation with Seth strikes her as "a kind of jockeying for place, a shifting about of the pieces on the board before the real game began" (*CCF*, p. 82). When she tries to ignore the unctuous Mybug, "he was forced to open the game with, 'Well?' (A gambit which Flora, with sinking heart, recognized as one used by intellectuals who had decided to fall in love with you)" (*CCF*, p. 101). Flora's reduction of social exchange to strategic calculation wholly concords with Simmel's analysis of metropolitan habits of mind: "The calculating exactness of practical life which has resulted from a money economy corresponds to the ideal of natural science, namely that of transforming the world into an arithmetical problem."[42]

Indeed for Simmel (as for Benjamin after him) the experience of modernity is figured as a traumatic shock, characterized as it is by "the unexpectedness of violent stimuli,"[43] and the blasé attitude is a direct response to this shock. Thus an emblematic modern figure is the traumatized veteran of the Great War, central to texts such as *Mrs. Dalloway*, *Beyond the Pleasure Principle*, *The Sun Also Rises*, and, as we saw, *Antic Hay*. Gibbons plays on this trope in the description of Flora's London friend Claud, who "had served in the Anglo-Nicaraguan wars of '46"

(*CCF*, p. 160), and whose resigned acceptance of life's follies and injustices matches any of Hemingway's wounded and stoic soldiers: "He had seen his friends die in anguish in the wars. For him, the whole of the rest of his life was an amusing game which no man of taste and intelligence could permit himself to take seriously" (*CCF*, p. 160). Behind Claud's formulation of social relations as a game of strategy or an arithmetical problem lie very real human stakes. Yet the narrator, equal to or exceeding Claud in indifference, gives no further hint of those stakes, and even implies that the traumatized veteran shocked into aloofness is itself a narrative convention worthy of spoofing.

Still, to say that Flora, like Claud, regards social relations as a game is not to say that she cannot experience heightened emotional states, only that she makes every effort to avoid such heightened states or to restore herself to a state of calm – that is, that she believes "her own conduct must be carefully regulated" (*CCF*, p. 155). When cousin Amos, a preacher in the Church of the Quivering Brethren, describes physically striking a female congregant with a Bible in order "to let the devil out of her soul," Flora seems disturbed by the misogynistic violence, but soon regains her poise: "'And did it come out?' asked Flora, endeavouring with some effort to maintain the proper spirit of scientific enquiry" (*CCF*, p. 90). When Judith, speaking of Meriam's yearly pregnancies, claims, "'Tes the hand of Nature, and we women cannot escape it," Flora is irritated, but maintains her outer calm, as we learn in a parenthetical aside: "('Oh, can't we?' thought Flora, with spirit, but aloud she only made such noises of tut-tutting regret as she felt were appropriate to the occasion")" (*CCF*, p. 64). Or again, when Urk intercepts a letter for her – importantly, one from her cousin Charles with whom she is (against her pragmatic beliefs about marriage) falling in love – she experiences "a start of indignation" but allows her anger to come through only in her "crisp" tone of voice and a short wisecrack (one that itself is facetiously censured by the even more blasé narrator):

"Who's writing to you from Howchiker?"
"Mary, Queen of Scots. Thanks," said Flora, with deplorable pertness, and twitched
    [the letter] out of his hand. (*CCF*, p. 140)

As a general rule, much of the comedy of the novel sets Flora as a "straight man" in exactly this way, as she determinedly keeps her cool amid the astonishing and outrageous excesses of life at Cold Comfort. At the same time, she seeks to minimize any other possible source of excitation, which might distract her from her reformative project. For this reason she chooses not to have Charles come out from London to escort her to a ball: "if Charles came to partner her she would be conscious of a certain interest in their own personal relationship, a current of unsaid speeches, which would distract her feelings and perhaps confuse a little her thoughts" (*CCF*, p. 137). Even in the narration, the "speeches" must be "unsaid" – like Flora's unspoken parenthetical thoughts in the exchange with Judith cited above – and Flora only owns up to the possibility of "a little" confusion. Her erotic attachment is acknowledged only to be deemed impermissible in the next clause; like a boxer before a championship bout, Flora regards libidinal excitation as a dangerous distraction from her disinterested professional goals.

Flora then embodies internally the same struggle to master affect that the novel more generally dramatizes; on both counts, by and large, she succeeds. Flora not only acknowledges her desire for this success but in fact presents it to herself as a struggle between competing world views: "It would be a triumph of the Higher Common Sense over Aunt Ada Doom. It would be a victory for Flora's philosophy of life over the sub-conscious life-philosophy of the Starkadders" (*CCF*, p. 134). In defeating Aunt Ada, Flora sees herself as triumphing over female sentimental excess. Her conviction of the rightness of her cause is bolstered by her recognition that the sentimental itself serves as a cover for power relations, a kind of *ressentiment*, or, to use Sedgwick's neologism, ressentimentality.[44] Through this ressentimentality Aunt Ada transforms her own vague sense of injury (from having seen that something nasty in the woodshed) into a tyrannical ability to subject others to her will: "It struck her that Aunt Ada Doom's madness had taken the most convenient form possible" (*CCF*, p. 119). Flora articulates the modernist hermeneutic of suspicion as directed toward affective life. The blasts of emotion emanating from the matriarch are interpreted as tools of domination, and Aunt Ada's long-nurtured wound is ironically redescribed as an exercise in aggrandizing self-deception. To be sure, the men at Cold Comfort Farm can be equally excessive in their emotions, and equally exploitive, but in making the tyrant of the farm a matriarch, Gibbons suggests that Flora's battle is not merely over the sentimental but over the representation of the female *as* sentimental.

TOLERABLE COMFORT

It is this triumph of the Enlightenment maxims of the Abbé Fausse-Maigre over the *ressentiment* of the Brontëan madwoman in the attic[45] that Gibbons signals in her choice of the novel's epigraph, Jane Austen's famous first-person intrusion in the first line of the last chapter of

Mansfield Park: "Let other pens dwell on guilt and misery." Gibbons implies – to resituate the epigraph in its original context – an Austenian desire to "quit such odious subjects," "to restore everybody ... to tolerable comfort," and "to have done with all the rest."[46] It is crucial here to discern the importance of Gibbons's choice of Austen's comic-satiric mode of writing as a means of achieving the desired "tolerable comfort." Bored with, or uninterested in, the emotional wallowings of Aunt Ada and her ilk, Gibbons deliberately deploys a tonal approach to her subject – a sensibility – that can both represent and master the affective surplus that Cold Comfort Farm provides. This approach is nothing less than satire itself. In Gibbons's Foreword, the author distinguishes the comic-satiric mode of her own book, which is "meant to be ... funny" (Gibbons's ellipses) from Pookworthy's more ambitious literary endeavors, which are "not ... funny" (*CCF*, p. 6) and which she describes as "records of intense spiritual struggles, staged in the wild settings of mere, berg or fen ... more like thunderstorms than books" (*CCF*, p. 6). (That cliché of the sublime, the thunderstorm, should also recall Aunt Ada's pleasure in emotionally stormy weather.) Gibbons's satiric provocation of laughter is an alternative, even an antidote, to the emotional deluges of sentimental fiction, including those of sentimental modernism.

By disciplining the affect of Cold Comfort Farm, then, Gibbons-as-Flora achieves the kind of emotion-free state that Henri Bergson sees as necessary to the production of the comic. The comic for Bergson, like the urban for Simmel, is characteristic of the intelligence rather than the passions. Bergson notes "the absence of feeling which usually accompanies laughter," and argues that, for comedy to succeed, something quite like the blasé attitude is required: "It seems as though the comic could not produce its disturbing effect unless it fell, so to say, on the surface of a soul that is thoroughly calm and unruffled ... Laughter has no greater foe than emotion."[47] Bergson's concluding formulation is striking: "the comic demands something like a momentary anaesthesia of the heart."[48] Like Simmel, too, the post-Darwinian Bergson notes that life requires the organism to respond to stimuli and adapt to a changing environment: "What life and society require of each of us is a constantly alert attention that discerns the outlines of the present situation, together with a certain elasticity of mind and body to enable us to adapt ourselves in consequence."[49] This "elasticity of mind," like Simmel's "intellectualistic" mental character of the metropolitan, is for Bergson a characteristic of the human, as opposed to the rigidity that makes people mechanical or thing-like. It is precisely such intelligent or abstract adaptability that Flora demonstrates in achieving her reformative goals. Never in thrall to her passions, she is steady but never mad in pursuit, dogged but never obsessed. Thus the novel itself, in imposing Austenian tidiness on the Brontëan countryside, preserves just enough of the unruly emotions of the Starkadders to cause pleasure, but never so much as to incite revulsion or violence.

There is, however, a significant glitch in this reading of the novel as a story of the affective modernization of Cold Comfort Farm, and that is the novel's ending. This ending imposes on an otherwise idiosyncratic narrative a highly conventional marriage plot in which Flora, after arranging her cousin Elfine's wedding, agrees to marry her handsome cousin Charles, who then whisks her away from Sussex in his airplane, the *Speed Cop II*. As the propellers begin to roar, Flora leans against Charles and puts aside her cares: "Like all really strong-minded women, on whom everybody flops, she adored being bossed about. It was so restful" (*CCF*, p. 232). Such an ending seems to indulge all of the sentimental tendencies – the reader's and the heroine's – so professionally kept at bay for the course of the novel. The cool exterior in fact begins to crack a bit earlier when Flora concedes a "something strangely like affection" (*CCF*, p. 203) for the farm, and the narrator (with no ironic Baedeker-style asterisks) lavishes praise upon the beauty of the countryside, which now is beginning to resemble a landscaped English garden more than a Brontëan moor: "There were no clouds in the blue sky, whose colour was beginning to deepen with the advance of night, and the face of the whole countryside was softened by the shadows which were slowly growing in the depths of the woods and hedgerows" (*CCF*, p. 203). The apparently conventional ending seems lifted straight out of Hollywood romances, and appears to give in to exactly the kind of sentimentality that women are accused – even by Gibbons – of producing and consuming. Does this conventional ending represent a capitulation to sentimentality? Or is it, as Reggie Oliver suggests, merely a compromise-formation, in which a modicum of affection can be admitted only after author and heroine alike have proven themselves sufficiently tough-minded? It must also be asked what are the consequences of this ending for the novel's feminist possibilities. Is this reversion to sentiment a feminist affirmation of the value of feeling? Or, conversely, by acknowledging the sentimental in Flora does it reinstate the hierarchies that the blasé Flora and the satiric Gibbons had seemed so successful at overturning?

Those critics who do comment on the ending tend to see it as a move away from satire toward "nostalgia and romance,"[50] and Parkins sees a reversion to a nineteenth-century "narrative of the woman as domestic manager."⁵¹ Now it may be that this critical suspicion of the romantic happy ending is a result of the triumph of modernist aesthetics, a suspicion that makes love itself appear as sentimentality. As Suzanne Clark writes: "Episodes of love . . . appear in the modern, rational conversation, the discourse of our times, as something to be gotten over, grown out of."⁵² The questions, then, about how to interpret the ending of *Cold Comfort Farm* only replicate the larger debate about the sentimental in culture more generally, distilled in the still-volatile 1980s debate within feminism between Douglas (who contends that the sentimental is complicit with patriarchy) and Tompkins (who argues for its aesthetic value and political force). Indeed, Rita Felski has shown persuasively that women within modernism were paradoxically represented as both *outside* of modernity – primitive and pre-cultural – and *emblematic* of it – though generally emblematic of the "demonized" aspect of a cultural formation characterized by needless and mindless consumption. Gibbons, in this light, may be said to face a double-bind in her theorization of the modern. In rejecting the misogynist characterization of the female as primitive, emotional, and outside of culture, she makes Flora an agent of civilization. But she then finds herself running up against the equally misogynist cliché of the woman as representative of the "vulgar materialism brought about by capitalist development."⁵³

To a degree then, any critical suspicion of the affective stances prompted in the novel's final pages ultimately signals a more fundamental double-bind in theorizing what Felski calls the gender of modernity. However, there is yet another interpretive possibility I want to introduce. That possibility begins with Regina Barreca's reading of *Mansfield Park*'s final marriage – a marriage that has historically produced similar dissatisfaction among readers. Writes Barreca about Fanny Price's all-too-perfect union with Edmund Bertram: "Austen refuses to provide the final satisfaction of a romance achieved through routes other than the path dictated by the textual necessity of a happy ending."⁵⁴ Austen acknowledges her reader's desire for, or the generic demand for, the marriage between Fanny and Edmund, but she provides it in such a cursory way as to signal the weakness of her own commitment to such conventions. It is hardly a stretch to believe that Gibbons uses the identical strategy in *Cold Comfort Farm*, or even that she learned such a strategy from *Mansfield Park*. Gibbons draws her epigraph from that novel and has Flora read the book "to refresh her spirits" (*CCF*, p. 206) as *Cold Comfort Farm* nears its climax. Flora Poste shares the initials of her name with Fanny Price, and, like Fanny, her chosen mate is a cousin who anachronistically plans to be a country parson. (Gibbons's own husband was, just as anachronistically, himself a country parson; but all that tells us is that Gibbons modeled her own life, as well as her character's, after a Jane Austen novel.[55]) The prominent allusions serve not only to invoke a general Austenian aesthetic of tidiness but also to recognize Austen's own duplicity in the use of the marriage plot. Thus, rather than simply surrendering her agency to a husband, Flora agrees to be bossed around by Charles for the simple reason that Gibbons/Flora has already exerted such mastery in designing Charles as the cliché of the perfect husband. Charles is a machine Flora has built, another modern appliance – like the new brush she gives Adam to replace the thorny twig he uses to clean the dishes – that can relieve her of one more wearying task of domestic management.

The feminist possibilities of the novel then can survive this parodic but perhaps not wholly cynical concession to romance.[56] Flora, inarguably, has shown herself a model of a modern, educated woman. She advocates birth control to Meriam, the hired girl, and thus frees her from the yearly spring pregnancies that have come upon her seemingly as naturally as the budding of the sukebind flowers. (That Flora possesses the knowledge of how to instruct Meriam in contraception suggests too that she is not herself inexperienced sexually.) She quietly bristles at the pet theories of the misogynistic Mybug, who suggests that women lack souls and that Branwell Brontë was the real author behind his sisters' successes. And Flora's Enlightenment values certainly include the sexual liberation of women:

There they all were. Enjoying themselves. Having a nice time. And having it in an ordinary human manner. Not having it because they were raping somebody, or beating somebody, or having religious mania or being doomed to silence by a gloomy, earthy pride, or loving the soil with the fierce desire of a lecher, or anything of that sort. No, they were just enjoying an ordinary human event, like any of the other millions of ordinary people in the world. (*CCF*, p. 217)

Literary studies have become so used to knee-jerk critiques of Enlightenment that the liberatory claims of Flora's reforms can easily seem a Foucauldian ruse of power. To be sure, disciplining those labeled deviant, even through apparently benign mechanisms, has historically caused much suffering. But in speaking in favor of liberal, reformist feminism, in siding with the politics of Marie Stopes rather than Flem Snopes, Gibbons also speaks for social organization as a triumph of not only the human, but also the humane. For Enlightenment may be an incomplete project, but it is not a misguided one. Indeed, in this valorization of the ordinary and the normal, in the linking of the reformed Starkadders to millions of others, Flora – as a comedian and a satirist within the text – enacts a leveling of distinctions and renders the Starkadders "ordinary," merely a few among "millions." Such a leveling is, more than anything, blasé: "The essence of the blasé attitude is an indifference toward distinctions between things."[57]

CHAPTER 6

Nathanael West and the mystery of feeling

Understanding the place of satire within modernism entails, I have been arguing, attention to the ways in which modern feeling can take on surprising new guises. Every bit as much as Waugh and Gibbons, Nathanael West explicitly thematizes problems of feeling throughout his writing. Often in his work, the mere experience of particular emotions, especially in response to scenes of suffering, becomes a source of conflict for characters and readers alike. As Justus Nieland has observed, West "regularly refuses to provide the affective codes that might give his reader a clue about how to feel."[1] Such conflict arises because even as West's fiction subjects sentimental expressions of feeling to intense satiric scrutiny, it is no less searching in its scrutiny of satire itself, and of the ironic or joking postures that accompany it. In fact, the artistic quests of virtually all West's protagonists can be seen very simply as efforts to resolve the tension between the claims of satire and those of sentiment. West's fiction at once manifests and resists a satiric impulse, and the push and pull of this ambivalence constitute the central dynamic of his work.

At the age of nineteen, writing in the Brown University literary magazine, West already discerns this conflict: "In reading Euripides, we find ourself ready to classify him at moments as a satirist and at other moments as a man of feeling. Of course he was both. Sometimes he seems like a religious man and again like a charlatan. Of course he was neither. He was a great playwright."[2] In this formulation, wry in its own tone if bland in its conclusions, satire negates feeling, and both pose risks for the writer: excessive feeling leads to religion and mysticism, while excessive satire leads to performance and charlatanry. In *The Dream Life of Balso Snell,* similarly, John Gilson remarks: "I always find it necessary to burlesque the mystery of feeling at its source; I must laugh at myself, and if the laugh is 'bitter,' I must laugh at the laugh. The ritual of feeling demands burlesque."[3] Feeling for Gilson is mere ritual, empty adherence to a prescribed norm; both sentimental feelings and the bitter negation of those feelings must be rejected. In contrast to this ever-more-ironic suppression of feeling stands "mystery," a term that gestures at the unknowable and the authentic, and which, I will argue, is never wholly negated in West.

What follows is an exploration of this "mystery of feeling" in West's writing, the need to burlesque this mystery, and indeed the need to burlesque the burlesque. I examine West's extra-fictional writings and his fate among his critics, and find within them a tension between self-definition and political commitment – a tension which fundamentally structures West's last novel, *The Day of the Locust*, producing a dominant mood that has been called grotesque. West deploys two distinct valences of the grotesque: the grotesque as the sign of tormented interiority (derived in part from Sherwood Anderson) and an externalist grotesque that depicts the human as mechanical (in the manner of Wyndham Lewis). The West that emerges in my reading is thus neither (quite) the modernist-as-expressionist who gives words to the agony of existence, nor the modernist-as-ironist who regards such agony with cold-eyed detachment. Ultimately, West's grotesque representations provoke an uncanny dread, and paradoxically affirm the importance of the feeling they set out to negate.

THE TERRIBLE SINCERE STRUGGLE

In moving across the Atlantic, from Waugh and Gibbons to West, many of the dynamics of late modernist satire remain clearly recognizable. But there is no doubt that West operates on a wider social canvas than the English contemporaries I have treated, and abandons the subgenre of the comedy of manners. Consequently, a broader public – which in Waugh appears as a disembodied force of public opinion vaguely impinging on an insular upper-class world – is in the American writer addressed directly, as a massive if still often anonymous social entity. This obvious concern with working-class suffering has been crucial to the attempt of recent critics to claim West for a progressive strain of experimental literature that descends from a Continental "avant-garde," and to attenuate his connection to a putatively more formalistic, apolitical "modernism."[4] According to critics such as Rita Barnard and Jonathan Veitch, such a depoliticized, "modernist" version of West was created by a post-war liberalism that took the suffering of his angst-ridden, sexually frustrated, Dostoevskian heroes, and their withdrawal into dream, delusion, and art, as symptomatic of a vaguely existentialist human condition – a "metaphysical sense of the helplessness of man trapped in an unstable universe."[5] In contrast, Barnard, Veitch, and others have related West's work to consumerism, professionalization, and mass media, resituating his novels within the historical and ideological context of 1930s America and finding in them a critique of a world permeated by simulacrum and commodity-fetishism.[6]

As it turns out, this politically refurbished version of West conforms well to the once-standard narrative of literary history in which the 1930s mark a return to politics from the formalistic concerns of the 1920s.[7] Whatever the flaws in that narrative, the enormous political and economic upheavals of the decade undoubtedly registered on some of its most aloof wits, as Dorothy Parker attested in 1937:

> I want to say first that I came to Spain without my ax to grind. I didn't bring messages from anybody, nor greetings to anybody. I am not a member of any political party. The only group I have ever been affiliated with is that not especially brave little band that hid its nakedness of heart and mind under the out-of-date garment of a sense of humor. I heard someone say, and so I said it too, that ridicule is the most effective weapon. I don't suppose I ever really believed it, but it was easy and comforting and so I said it. Well, now I know. I know that there are things that never have been funny, and never will be. And I know that ridicule may be a shield, but it is not a weapon.[8]

West was friendly with Parker and had familial connections to her celebrated circle of wits; his sister, Laura, married and wrote screenplays with S. J. Perelman, while his wife, Eileen McKenney, was the subject her own sister Ruth's stories in the *New Yorker*. Yet if these biographical links suggest particular geographic or institutional locations for late modernist satire, the more fundamental similarity between West and Parker is the shared notion that satire can be outgrown, that irony can be and must be put aside when political commitment finally calls.

Yet there is a crucial difference. While Parker avers with confidence that "there are things that never have been funny, and never will be," West struggles to make such a renunciation. Thus, even those who aim to recover a political West must concede that his is a peculiar case. His politics were progressive, and in the later 1930s he attended meetings of the Hollywood anti-Nazi League, but he had, by the spring of 1939, rejected the mode of the prominent leftist writers of the day.[9] In a letter to Malcolm Cowley, he describes himself as divided – committed to the cause but unable to accept its literature:

Take the "mother" in Steinbeck's swell novel – I want to believe in her and yet inside myself I honestly can't. When not writing a novel – say at a meeting of a committee we have out here to help the migratory worker – I do believe it and try to act on that belief. But at the typewriter by myself I can't.[10]

Whereas Parker self-importantly renounces her comic tendencies, West worries that he can't escape his: "I'm a comic writer and it seems impossible for me to handle any of the 'big things' without seeming to laugh or at least smile."[11]

His uncontrollable comic proclivities, he fears, are also hurting him commercially. To Edmund Wilson and F. Scott Fitzgerald, he voices the identical complaint:

Somehow or other I seem to have slipped in between all the "schools." My books meet no needs except my own, their circulation is practically private and I'm lucky to be published. And yet I only have a desire to remedy all that *before* sitting down to write, once begun I do it my way. I forget the broad sweep, the big canvas, the shot-gun adjectives, the important people, the significant ideas, the lessons to be taught, the epic Thomas Wolfe, the realistic James Farrell – and go on making what one critic called "private and unfunny jokes."[12]

A private and unfunny joke is something of an oxymoron, since, as Freud and Bergson both note, jokes are inherently social. Yet West's jokes are unshared and noncathartic, achieving no therapeutic release.[13] His joking style thus defeats any political impulse. He mentions to Cowley an excised scene from *The Day of the Locust*: "I tried to describe a meeting of the Anti-Nazi League, but it didn't fit and I had to substitute a whorehouse and a dirty film. The terrible sincere struggle of the League came out comic when I touched it and even libelous."[14] A Midas of irony, everything West touches turns into a joke.

West's letters, in short, articulate a rift between his ethical-political ambitions ("the terrible sincere struggle") and the aesthetic constraints of his sensibility ("private and unfunny jokes"), a rift that has been reproduced in the critical debate over the meaning of his work as political or ironic.[15] Could West reconcile his political beliefs and his comic mode of writing? In a letter of June 1939, West articulates a solution to his friend Jack Conroy:

As I understand it, Balzac, Marx thought, was the better writer, even revolutionist, than [Eugène] Sue, despite the fact that Sue was a confirmed radical while Balzac called himself a royalist. Balzac was the better because he kept his eye firmly fixed on the middle class and wrote with great truth and no wish-fulfillment. The superior truth alone in Balzac was sufficient to reveal the structure of middle class society and its defects.[16]

His own "great truth," West implies, is superior to the "wish-fulfillment" that the neonaturalists trade in. Of course, many readers have found that in West's novels the very problem with a modern, artifice-ridden culture lies in its false promise of just such an easy wish-fulfillment – what is elsewhere named sentimentality. By implication, the neonaturalist aesthetic would be a symptom of the same sentimental culture it denounces, and the rejection of the wish-fulfillment it proffers would be necessary for any legitimate political critique.[17]

What is the role for satire in this formula? If one accepts the assumption that satire is a normative, moralistic mode, its function seems clear enough: comic ridicule (technique) works in the service of social criticism (content). But, as I've tried to demonstrate, satire's moral impulse can mask, even license, more primitive energies; satire, by delighting in the representation and ridicule of vice, unleashes the moral entropy it purports to decry. Even if West at times can be seen as excoriating vice, the anarchic power set free by his satire regularly exceeds the aims of moral correction. The problem is not simply that the author himself claimed to have "no particular message for a troubled world (except possibly 'beware')."[18] It is that West employs the same satiric method in treating causes with which he claims sympathy (like the struggle of the anti-Nazi League) as in treating ideologies he rejects.

For example, in *A Cool Million*, the simple-minded hero, Lemuel Pitkin, witnesses a didactic Communist "playlet" that shows an old grandmother defrauded of her life savings by ruthless capitalists.[19] But it is impossible to read West's presentation of this play as an indictment of capitalism. We laugh at the clichéd symbolism with which the salesman entices the grandmother to surrender her money, but the play itself relies on a symbolism no less inert. From the "old white-haired grandmother knitting near the fire" in "a typical American home," to the "sleek, young salesman" with the "rich melodic voice," to the "idle breeze [that] plays mischievously with the rags draping the four corpses," the entire drama is written to highlight its own predictability; it treats the reader as if she were as mentally under-equipped as Lem himself.[20] While it is true that Lem – to our surprise and delight – is profoundly upset by the play, this sensitivity is less a sign of his ethical convictions than of his stunning idiocy. Rather than engaging our sympathy for the grandmother's plight, the comedy disengages us. The delight the novel takes in its depiction of the Marxist morality play suggests a sensibility that puts aside political concerns for comic indulgence.

An even more tangled treatment of Marxist theory occurs in *Miss Lonelyhearts*, where the editor Shrike distributes to partygoers letters that the advice columnist Miss Lonelyhearts has received:

This one is a jim-dandy. A young boy wants a violin. It looks simple; all you have to do is get the kid one. But then you discover that he has dictated the letter to his little sister. He is paralyzed and can't even feed himself. He has a toy violin and hugs it to his chest, imitating the sound of playing with his mouth. How pathetic! However, one can learn much from this parable. Label the boy Labor, the violin Capital and so on ...[21]

What first appears as an economic problem, satisfying a wish for a commodity, becomes instead an example of brute, irremediable suffering. The boy desires not a violin, but the ability to play one, and his inability to reproduce the beauty of music renders his suffering all the more acute. Yet, with a single sentence, "How pathetic!", Shrike at once sums up and dismisses the emotional appeal of the boy's longing. Instead he reads the story as a "parable" of capitalism – a reading that, in its attempt to recover a political meaning, becomes an empty rhetorical exercise. As the "and so on ..." suggests, the Marxist metanarrative is reduced to a predictable cliché. The very gesture of interpretation is here literally no more than a parlor game in which a case of suffering is "a jim-dandy" because and only because it offers a significant interpretive challenge.

Thus it is that despite their indifference to the boy's pain, Shrike's verbal pyrotechnics – he speaks like a "circus barker"[22] and fills his sentences with rhymes and rhetorical ornaments – afford the reader of *Miss Lonelyhearts* considerable pleasure. They constitute a form of verbal play that Ronald Paulson has seen as central to the comic: "the recovery of a transgressive category (imagination, ridicule) by turning it into an aesthetic object – that is taking it out of a moral discourse ... and into an aesthetics of pleasurable response."[23] Shrike reduces Marxist analysis to a smug metaphor-making (or literary criticism) in which imposing a theoretical vocabulary affords aesthetic pleasure but remains sundered from experience. If his previous novels are any indication, then, West had no choice but to eliminate the meeting of the anti-Nazi League from *The Day of the Locust*. Had he left it in, it would never have withstood his own satiric powers.

This opposition between the ironic (private, theoretical, aesthetic) and the sincere (public, experiential, ethical-political) constitutes not just an obstacle in West's search for artistic principles, but the basic conflict of his major works, *Miss Lonelyhearts* and *The Day of the Locust*. For the two novels are in many ways versions of the same story. In both, the hero confronts widespread human suffering: Miss Lonelyhearts is psychically overwhelmed by the tales of poverty, rape, disease, and disfigurement he encounters in the letters of his readers, while in *The Day of the Locust*, Tod Hackett is haunted by the "starers," the anonymous unfulfilled Midwesterners who "had come to California to die" (*DL*, p. 242). These heroes both experience their own spiritual and sexual longing, an inner emptiness that had by West's day already become an emblem of the modern hero. The suffering of West's protagonists is thus amplified by or even produced from the suffering of those around them: Shrike observes that the advice columnist is himself one of the letter-writers, and Tod thinks that he might "suffer from the ingrained, morbid apathy he liked to draw in others" (*DL*, p. 336). In both novels, finally, the fulfillment of characters' ethical-political ambitions curiously resides in aesthetic solutions. Like West himself, Miss Lonelyhearts (writing columns) and Tod Hackett (painting canvases) seek rhetorical modes adequate to the task of representing or relieving the pain of the masses.

This division parallels the split between what Richard Rorty has called "private irony" and "liberal hope." Private irony, according to Rorty, is the work of breaking free from ideological constraints symbolically to forge one's identity, while liberal hope describes the ambition to create a social order in which pain and cruelty are relieved. The first aspires to maximize personal freedom, the second to minimize collective suffering. In *Lonelyhearts*, the advocate of private irony is Shrike; in a famous passage, he rewrites "The Vanity of Human Wishes" in order to demolish every set of ideals (pastoral retreat, hedonism, art, religion) that Miss Lonelyhearts might offer his readers. A Rortian ironist, Shrike is skeptical of all "final vocabularies," of all "set[s] of words which [people] employ to justify their actions, their beliefs, and their lives." Shrike believes that "anything can be made to look good or bad by being redescribed,"[24] and he makes Miss Lonelyhearts' beliefs look bad by ironically redescribing them. Or, to use Paulson's term, he *aestheticizes* them: by moving the question of suffering from a moral to an aesthetic register he allows pleasure in the verbal presentation of a painful situation. Miss Lonelyhearts, taught by Shrike "to handle his one escape, Christ, with a thick glove of words," has therefore become a reluctant ironist as well, doubting all final vocabularies.[25] Hence the novel begins with a case of writer's block, with the columnist deprived of words that he finds "sincere."[26] But whereas Shrike (like Rorty) seems confident, even smug, in his ironism, Miss L. longs for something pre- or extra-rhetorical; in Rorty's terms, he wishes to be a "metaphysician" again.[27]

Does this mean that West believed suffering could be ameliorated if only we could still take seriously the "final vocabularies" that the Shrikes of the world render untenable? Such a view would again square with the idea of satire as a conservative mode that calls for an end to practices that destabilize communal values, a reading in which the ironic Shrike becomes the primary target of the author's scorn. But it is a mistake to read *Miss Lonelyhearts* as a lament for a bygone world of stable beliefs. Miss Lonelyhearts may think, "If only he could believe in Christ ... then everything would be simple and the letters extremely easy to answer,"[28] but his final religious experience must be taken as parodic: it leads him to misconstrue the intention of the cripple Doyle, who arrives at the apartment of the delusional columnist not to receive healing but to kill him. The novel is as uncomfortable with the hero's sentimental relapse into religiosity as with Shrike's belligerent assertion of irony. This stalemate suggests a fault line within West's sensibility and his conception of his role as an artist. It is a more extensive tracing of this fissure that I undertake in turning to *The Day of the Locust*.

THE SUN IS A JOKE

The Day of the Locust differs from *Miss Lonelyhearts* in that, unlike his predecessor, Tod Hackett has relinquished the goal of *relieving* the suffering of the masses, and seeks instead only to *represent* it. If for Miss Lonelyhearts the failure to produce a successful public rhetoric becomes a private crisis in which he can neither alleviate nor forget the suffering he faces, Tod conversely begins by seeking a private, painterly rhetoric that becomes entwined with his concern for a suffering public. Approaching the problem from the other side, Tod ends up with the same dilemma: what demands to make of his art. When he contemplates his magnum opus, then, he is caught between two views of his function as a painter: "He told himself that ... he was an artist, not a prophet. His work would not be judged by the accuracy with which it foretold a future event but by its merit as painting. Nevertheless, he refused to give up the role of Jeremiah" (*DL*, p. 308). To see the painting as prophecy is to see it as political, an insight into the destructive energies of the mob, a warning about the decline of civilization. (Such a view has become the enduring popular conception of West, a herald of the apocalyptic violence which his novel's conclusion enacts.) To judge the work on "its merit as painting," on the other hand, rejects the importance of its political insight for presumably formal concerns. And, although the prophetic role is already a curtailment of the role of savior that Miss Lonelyhearts assumes, in the internal debate over the function of Tod's art we see the same clash between public, ethical imperatives and private, aesthetic ones that structures the earlier novel.

As a modern artist, seeking to reconcile these imperatives, Tod renounces the naturalistic painting of "fat red barn[s], old stone wall[s]," and "sturdy Nantucket fisher[men]," and concludes that "neither

Winslow Homer nor Thomas [*sic*] Ryder could be his masters" (*DL*, p. 242).²⁹ The old, fat, sturdy subjects of Tod's earlier art signify perman- ence, tradition, and Yankee pastoral values, but since this stability is of little use to the artist of the modern metropolis, Tod must find a new model in the satirical cartooning of Goya and Daumier. Yet Tod's aesthetic search is hardly restricted to moments when he thinks about his painting. When he tries to persuade the aspiring starlet Faye Greener not to resort to prostitution, he is at a loss for words: "He had to say something. She wouldn't understand the aesthetic argument and with what values could he back up the moral one? The economic one didn't make sense either. Whoring certainly paid" (*DL*, pp. 319–20). Like Miss Lonelyhearts facing the blank page, Tod can find no final vocabulary, no "argument" or "values," whether moral, aesthetic, or economic, to justify his desire to keep Faye from prostitution. And when he finally finds speech his words are laughable: "Suddenly he began to talk. He found an argument. Disease would destroy her beauty. He shouted at her like a Y.M.C.A. lecturer on sex hygiene" (*DL*, p. 320). Tod himself cannot believe in this language, borrowed en masse from an outworn discursive system, and the narratorial voice slides into ridicule.

Thus, much as Tod's desire to do aesthetic justice to the starers drives him toward the cartoons of Goya and Daumier, so the rhetorical poverty he faces in his exchange with Faye attracts him to the screenwriter Claude Estee's way of sneering at the world: "Tod liked to hear him talk. He was master of an involved comic rhetoric that permitted him to express his moral indignation and still keep his reputation for worldliness and wit" (*DL*, p. 255). This description of an "involved comic rhetoric" seems to suggest a model for both Tod and West himself – a satiric mode that offers the promise of combining the two classical strains of satire, Juvenalian outrage and Horatian urbanity. If Shrike's imitators are "machines for making jokes,"³⁰ then Claude is a machine for making metaphors. When Tod declines to attend a brothel because he finds them "depressing . . . like vending machines" (*DL*, p. 255), Claude elaborates on the "lead" Tod feeds him:

Love is like a vending machine, eh? Not bad. You insert a coin and press home the lever. There's some mechanical activity inside the bowels of the device. You receive a small sweet, frown at yourself in the dirty mirror, adjust your hat, take a firm grip on your umbrella and walk away, trying to look as though nothing had happened. (*DL*, pp. 255–56)

Claude revels in the construction of the rhetorical trope; he responds not to Tod's expressed emotion but to the inventiveness of the simile. Like Shrike, Claude transforms a call for sympathy into a pleasurable verbal artifact.

In his preference for play with metaphor over immersion in feeling, Claude has a long line of precursors in West's work, up through and including Shrike. (West himself, in a 1934 application for a Guggenheim fellowship, referred to "the impossibility of experiencing a genuine emotion" and to "the necessity of laughing at everything, love, death, ambition, etc."[31]) This kind of private joking is an under-appreciated aspect of West's own narrative style. For example, his description of Romola Martin seems more a linguistic experiment in the manner of Gertrude Stein than an effort at mimesis: "Her youthfulness was heightened by her blue button eyes, pink button nose and red button mouth" (*DL*, p. 270). Whatever shred of representational value might exist in a phrase such as "button nose" becomes merely an opportunity to explore how the figure of the button might be deployed. Like Stella Gibbons playing with the descriptions of landscape in *Cold Comfort Farm*, West forsakes mimesis and embraces a pleasure found in non-sensical jesting with words.

But before we take Claude's "involved comic rhetoric" as the author's aesthetic prescription, we should note that "worldliness and wit" themselves come under attack in *The Day of the Locust*, just as the satirist Shrike is himself satirized in *Lonelyhearts*. West mocks the fashion-following style of the sophisticates Tod meets at a party at Claude's house. Like the partygoers whom Shrike entertains with the letters in *Miss Lonelyhearts*, or like Brenda Last's coterie in *A Handful of Dust*, these celebrants take a certain moral indifference as essential to their code of sophistication. One woman, Joan Schwartzen, speaks in "a loud, stagey whisper" (*DL*, p. 253) and feigns delight at the pretensions of her hosts. When Tod meets her, she is discussing tennis:

"How silly, batting an inoffensive ball across something that ought to be used to catch fish on account of millions are starving for a bite of herring."

"Joan's a female tennis champ," Alice explained. (*DL*, p. 252)

Delighting in the silliness of her pretended radicalism, Joan pre-emptively mocks any critique of her bourgeois values. Tod and West may tell us that Claude can combine witty worldliness with moral indignation, but for Joan one comes precisely at the expense of the other. West is too thoroughly modern, too worldly, to accept any simple appeal to earnest sentiment, yet he is suspicious enough of his own ironic temperament to show worldliness at its worst.

One might surmise that in West's novels (as elsewhere) there are good ironists and bad ones, and that Joan is simply a less original and less successful wit than Claude. But even Claude is implicated in the culture of artifice and pretense that pervades Tod's universe; he lives in "an exact reproduction of the old Dupuy mansion near Biloxi, Mississippi," "teeter[s] back and forth on his heels like a Civil War colonel and [makes] believe he [has] a large belly" (*DL*, p. 252). Faye too adopts worldliness as a pose; after her father's death she and a friend start speaking in a gangsterish slang which "[makes] them feel worldly and realistic, and so more able to cope with serious things" (*DL*, p. 317). Faye's father, the aging vaudevillian Harry Greener, "clown[s] continuously" because joking has become "his sole method of defense" (*DL*, p. 261). The joking persona becomes a mask one never takes off. Even the dwarf Abe Kusich seems trapped in his combative role: "Abe's pugnacity was often a joke" (*DL*, p. 248).

The very idea of the joke, in fact, associated throughout the novel with sophistication, implies a coarsening of the capacity to experience feeling that lies at the heart of the plight of the starers. For in their own way what these transplanted Midwestern hicks suffer from is – paradoxically – an excess of worldliness: "Both [the newspapers and the movies] fed them on murder, sex crimes, explosions, wrecks, love nests, fires, miracles, revolutions, wars. This daily diet made sophisticates of them. The sun is a joke. Oranges can't titillate their jaded palates" (*DL*, p. 381). The starers themselves endure the same fate as West's heroes. The vicarious experience of horrors with which the mass media inundate them fails to satisfy their "palates." These lowbrow "sophisticates" are like Beagle Darwin of *Balso Snell*, who has from too much reading assumed in his thought and speech a "literary coloring" that "is a protective one – like the brown of the rabbit or the checks of the quail."[32] Like Beagle, the characters of *The Day of the Locust* disappear into the ironic or joking roles that they enact.

For so many of West's characters, then, in *The Day of the Locust* and elsewhere, the joke, the laugh, or the "involved comic rhetoric" run the risk of trapping their user in a jaded, ironic role, shutting off the capacity for experience. To make things worse, it doesn't always work. The rhetorical play that Claude indulges in fails as a defense against pain when Tod tries it out:

[Faye's] invitation wasn't to pleasure, but to struggle, hard and sharp, closer to murder than to love. If you threw yourself on her, it would be like throwing yourself from the parapet of a skyscraper. You would do it with a scream. You couldn't expect to rise again. Your teeth would be driven into your skull like nails into a pine board and your back would be broken. You wouldn't even have time to sweat or close your eyes.

He managed to laugh at his language, but it wasn't a real laugh and nothing was destroyed by it. (*DL*, p. 251)

As Tod equates sex with a suicide leap, he begins to enjoy the excesses of his own linguistic conceit. The elaborate figure of speech spawns its own figures, as the vehicle becomes the tenor of secondary metaphor (teeth are nails, the skull a pine board – hints of a crucifixion?). But the attempt to aestheticize experience misfires; laughter fails to "destroy." If ever there was a private and unfunny joke, this is it. Tod shares it with no one and it is too weak to destroy any authoritarian presence. Like Claude's elaboration of the love-as-vending-machine metaphor, or Shrike's elaboration of the boy-as-Labor metaphor, Tod's "joke" entails a writer's delight in the construction of analogies – only now presented as a noncathartic internal reverie that leaves his world unchanged.

THE BOOK OF THE GROTESQUE

Having displayed its suspicion of worldliness and wit, it is not surprising that *The Day of the Locust* periodically attempts to affirm the value of sentiment against irony, to transpose aesthetic judgments back into ethical terms. Early in the novel, Tod passes two houses with incongruous architectural styles, "a miniature Rhine castle with tarpaper turrets pierced for archers" and "a little highly colored shack with domes and minarets out of the Arabian Nights" (*DL*, p. 243). But although just a moment before Tod has considered destruction by dynamite as the only recourse against such ugliness, he responds differently here:

Both houses were comic, but he didn't laugh. Their desire to startle was so eager and guileless.

It is hard to laugh at the need for beauty and romance, no matter how tasteless, even horrible, the results of that need are. But it is easy to sigh. Few things are sadder than the truly monstrous. (*DL*, p. 243)

Instead of destroying or deriding, Tod finds pathos in the "guileless" sincerity of the houses. The homeowners have money; their struggles are not material, but aesthetic or spiritual – a "need for beauty and romance" that recalls the paralyzed boy in *Miss Lonelyhearts* who simply wishes to play the violin. Of course these houses, in their eclectic appropriation of historical styles, have exemplified for critics the disfiguring of reality by simulacrum rife throughout West's fiction – what Alvin Kernan has called "a grotesquely phony and pitifully illusory world."[33] But the apprehension of the discordant forms that Kernan calls grotesque and that West calls monstrous inspires compassion in Tod.

Tod shares this need for beauty and romance. Just before noticing the houses, he has observed the environment around him, with his characteristic painter's eye: "The edges of the trees burned with a pale violet light and their centers gradually turned from deep purple to black. The same violet piping, like a Neon tube, outlined the tops of the ugly, humpbacked hills and they were almost beautiful" (*DL*, p. 243). The "almost" here is telling; nature (seen as it is through comparison to the technologies of advertising) aspires yet fails to achieve beauty. But, because Tod's eye seeks out beauty amid the ugliness of nature he can recognize the aspiration toward beauty even in the hideous melange of architectural styles. The desire of the houses to satisfy a need for beauty and romance is touching in its innocence and nearly tragic in its failure – as if the gulf between the ethical urge to recognize this need and the aesthetic urge to reject its results is unbridgeable.

The same affective pattern emerges when Tod considers Faye's mannerisms:

Being with her was like being backstage during an amateurish, ridiculous play. From in front, the stupid lines and grotesque situations would have made him squirm with annoyance, but because he saw the perspiring stagehands and the wires that held up the tawdry summerhouse with its tangle of paper flowers, he accepted everything and was anxious for it to succeed. (*DL*, p. 292)

In going "backstage," Tod recognizes the labor ("the perspiring stagehands") behind the performance and surrenders his critical stance for a sympathetic one. What would from an aesthetic standpoint appear "ridiculous" instead stirs compassion. Again, a grotesque situation – here it is West's own word – no longer provokes ridicule because aesthetic terms are translated into ethical ones.

Although this oscillation between the claims of satire and feeling tends, as in *Miss Lonelyhearts*, to produce a frustrated stand-off, as the novel progresses Tod begins to apprehend a third option for his art: "He had lately begun to think not only of Goya and Daumier but also of certain Italian artists of the seventeenth and eighteenth centuries, of Salvator Rosa, Francisco Guardi and Monsu Desiderio, the painters of Decay and Mystery" (*DL*, p. 325). Attending a meeting of one of California's many religious cults, Tod sees in the masses he will paint the exaggeration, decadence and disorder typical of a grotesque aesthetic:[34]

As he watched these people writhe on the hard seats of their churches, he thought of how well Alessandro Magnasco would dramatize the contrast between their drained-out, feeble bodies and their wild, disordered minds. He would not satirize them as Hogarth or Daumier might, nor would he pity them. He would paint their fury with respect, appreciating its raw, anarchic power and aware that they had it in them to destroy civilization. (*DL*, p. 337)

One night a man stands up and spews "a crazy jumble of dietary rules, economics, and Biblical threats" (*DL*, p. 337). In representing the scene, Tod rejects both satire and sentimentality: "Tod didn't laugh at the man's rhetoric. He knew it was unimportant. What mattered were his messianic rage and the emotional response of his hearers" (*DL*, p. 338). The man's rhetoric may be laughable, but his emotion, and that of his audience, is not. Tod can now recognize a value in the "emotional response" – the mystery of feeling – that a "crazy jumble" of rhetoric can provoke. He finds in the emotion of the cultists a cathartic capacity to "destroy" that his private, ironic metaphor-making lacks. And, by acknowledging rather than ridiculing this emotional response, he moves away from John Gilson's impulse to "burlesque the mystery of feeling at its source." Mystery, rather, is precisely what he values in his new artistic masters. He recognizes feeling, not in the form of pity, but in the form of anger and terror. These aversive feelings offer an alternative to both sentimental pity and satiric ridicule – a grotesque aesthetic that reinstates feeling as a guarantee of authenticity.

No doubt, such a reading is at least partly assimilable to a common view of *The Day of the Locust* that sees West as rehearsing a familiar, if extreme, version of a basic modernist narrative: the corroded pillars supporting civilization finally crumble to expose the fundamental barbarism of humanity. If this violence is not endorsed, it is recognized as inevitable, and somehow more real than the illusions of modernity. The novel's most famous scenes – the bloody cockfight and the concluding riot – are thus only eruptions of a simmering violence, eruptions that result from repeated frustrations of desire. West is hardly subtle in punctuating the novel with scenes of imitated violence as well – carnage on the studio lot when a movie set collapses, the "mock riot" that Claude's friends stage when their "dirty film" is interrupted – that suggest a capacity for violent play to spill over into something more threatening. But while I would hardly deny that in West frustration often gives way to violence, neither am I content to rest with this (relatively obvious) recognition. What is perhaps less obvious, and more telling, is the underlying pattern of frustration and eruption, and the way in which that pattern itself emerges from the stalemate of contradictory imperatives – the imperative to articulate sympathy for suffering masses, and the imperative to aestheticize suffering through satire.

Moreover, if a violence born of frustration is the only catharsis available in West's fiction, it is hardly one with great political promise. To be sure, the pessimism of this relatively widespread "regressive" reading of West can be countered by the claim that Tod's art offers a more positive model – the grotesque aesthetic – for managing the violence he perceives. Yet before upholding "The Burning of Los Angeles" as a triumph of modern art, we must first observe that Tod's aesthetic ambitions are only realized in (a description of) an unfinished painting that no real reader ever sees. Whatever power or success one wants to grant the artist who finds a visual form to represent modernity, the question as to how, or whether, West *himself* realizes a grotesque aesthetic remains more or less unanswered.

How then might West more usefully be understood as a writer of the grotesque? Theoretical formulations of the mode overlap significantly with Fredric Jameson's famous description of modernism (indebted to Lukács) as characterized by a discord between inner and outer worlds. For Jameson, such discord is evident in a work like Edvard Munch's *Scream*, whose depiction of a disfigured, agonized human face constitutes "a canonical expression of the great modernist thematics of alienation, anomie, solitude, social fragmentation and isolation."[35] Munch's "expressionist" aesthetic "presupposes," in Jameson's analysis, a view of the subject as divided, a view on which rests "a whole metaphysics of the inside and outside, of the wordless pain within the monad and the moment in which, often cathartically, that 'emotion' is then projected out and externalized, as gesture or cry, as desperate communication and the outward dramatization of inward feeling."[36] West undoubtedly draws on such "modernist" deployments of the grotesque as "wordless pain" and "inward feeling"; however, I want to argue that, arriving to modernism a generation late, he also refashions these paradigms in ways that question Jameson's expressivist model.

West's novel features an abundance of grotesque representations of physically and comically malformed bodies – a funeral director with "a face like a baked apple, soft and blotched" (*DL*, p. 315), an "old woman with a face pulled out of shape by badly fitting store teeth" (*DL*, p. 321), and many other satirical cartoons worthy of Hogarth, Goya, or Daumier. Yet in other cases the cause of grotesquerie seems harder to locate. Homer Simpson's body, for example, is first described as something closer to the Bakhtinian classical ideal; he is "well proportioned," "his muscles [are] large and round," and "he has a full heavy chest" (*DL*, p. 268). Nonetheless, his physical appearance induces unease: "Yet there was something wrong. For all his size and shape, he looked neither strong nor fertile. He was like one of Picasso's great sterile athletes, who brood hopelessly on pink sand, staring at veined marble waves" (*DL*, p. 268). The outlandish metaphors that render the secondary characters grotesque give way in Homer's case to a more vague intimation of "something wrong."

Significantly, that same phrase is also used in *Winesburg, Ohio*, Sherwood Anderson's own "Book of the Grotesque," to describe his character Wing Biddlebaum. When George Willard looks at Wing, he thinks: "There's something wrong, but I don't want to know what it is. His hands have something to do with his fear of me and of everyone."[37] The comparison between Wing and Homer has been made before, but the points of contact are worth examining.[38] Both men possess nervous, overactive hands; Homer comes from Wayneville, Iowa while Wing lives in Winesburg, Ohio; both men lose their shyness when shown sympathy. More generally, *The Day of the Locust*, like *Winesburg, Ohio*, is a series of character sketches, verbal correlatives of the "set of lithographs" which Tod works on in preparation for his grand canvas.

Anderson's use of the grotesque, in which the grotesque body is viewed as a symptom of a crippled or deformed psyche, clearly conforms to Jameson's description of a depth-oriented "expressivist" modernism. The stories of *Winesburg, Ohio* in general, and "Hands" in particular, offer a narrative about the psychic costs of repression. Biddlebaum, as "the town mystery," desires to keep "hidden away" his hands, which, we are told, "made more grotesque an already grotesque and elusive individuality."[39] Ultimately we learn the story of the hands: the schoolteacher Wing used to "[caress] the shoulders of the boys, playing about the tousled heads" with his active hands, but when he is falsely accused of "unspeakable things" and driven from town by an angry mob, he must live out his life in fear of human contact.[40] The hands are the physical manifestation of a repressed, transgressive, and ultimately tragic sexuality. Like the other grotesques of Winesburg, Wing struggles with what Jameson calls "wordless pain," which results in this case from the confining codes of a small-town Victorian morality. Most crucially, Wing is not primarily rendered in satiric terms: in presenting his characters' psychic deformities Anderson seeks to elicit not laughter but pity or sympathy.

Twenty years later, West still relies to a degree on this "depth" model of a "modernist grotesque" character whose outward features are only symptoms of a damaged interior state. Like his precursor Wing, Homer is, in his experience of "wordless pain," a modernist paradigm; we are told he experiences an "anguish" that "is basic and permanent" (*DL*, p. 291). Homer's overactive hands, like Wing's, are a classic illustration of the Freudian idea that a somatic symptom inevitably reveals the illness of the psyche; we easily surmise that Homer's "anguish" stems from repressed lust – at one point Homer's "fingers twined like a tangle of thighs in miniature" (*DL*, p. 290). Like Wing too, Homer is mistaken for a pedophile and attacked by an angry mob, and, like Wing, he has been traumatized by his own sexual desires. In his compulsive symptomatology and his tormented struggle with his memories, then, Homer seems a textbook case of repressed sexuality, and it is only fitting that when Tod sees Homer curled up asleep he is reminded precisely of "a book of abnormal psychology" (*DL*, p. 372). *The Day of the Locust* too is "a book of abnormal psychology," offering, like *Winesburg, Ohio*, a series of case studies. Indeed, Tod himself is introduced as a contrast between inner and outer, between an "almost doltish" appearance and a complex interior, with many "personalities" stacked up "like a nest of Chinese boxes" (*DL*, p. 242), and his deep, irrational lust for Faye is depicted as the modernist *angst* that Jameson finds in Munch's painting: "He shouted to her, a deep, agonized bellow, like that a hound makes when it strikes a fresh line after hours of cold trailing" (*DL*, p. 308). And of course the novel ends with another famous scream, as Tod, carried off from the riot in a police car, "began to imitate the siren as loud as he could" (*DL*, p. 389).

THE REFUSE OF FEELING

Both Tod and Homer thus exemplify a kind of grotesque character that, often explicitly, illustrates the modernist story of latent internal struggle finding its way to the body's surface. But if in this deployment of a depth-psychological model West works within a "high" modernist world view, it is crucial to note that he not only borrows but also reworks Anderson's material. For West's is a world in which modernism itself is already a too-familiar story, where the Hollywood madam Audrey Jenning displays her impeccable "refinement" by "discussing Gertrude Stein and Juan Gris" (*DL*, p. 257) with her clients. The transgressive sexuality so fundamental to Lawrence or Joyce is for West already – like everything else – a joke. The "dirty film" with which West replaced the meeting of the anti-Nazi League arouses in its viewers not desire but a parody of desire; when the cameraman fails to focus the projector, the crowd "imitated a rowdy audience in the days of the nickelodeon" (*DL*, p. 258), whistling and stomping. The film itself is described as a series of clichés as banal as the Communist stage play in *A Cool Million*:

After some low comedy with the father's beard and the soup, the actors settled down seriously to their theme. It was evident that while the whole family desired Marie, she only desired the young girl. Using his napkin to hide his activities, the old man pinched Marie, the son tried to look down the neck of her dress and the mother patted her knee. Marie, for her part, surreptitiously fondled the child. (*DL*, p. 259)

The film plods along in an equally deliberate manner until, as it nears its dramatic climax, the machine jams, in a moment reminiscent of the film screening in *Vile Bodies*: "there was a flash of light and the film whizzed through the apparatus until it all had run out" (*DL*, p. 239). The "theme" that the "actors" treat "seriously" is of course not an iota more serious than the lame beard-in-the-soup gag, and the depiction of incest, lesbian-ism, and pedophilia hardly even ruffles the audience of sophisticates.

    Similarly, in the final riot, members of the mob, on hearing that "a pervert attacked a child," seem amused and make jokes about another "pervert" who "ripped up a girl with a pair of scissors." One man asks, "What kind of fun is that?", while another jokes that a pair of scissors is "the wrong tool" (*DL*, p. 386). West refuses to exalt sexual transgression to a status of authenticity and deprives it of its capacity to shock. Thus even as his novel leans on an idea of alienated man, warped by lust, defined by an inner experience of pain, it elsewhere questions these very modernist assumptions. West layers onto his tormented grotesques an involved comic rhetoric utterly lacking from Anderson's sketches. (Susan Hegeman calls Homer "a caricature of a Sherwood Anderson charac-ter."[41]) Even as he deploys Anderson's still affectively powerful techniques to evoke a wordless pain, West indulges a satiric tendency in which the grotesque is less about inwardness than about adherence to the external. The grotesque, the violent, the regressive: these categories, it turns out, are subject to the same dialectical shuttling – are they cause for compassion or cause for laughter? – as everything else in West's work.

    In contrast to Anderson's "internalist" grotesque, then, *The Day of the Locust* also deploys Lewis's "externalist" one. As Tim Armstrong observes, "throughout the text, bodies are mechanical, with a matching artificiality of voice."[42] Such a pattern of "human bodies reduced to puppets, mario-nettes, and automata" is, as Wolfgang Kayser observes in his seminal study, "among the most persistent motifs of the grotesque."[43] Indeed,

West repeatedly describes human bodies as robotic or puppet-like: Abe "look[s] like a ventriloquist's dummy" (*DL*, p. 354); Earle Shoop resembles "a mechanical drawing" (*DL*, p. 299); Homer is compared to "a poorly made automaton" or a "badly made automaton" (*DL*, pp. 267, 381); Harry Greener acts like a "mechanical toy which had been over-wound" (*DL*, p. 279). Clearly, West is drawing on the association of the comic and the mechanical that had been already postulated by both Bergson and Lewis. For Lewis, as we have seen, the resemblance of the human to the machine does not result in Bergson's affirmation of human adaptability, but in an antihumanism. Writes Lewis: "'Men' are undoubtedly, to a greater or less extent, machines. And there are those amongst us who are revolted by this reflection, and there are those who are not."[44] West, in his repeated evocation of the puppet and the machine, is (to use Kayser's term) *reducing* the human, tacking away from Anderson to a more Lewisian aesthetic.[45]

Even when explicit comparisons between people and machines are absent from the novel, bodies still behave with a strange independence from the minds that inhabit them. The eight-year-old Adore Loomis performs a popular song, which he accompanies with "a little strut" and an "extremely suggestive" (*DL*, p. 335) bit of pantomime: "He seemed to know what the words meant, or at least his body and his voice seemed to know. When he came to the final chorus his buttocks writhed and his voice carried a top-heavy load of sexual pain" (*DL*, p. 336). The uncanny suggestion is that the sexualized body and voice are somehow more knowing than the innocent boy.[46] Faye Greener's body exhibits the same unconscious knowledge. As she chats with Claude, he and Faye's other admirers sit enraptured:

None of them really heard her. They were all too busy watching her smile, laugh, shiver, grow indignant, cross and uncross her legs, stick out her tongue, widen and narrow her eyes, toss her head so that her platinum hair splashed against the red plush of the chair back. The strange thing about her gestures and expressions was that they didn't really illustrate what she was saying. They were almost pure. It was as though her body recognized how foolish her words were and tried to excite her hearers into being uncritical. (*DL*, p. 357)

The extended recitation of Faye's various gestures highlights the mechanistic nature of her movements; there is indeed something "strange" – something uncanny – in the suggestion that her body might be operating on its own agenda.

Of course this convergence of the human and mechanical can be understood as a variation on the phenomenon, characteristic of theories of the postmodern, whereby experience disappears into representation, and performed roles overwhelm any possibility of an authentic self. *The Day of the Locust*, however, shows little postmodern comfort with such a loss of authenticity, but rather represents it as a fear – a fear that emerges in the reactions of characters to the uncanny prospect of a body reduced to automatism. When Homer witnesses Harry's seizure, "He was terrified and wondered whether to phone the police. But he did nothing" (*DL*, p. 279). The disturbing effect of Harry's "purely muscular" (*DL*, p. 279) behavior is enhanced by the continuity of the seizure with his "normal" conduct, as he slips undetectably from his clownish sales pitch into his mechanistic spasm. In the same scene, he uses a stage laugh, another muscular spasm, to frighten Faye: "This new laugh was not critical; it was horrible. When she was a child, he used to punish her with it. It was his masterpiece. There was a director who always called on him to give it when he was shooting a scene in an insane asylum or a haunted castle" (*DL*, p. 284). Harry's laugh is horrible rather than critical, prompting not ironic distance but visceral fear.

At a few crucial moments, moreover, *The Day of the Locust* explicitly suggests that this reduction of the human to an automatic bodily mechanism implies a disappearance of the interiority so central to (Jameson's version of) modernist aesthetics. By deliberately questioning characters' capacity for feeling, the novel dramatizes the uncanny anxiety latent in the representation of them as mere bodies. For example, when Homer sits on his shabby patio, dumbly watching a lizard catch flies, the narrator struggles to characterize his condition: "Between the sun, the lizard and the house, he was fairly well occupied. But whether he was happy or not is hard to say. Probably he was neither, just as a plant is neither" (*DL*, p. 276). The narrator's doubt about Homer's capacity for feeling is particularly striking because the narrator has confidently assumed omniscience at other moments in the novel; he has told us when Homer experiences fear, excitement, and lust. But he remains oddly tentative about whether to call Homer happy. The narrator's problem is not whether he can know Homer's mind – we have seen that he can – but whether Homer's condition can at all be described by conventional categories. We are told that Homer possesses "emotions," but that there is something odd about them:

He felt even more stupid and washed out than usual. It was always like that. His emotions curved up in an enormous wave, surging and rearing, higher and higher, until it seemed as though the wave must carry everything before it. But the crash never came. Something always happened at the very top of the crest and the wave collapsed to run back like water down a drain, leaving, at most, only the refuse of feeling. (*DL*, p. 273)

Like the elusive "something wrong" (*DL*, p. 268) in Homer's appearance, the "something" that "always happen[s]" to Homer, the failure of catharsis, defies naming. Despite Homer's deep anguish, what he feels is the *absence* of feeling, or "at most, only the refuse of feeling."

Tod entertains the same anxiety when he observes Harry suffering from chest pains. Even the man's physical agony, he notes, has become an antic performance:

Tod began to wonder if it might not be true that actors suffer less than other people. He thought about this for a while, then decided that he was wrong. Feeling is of the heart and nerves and the crudeness of its expression has nothing to do with its intensity. Harry suffered as keenly as anyone, despite the theatricality of his groans and grimaces. (*DL*, p. 311)

Here again is the problem of feeling and expression so ubiquitous in modernist treatment of affect: Tod's inability to find a correlation between *experience* and *expression* leads him to doubt the very existence of Harry's pain. Yet he steps back from this radical possibility and concludes that suffering retains a material, biological basis in "the heart and nerves" that is independent of the artfulness with which the sufferer communicates it. Just as the ugly houses in the foothills communicate a need for beauty and romance in spite of their outlandish architecture, so Harry's theatricality still (just) manages to convey his pain.

But Tod's doubt is as important as his conclusion. Indeed, he is not the only one to question the reality of Harry's pain. In a review of a vaudeville performance Harry had given years back, a critic wrote: "The pain that almost, not quite, thank God, crumples his stiff little figure would be unbearable if it were not obviously make-believe. It is gloriously funny" (*DL*, p. 263). Knowledge of the fictionality of Harry's suffering transforms the audience's potential pity and horror into laughter. But the performance goes right up to the edge of the "unbearable," the power of its comedy deriving precisely from the magnitude of the pain that it ultimately assures us is unreal. In other words, comic laughter, infused with sadism, depends upon a point of view that confines the suffering to a fictional space. But since the reader has already been told that Harry's clowning is a deliberate attempt to hide real-life pain – "It was his sole method of defense" (*DL*, p. 261) – she cannot be as confident about the "make-believe" nature of Harry's pain as is the reviewer. Thus the inescapable *mediation* of all feeling through expression, whether onstage or off, renders indeterminate the nature of Harry's suffering and creates the perception that his capacity for experience hovers uneasily – uncannily – between fiction and reality. For the reviewer, Harry's aesthetic triumph causes make-believe pain to appear real, while for Tod, Harry's aesthetic failure causes real-life pain to appear make-believe. In both cases, however, an ethical judgment must be suspended so that an aesthetic one can be rendered.

In this surrender of ethical standards of judgment for aesthetic ones lies the very dynamic of the satirical impulse – at least as formulated by Lewis in his valorization of the mechanical and the inhuman. West – or that part of his sensibility that finds expression in Shrike and Claude, his machines for making jokes – can reduce his characters to automata and reject the experiential appeal of suffering in favor of the pleasures of metaphor-making. But for West, unlike the brasher Lewis, this automatism brings an uncanny fear. The idea that the characters of *The Day of the Locust* have no feelings to be sympathized with but only bodies to be laughed at reveals itself as a fear of the consequences of satire. Ironic aloofness collapses into uncanny dread when satire recoils in the face of its own dehumanizing representations.

The novel contains at least one other crucial moment where it denies the capacity of its characters to suffer pain. Just before the final riot, Tod speculates on what will become of Faye:

Tod wondered if she had gone with Miguel. He thought it more likely that she would go back to work for Mrs. Jenning. But either way she would come out all right. Nothing could hurt her. She was like a cork. No matter how rough the sea got, she would go dancing over the same waves that sank iron ships and tore away piers of reinforced concrete. (*DL*, p. 375)

In assuring himself that "nothing could hurt" Faye, Tod is defending himself against the fear – also a fantasy – that Faye will become a prostitute. Again, Tod lets his metaphorical imagination carry him away, delighting in the conceit of Faye as an object impervious and insensate:

It was a very pretty cork, gilt with a glittering fragment of mirror set in its top. The sea in which it danced was beautiful, green in the trough of the waves and silver at their tips. But for all their moon-driven power, they could do no more than net the bright cork for a moment in a spume of intricate lace. Finally it was set down on a strange shore where a savage with pork-sausage fingers and a pimpled butt picked it up and hugged it to his sagging belly. Tod recognized the fortunate man; he was one of Mrs. Jenning's customers. (*DL*, pp. 375–76)

The free-associative linguistic play – reveling in its own powers of invention, keeping at bay an anxious compassion – literally runs aground with one of the novel's most arresting images of the grotesque. As Tod's painterly progress culminated in a grotesque aesthetic, so his personal internal language comes to rest in imagery that evokes neither irony nor pity but rather revulsion. The primitive "savage" returns us to an uncanny space ("a strange shore") that turns out to be the whorehouse, this novel's familiar and unfamiliar space of sexuality; the savage's corporeality – his "pork-sausage fingers" and "pimpled butt" and "sagging belly" – remind Tod of Faye's own corporeality, and render the prospect of her prostitution horrifying. Unlike Lewis, Tod indeed is revolted by the idea of regarding Faye as merely a body. As when he imagined sex with Faye as a suicide leap, Tod's language again fails to destroy. The ethical claims of Faye's humanity remain. A grotesque image of the human body – meaty, pock-marked, excessive – serves to reaffirm, through the revulsion it elicits, Tod's human relation to Faye.

CHAPTER 7

Nightwood *and the ends of satire*

One contention of this book has been that far from being simply anti-modern, satire occurs at the scene of modernity, that satire is dependent upon and symptomatic of the modern. For modernity implies not only newness but also a degenerate culture against which the modern orients itself. Matei Calinescu has described this dynamic in his analysis of progress and decadence, terms which, he argues, "imply each other so intimately that, if we were to generalize, we would reach the paradoxical conclusion that progress *is* decadence and conversely, decadence *is* progress."[1] For Michael Seidel, similarly, satire at once marks the disruptive emergence of novelty and the senescent decline of tradition. Its irony is both a symptom and a cause of the weakening of literary inheritance: "In satiric narration, irony is ... a negation of that phase of narrative that counts on making such things as saga, legend, myth, fable, and determinative allegory *seem* legitimate or authoritative ... Irony must come at the end of inheritable literary transmissions, so that irony is a step in the direction of revision."[2] Seidel extends this claim about literary forms to the thematics of satire; because of satire's concern with its own legitimacy, its anxieties about literary continuities find representation in figures of failed familial and biological inheritance. Seidel concludes: "Satire's actions depict the falling-off or exhaustion of a line ... The origin of satiric being is the absurd or suspect birth."[3]

In reading Djuna Barnes's *Nightwood* as satire, I therefore foreground its themes of cultural tradition, familial inheritance, and sexual generativity. In the novel, these phenomena are represented negatively: tradition is on the wane, inheritance is in jeopardy, sexual reproduction is in crisis, and all are represented through what I call anti-procreative imagery – sterility, impotence, infanticide, abortion. Thus, although Barnes, unlike Waugh, Gibbons, or West, is not generally described as a satirist, *Nightwood*'s strategies of stymieing inheritance manifest the miscarriage of generational continuity which Seidel recognizes as central to the mode.[4]

This is not to deny two interrelated factors that strongly *prevent* the comfortable classification of *Nightwood* as satire, a mode to which malice and wit have been seen as essential. First, despite Barnes's sense of humor, the reader's need to devote great cognitive energy to the interpretation of symbolic meanings and syntactical structures is likely to impede the psychic release that constitutes laughter. Second, while the novel represents many characters with decided mockery – joking about Felix Volkbein's pomposity, Jenny Petherbridge's stupidity, and Matthew O'Connor's stinginess – the two central characters, Nora Flood and Robin Vote, are largely treated without such derision. Robin is a cipher; because she is understood in a symbolic rather than a psychological framework, it is almost impossible to satirize her. Nora does appear susceptible to moral and psychological judgment, but although her grief over Robin's desertion has sometimes been regarded as excessive (hysterical, obsessive, melancholic) the implied author's judgment upon her never takes the shape of pointed ridicule.[5]

But if *Nightwood* sits uncomfortably on the fringe of the satiric, there seems to be consensus that the novel fully belongs to the related tradition of the grotesque.[6] As many have noted, it upends traditional hierarchies such as male/female, day/night, human/animal, and reason/unreason in a "process of hybridization or inmixing of binary opposites" that has been taken as definitive of the mode.[7] Indeed, the presence of the grotesque, with its ambivalent, uneasy laughter, may, more than any other factor, account for the repeated linking of Barnes with West – from their joint 1946 publication in the New Directions New Classics series, to their juxtaposition by John Hawkes and Stanley Edgar Hyman in the 1960s as precursors of postmodernism, down to an array of recent scholarly treatments.[8] To be sure, *Nightwood*'s cast of transvestites, circus performers, and others on the social margins may strike some readers, as T. S. Eliot feared, as "a horrid sideshow of freaks."[9] The characters are certainly compared to freaks: O'Connor likens himself to "the bearded lady" (*N*, p. 100), Robin to "the paralysed man in Coney Island ... who had to lie on his back in a box" (*N*, p. 146), Felix to a legless girl who "used to wheel herself through the Pyrenees on a board" (*N*, p. 26). Such grotesque figuration not only opens a critique of patriarchal or heterosexist norms (as numerous feminist and queer readings have shown) but interrupts and ironizes historical continuity as such. *Nightwood* is therefore both radically modern and exceptionally anti-modern. It discards not only tradition and history but also such consolations as narrative and love, yet it also represents the modern as a scene of unredeemed cultural wreckage. Thus I mean my title "the ends of satire" to suggest both the aims of satire and its limits, the work satire does and the points at which it becomes no longer tenable.

GREAT DEFAMING SENTENCES

A reading of *Nightwood* as satire must begin with Dr. Matthew Dante O'Connor, the homosexual transvestite whose talk dominates the novel. Like Eliot's androgyne Teresias, O'Connor possesses long experience of suffering that he expresses in weary, prophetic tones;[10] like a psychoanalyst, he is a doctor to whom ailing patients turn for knowledge of dreams, sexuality, and the unconscious;[11] like Dante's Virgil, he leads characters and readers through the dark wood of the novel. Yet he is also a kind of satirist. The plots of most satires, Alvin Kernan points out, "lack a conventional story, intricately contrived and carefully followed,"[12] and O'Connor's speech is full of narrative digressions: "I have a narrative, but you will be put to it to find it" (*N*, p. 97). His torrent of epigrams, anecdotes, and philosophical pronouncements often has little to do with the core "story" of the novel and instead takes place at the level of discourse; this discourse is marked less by conventional norms of narrativity than by the associative chains of Freudian primary process. After digressing onto the topic of the thick toenails of a friend's husband, he declares, "My mind is so rich it is always wandering!" (*N*, p. 105), and the word *wandering* is instructive. Like Robin's night-roaming, his wandering speech seems promiscuous in its affection for whatever riddling tale or fine-spun phrase crosses its path. His anecdotes often fail to deliver on their promises of meaning, and his free-associative mode surrenders sentimental attachment to bourgeois terms of reading much as Robin's nocturnal *flânerie* surrenders traditional erotic attachments. In his talk, satire's formal disruptions mirror its thematic ones.

A second characteristic that marks O'Connor as a satirist is what Alan Singer calls his "pontificatory idiom."[13] Like West's Shrike, O'Connor speaks in "great defaming sentences" (*N*, p. 158) characterized by a florid, histrionic, and ironic manner; he wins attention by shouting "some of the more boggish and biting of the shorter early Saxon verbs" (*N*, p. 15). This histrionicism raises the suspicion that O'Connor is nothing but bluster, and the doctor freely admits that he is "the greatest liar this side of the moon" (*N*, p. 135), counting himself among the Irish who possess "the power of the charlatan" (*N*, p. 31). The doctor is a charlatan in deed as well as word, as Felix recognizes when O'Connor is called to treat Robin, who has fainted: "Felix now saw the doctor ... make the movements common to the 'dumbfounder,' or man of magic; the gestures of one who, preparing the audience for a miracle, must pretend that there is nothing to hide." O'Connor distracts his audience with a show of mock-honesty "while in reality the most flagrant part of [his] hoax is being prepared" (*N*, pp. 35–36). The "hoax" the doctor is preparing here is the theft of some cosmetics and 100 francs – part of a pattern by which the impoverished O'Connor himself is satirized as a fraud and a sponge who is constantly cajoling others into paying for his drinks, unable, when invited to dine with Felix, to think of anything but what he will order. Yet Felix does not disdain the doctor's fraudulence: "Felix thought to himself that undoubtedly the doctor was a great liar, but a valuable liar" (*N*, p. 30). For all their flourishes and embellishments, O'Connor's "every jest and malediction" conceals "seriousness" and "melancholy" (*N*, p. 39). I will return to the way in which this satiric jesting suppresses O'Connor's own melancholic affect, but the "seriousness" of the jest also denotes the tendentious work of satire.

This tendentious work is, specifically, the de-idealization of false values, a task particularly appropriate to O'Connor's medical profession. Introduced as "a middle-aged 'medical student' ... whose interest in gynaecology had taken him half way around the world" (*N*, p. 14), he works as an abortionist. While the critical tendency has been to interpret O'Connor's medical role as a sign of his function as a healer, it continues the association of surgeon and satirist that we've seen in Pound, Lewis, and Joyce. Like the satirists before him, O'Connor asserts the material basis of human existence: "I, as a medical man, know in what pocket a man keeps his heart and soul, and in what jostle of the liver, kidneys, and genitalia these pockets are pilfered. There is no pure sorrow. Why? It is bedfellow to lungs, lights, bones, guts and gall!" (*N*, pp. 21–22). As Joyce's Buck Mulligan reduces death to the failure of cerebral lobes, so O'Connor situates hearts and souls within the "confusions" (*N*, p. 22) of the material body. Or, as he later remarks: "Even the contemplative life is only an effort, Nora my dear, to hide the body so the feet won't stick out" (*N*, p. 134). Even as he ruthlessly exercises his own intelligence, O'Connor reminds his interlocutors that the "contemplative life" valued by Western philosophy is little more than a strategy to repress or sublimate bodily drives.

To each character, O'Connor debunks a chosen ideal. To Felix, the lover of nobility, he scoffs that a king is revered only because "he has been set apart as the one dog who need not regard the rules of the house." While royal subjects are "church-broken, nation-broken," their rulers "may relieve themselves on high heaven" (*N*, p. 39). Similarly, to the lovesick Nora, O'Connor explodes the notion of sexual fidelity. He suggests that dream-life and desire are inherently promiscuous, and that love itself is mere sentimentality:

For what is not the sleeper responsible? What converse does he hold and with whom? He lies down with his Nelly and drops off into the arms of his Gretchen. Thousands unbidden come to his bed ... Girls that the dreamer has not fashioned himself to want scatter their legs about him to the blows of Morpheus. (*N*, pp. 86–87)

The sleeper's lover, moreover, lying beside him, is guilty not only of infidelity but of every horror known to the House of Atreus:

When she sleeps, is she now moving her leg aside for an unknown garrison? Or in a moment, that takes but a second, murdering us with an axe? Eating our ear in a pie, pushing us aside with the back of her hand, sailing into some port with a ship full of sailors and medical men? (*N*, p. 87)

O'Connor revels in his own rhetoric, decorated with the neat counter-point of Nelly and Gretchen, the faux-poetic invocation of Morpheus, the shining comic-surrealist touches like the ear in the pie. As in Freud's description of tendentious jokes, the form of O'Connor's speech provides a pleasure which circumvents censorship and allows the hearer to enjoy its transgressive substance.

This debunking of values sometimes leads to an outright advocacy of decadence. Discussing Robin, the novel's most central figure of the archaic, the doctor claims, "In the acceptance of depravity the sense of the past is most fully captured" (*N*, p. 118), invoking a primordial state of confusion prior to the establishment of rational categories. He maintains that "cleanliness is a form of apprehension," a fear of the disorderliness of our primitive beginnings (*N*, p. 118). We regain contact with this primitive disorder, he claims, when we read of murder and violence in the newspaper, and the vicarious emotion we experience is "a way to lay hands on the shudder of a past that is still vibrating" (*N*, p. 119). Having lost our animal nature, we gain a "tension in the spirit which is the contraction of freedom" (*N*, p. 119). O'Connor thus insists upon our proximity to our animal origins, and discerns the psychic toll we pay for the repressions we have undergone in attempting to rise above them.

O'Connor himself is represented as physically malformed or grotesque; like *Vile Bodies'* Father Rothschild, he is marked as a satirist by his ugliness. O'Connor has a "small slouching figure" (*N*, p. 29) and describes himself as "the funniest-looking creature on the face of the earth" (*N*, p. 98), "born as ugly as God dared premeditate" (*N*, p. 153), with "a face on me like an old child's bottom" (*N*, p. 91). Part of the novel's pervasive dog motif, he himself appears canine, holding his hands "like a dog who is walking on his hind legs" (*N*, p. 32), hailing a cab with "a bulldog cane" (*N*, p. 24). To Felix, O'Connor's crude habits parody the manners of a bygone aristocracy: "His manner was that of a servant of a defunct noble family, whose movements recall, though in a degraded form, those of a late master" (*N*, p. 30). O'Connor thus embodies decadence even as he advocates it. "To be satirically conceived is to be rendered monstrous – too singular, too materially degenerate to carry on," writes Seidel,[14] and O'Connor affirms his own sterile status: "I'm the last of my line" (*N*, p. 139).

Thus an anti-procreative imagery surrounds O'Connor, suggesting a degenerative process less moral than biological. Like other men in the novel, O'Connor is associated with impotence. He tells Nora of a night in which, wishing he had been born a woman, he entered a church and spoke to his penis, which "was lying in a swoon": "And there I was holding Tiny, bending over and crying, asking the question until I forgot and went on crying, and I put Tiny away then like a ruined bird, and went out of the place" (*N*, pp. 132–33). Karen Kaivola describes this scene as "delightful and liberating" because it stages "an undoing of the sign of male power and privilege."[15] But if this imagery contributes to a feminist sexual politics, it can only be a satirical politics that locates itself in the suffering of a character himself socially marginalized.[16] Moreover, O'Connor is associated not only with the failure to produce life, but – as an abortionist – with the undoing of it. (Wyndham Lewis, recall, likens the material of satire to an aborted fetus: "This *matière* which composes itself into what you regard I daresay as abortions, is delightful to us, *for itself*."[17]) O'Connor thus articulates an abortive rhetoric, a language that thwarts cultural and biological transmission. In one gruesome riff, he speculates on a world in which aging is reversed:

How more tidy had it been to have been born old and have aged into a child, brought finally to the brink, not of the grave, but of the womb; in our age bred up into infants searching for a womb to crawl into, not to be made to walk loth the gingerly dust of death, but to find a moist, gillflirted way. And a funny sight it would be to see us going to our separate lairs at the end of day, women wincing with terror, not daring to set foot to the street for fear of it. (*N*, pp. 98–99)

Although the image initially suggests a gentle return to the womb, O'Connor finds a cold laughter in the terror of the women who would undergo this reverse-delivery, and reveals the regressiveness, if not the sadism, of his vision.[18]

Yet although he is an abortionist in rhetoric and trade alike, O'Connor also harbors an unrealizable fantasy of a life as an extravagantly fertile woman. He imagines a past life as "a girl in Marseilles thumping the dock with a sailor" (*N*, p. 90), announcing his wish for "a womb as big as the king's kettle, and a bosom as high as the bowsprit of a fishing schooner": "God, I never asked better than to boil some good man's potatoes and toss up a child for him every nine months by the calendar" (*N*, p. 91). He even suggests that his desire for motherhood has caused him to claim his brother's children for his own, "to adopt his brother's children to make a mother of himself" (*N*, p. 73), to "[sleep] with his brother's wife to get him a future" (*N*, p. 73). Later, he drunkenly hints that he has fathered these children. In contrast to his abortive rhetoric, then, stands an explicit womb envy that seeks a "future" through procreation.

O'Connor, however, recognizes this fantasy as a cliché, itself already satirized. Thumping the dock with a sailor, boiling a good man's potatoes, tossing up a child every nine months – O'Connor emphasizes the banality of his fantasy of motherhood with a double-edged effect. He underscores the modesty of his desires, even as he ridicules their outrageous impossibility. Andrea Harris points to the estranging effect of O'Connor's cross-dressing as a species of parody (Nora discovers him sleeping in a blonde wig and woman's nightgown), viewing it as a de-naturalizing of gender roles, and implicitly attributing a kind of satiric work to O'Connor's transvestism or travesty.[19] But while O'Connor is surely mocking norms of femininity he is also mocking his own longing for it. Merely finding words for his desire reduces it to banality. By inflecting his lament for his never-born children with self-satire, O'Connor posits generational continuity as ludicrous.

What results is pathos, although a peculiar kind, similar to the intense but hesitant sympathy that West's heroes feel for the masses. The misery O'Connor expresses for the impossibility of his fantasy coexists with an equally persuasive laughter at that fantasy. Therefore, although the doctor, like West's Shrike, redescribes cherished ideals as sentimental pieties, as the novel progresses he becomes a Miss Lonelyhearts, overwhelmed by his compassion for others.[20] As in West too, this compassion transmutes into angry frustration at those who seek solace from him. To Robin, he cries: "And I was doing well enough . . . until you kicked my stone over, and out I came, all moss and eyes; and here I sit, as naked as only those things can be, whose houses have been torn away from them to make a holiday, and it my only skin – labouring to comfort you" (*N*, p. 153). Felix's intuition that the jests and maledictions of the doctor conceal melancholy turns out to be well-founded. Satiric derision gives way to pathos. Of course, how one assesses Barnes's provocation of that pathos will vary, since norms of sentimentality vary widely. Yet readerly affect here is especially unstable. While the other patrons of the cafe scorn the doctor's tirade as boozy sentimentality – "'Drunk and telling the world,' someone said" (*N*, p. 164) – their scorn also separates the reader's position from that of the fictional characters and rewards the reader for possessing greater sympathy. In any case, O'Connor's own affect undergoes a marked shift, as his ironism doubles back on itself. Hypersensitive to the suffering of the world, he expresses the desperation of one who has seen through all consolatory fictions including the pleasures of his own verbal skills. This fate is at least one of the ends of satire.

WE GO UP – BUT WE COME DOWN

With his ironic and histrionic speech and his emphasis on the bodily and the material, Dr. O'Connor is, then, the voice of satire in *Nightwood*; his ironic redescription of inherited values finds figural expression in the blockage of his and others' procreative impulse. But in a broader sense *Nightwood* as a whole can be understood as satiric, for Barnes's novel stages an end to the idea of familial inheritance secured through the continuity of fathers and sons. In this sense, *Nightwood*'s vision of modernity strongly resembles that of a work more conventionally recognized as satire, Waugh's *A Handful of Dust*. At first glance, of course, Barnes's ornate, winding sentences and her disjunctive leaps in time, space, and logic suggest an aesthetic practice worlds away from Waugh's sharply focused dissection of the English upper class. Thematically, however, both novels concern betrayed lovers, and both situate their explorations of erotic loss within a context of declining cultural traditions and waning sexual generativity.

In *A Handful of Dust*, recall, Tony Last is slavishly and sentimentally devoted to his family estate and to the aristocratic traditions with which it is associated. When Brenda says that keeping up the estate is "pointless," Tony responds: "*Pointless?* I can't think what you mean ... We've always lived here and I hope John will be able to keep it on after me. One has a duty toward's [*sic*] one's employees, and towards the place too. It's a definite part of English life which would be a serious loss" (*HD*, p. 19). Hetton represents for Tony the preservation of "English life" and *noblesse oblige*, and its survival rests upon the perpetuation of the family line. It is not Hetton that is maintained for John's sake, but John who has been born to preserve Hetton. In *Nightwood*, the Italian-Viennese Jew Guido Volkbein similarly reveres the aristocratic traditions of Europe. And while Barnes's treatment of Guido's "remorseless homage to nobility" (*N*, p. 2) may not be as mordant as Waugh's mockery of Tony, it retains a satiric bite. Guido, we learn, adopts the title of Baron in order "to span the impossible gap" (*N*, p. 3) between his Jewish descent and the Christian world in which he lives. To shore up his claim to his invented lineage, he marries an Austrian woman, Hedvig, who walks with a "goose-step of a stride" (*N*, p. 3) and embodies the martial virtues of her nation to the point of caricature. He even provides her with a house befitting his assumed nobility – a Viennese Hetton decorated with a false coat of arms and "life-sized portraits of [his] claim to father and mother" (*N*, p. 6) that are actually "reproductions of two intrepid and ancient actors" (*N*, p. 7). As in Waugh, much of the problem with revering tradition is that tradition is already saturated with what Waugh called the pseudo; when Guido attempts to assume Hedvig's Austrian goose-step, he appears with a Bergsonian rigidity that renders him "dislocated and comic" (*N*, p. 3).

Because Guido's ambitions are incomplete without a son to carry on his faux-aristocratic line, the novel begins with the problem of perpetuating the clan. The labyrinthine first sentence describes a birth:

Early in 1880, in spite of a well-founded suspicion as to the advisability of perpetuating that race which has the sanction of the Lord and the disapproval of the people, Hedvig Volkbein – a Viennese woman of great strength and military beauty, lying on a canopied bed of a rich spectacular crimson, the valance stamped with the bifurcated wings of the House of Hapsburg, the feather coverlet an envelope of satin on which, in massive and tarnished gold threads, stood the Volkbein arms – gave birth, at the age of forty-five, to an only child, a son, seven days after her physician predicted that she would be taken. (*N*, p. 1)

The second, a death:

Turning upon this field, which shook to the clatter of morning horses in the street beyond, with the gross splendour of a general saluting the flag, she named him Felix, thrust him from her, and died. (*N*, p. 1)

Just as the aging Hedvig has apparently entered into motherhood with suspicion, so the very syntax of the first sentence seems to postpone Felix's birth – and the birth of the novel – as if it fears its own death. From the beginning of this novel, death shadows birth, stalks it. The tremor produced by "the clatter of morning horses in the street beyond" is only the first occurrence of the novel's often sinister animal motif; as in a Dutch still life, horses, dogs, and cows assume the significance of omens.

Nightwood's first sentence thus describes a satiric origin, a suspect birth. As if in confirmation of this suspicion, the second sentence begins with a literal "turn" in which Hedvig "thrust[s]" away her son. Felix, born amid emblems of family and nation, is immediately thrust from them. These sentences, adorned as richly as Hedvig's bedding, intertwine the perpetuation of cultural institutions with the biological perpetuation of races and families. Yet they do so suspiciously, presenting birth as an omen, subtly sabotaging the continuity they describe.

Guido's determination to produce an heir who will secure the aristocratic affiliation of his own blood both succeeds and fails. In one sense, he succeeds triumphantly, as his son Felix inherits both the title of Baron and his father's "obsession for what he termed 'Old Europe'" (*N*, p. 9). Felix, like his father, recognizes the importance of biological succession, and desires a son "who would feel as he felt about the 'great past'" (*N*, p. 38). Yet, paradoxically, Felix's very need for a son, re-enacting his father's *anxiety* about succession, only points up the tenuousness of his own connection to the tradition whose survival he wants to ensure. Hence to O'Connor Felix betrays an acute awareness of the fragility of aristocratic traditions in a modern world:

"To pay homage to our past is the only gesture that also includes the future."
"And so a son?"
"For that reason. The modern child has nothing left to hold to, or, to put it better, he has nothing to hold with. We are adhering to life now with our last muscle – the heart." (*N*, pp. 39–40)

The exchange is cryptic, but it is clear that Felix considers procreation to be a "gesture" that "includes" both the past and the future. He expresses the same idea to Robin when he explains to her his desire "that she might bear sons who would recognize and honour the past" since "without such love, the past as he understood it, would die away from the world" (*N*, p. 45).

Whatever fun Barnes derives from Felix's fascination with the "great names" (*N*, p. 17) of the past, then, she recognizes that this fascination is less a denial of modernity than a considered, if quixotic, response to it. For Felix, the modern assault on tradition requires the very devotion that he recognizes as arbitrary. If the old motivations for maintaining a connection to the past have been exposed as false, then devotion must be warranted by love alone. Felix's position here is not far from Walter Benjamin's valorization of book-collecting, which he upholds as a way of undoing the work of modernity. As Benjamin puts it in his own quaint old-world manner, to buy a book is "to give it its freedom – the way the prince bought a beautiful slave girl in *The Arabian Nights*."²¹ The collector's loving relation to the collected objects has a custodial quality, rescuing them from promiscuous wandering through the marketplace. Collecting is less a practice of commodification than a protest against it. Felix too is something of a collector, a "taster of rare wines, thumber of rarer books" (*N*, p. 10) – although Barnes's phrasing here has a hint of that satire which is never fully absent from Felix's portrait, suggesting something both pathetic and risible in his indulgences. And Felix's father was a collector as well, having assembled for Hedvig the tokens of his false ancestry in "a fantastic museum of their encounter" (*N*, p. 5) that includes fragments of classical sculpture, coats of arms, grand pianos, Spanish rugs, studded desks, velvet curtains, and the portraits of Guido's "parents." Through their inheritability, such collected objects promise the Volkbein men, as they do Benjamin, a continuity preserved against the commercial forces of modernity. Indeed, when Felix is reintroduced, seven pages and thirty years after his birth, it is the fetish objects he has inherited – the paintings of his fictional grandparents – that have preserved for him his father's dream: "Felix . . . turned up in the world with these facts, the two portraits and nothing more" (*N*, p. 7).

Barnes's attention to problems of inheritance may also help to explain the meaning of her choice of a Jew as a central character – a choice which has been both applauded as sympathetic and deplored as bigoted.²² For the Jew, in Barnes's symbolic scheme, stands outside inheritance: "The step of the wandering Jew is in every son. No matter where and when you meet him you feel that he has come from some place . . . some country that he has devoured rather than resided in, some secret land that he has been nourished on but cannot inherit" (*N*, p. 7). Figures of ingestion – devouring, nourishing in secret – lend the Jew a vampiric coloring; stereotypical of the modern, he consumes instead of preserving. Yet, for Barnes, the Jew is not devoid of history, but rather *too* burdened with his history to render his own past as inheritable: "A race that has fled its generations from city to city has not found . . . enough forgetfulness in twenty centuries to create legend" (*N*, p. 10). The Jew must therefore reacquire his tradition second hand; he "becomes the 'collector' of his own past" only once "some *goy* has put it back into such shape that it can again be offered as a 'sign'" (*N*, p. 10). Barnes suggests a relation to the past necessarily mediated by meanings created not by the Jews themselves but by "Christian traffic in retribution." This traffic "has made the Jew's history a commodity; it is the medium through which he receives, at the necessary moment, the serum of his own past that he may offer it again as his blood" (*N*, p. 10). Like Benjamin's collector, Felix can find in these old stories, now figured as commodities, a defense against modernity. Tradition is factitious – a serum absorbed into the blood and passed off as the body's own.

Modernity spells the end for the Volkbein line, as it does for the Lasts in *A Handful of Dust*. In *A Handful of Dust*, Tony's young son John is killed during a fox hunt, ironically one of those very aristocratic traditions that Tony is so keen to preserve. In a similar irony, Felix's fascination with the traditions of his people's historical oppressors results in the aspiration of his son (also named Guido) "to enter the church" (*N*, p. 108) and consequently lead a sterile life. Guido, described as "mentally deficient and emotionally excessive" (*N*, p. 107), fulfills O'Connor's prediction that Felix's "aristocratic" line will end in decadence and "madness": "The last child born to aristocracy is sometimes an idiot, out of respect – we go up – but we come down" (*N*, p. 40). O'Connor here describes what Seidel calls the gravitational principle of satire, "the defeat of systematic and organic continuity,"[23] a principle evident in the novel's refrain of "going down" and "bowing down." O'Connor concludes with a characteristically scatological image: "In the king's bed is always found, just before it becomes a museum piece, the droppings of the black sheep" (*N*, p. 40), droppings that denote the earthbound direction of all satirical redescriptions.

But if Guido fulfills O'Connor's prediction that all noble lines produce their black sheep, the "emotionally excessive" boy also, ironically, fulfills his father's expectation that he adhere to tradition with the heart. O'Connor expresses this irony to Felix a decade after their first encounter: "'Aristocracy,' he said, smiling, 'is a condition in the mind of the people when they try to think of something else and better – funny,' he added sharply, 'that a man never knows when he has found what he has always been looking for.'" (*N*, p. 121). While Felix has perceived Guido's religious calling as "a demolition of his own life" (*N*, p. 108), O'Connor recognizes that the boy, because of his strangeness, is a breed apart, a shadow-image of the aristocratic exceptionality Felix has always sought. In Felix's devotion to the sensitive and vulnerable boy, Barnes again swerves from the satiric, finding poignancy alongside ridiculousness in the scenes of Felix dragging Guido from cafe to cafe, drinking heavily. The final image of Felix in the novel is a decidedly restrained image of fatherly affection: "'Come,' he said, taking the child's fingers in his own. 'You are cold.' He poured a few drops of oil and began rubbing Guido's hands"

(*N*, p. 123). Felix's aristocratic fantasies contain their own undoing, and he is left clinging to his future as well as his past with only his heart.

The Volkbein story is one of fathers and sons, and Felix's hopes of forging a meaningful relationship to the past rest on the perpetuation of patrilineal tradition. Robin, his wife, matters to him mainly as a vehicle for producing an heir. But Felix's tale is only one part of *Nightwood*, and Robin's resistance to Felix's scheme is crucial to the frustration of inheritance in the novel. Robin's role in this satiric task, however, cannot be understood without a broader discussion of her character, since Barnes's portrait of her renders uncertain the paradigms by which fictional characters are generally interpreted. Because Robin's motives are enigmatic, her frustration of inheritance cannot readily be understood as any kind of conscious decision. It can be made sense of, on the contrary, only as the work of the novel itself, or as part of the modernity that the novel takes as its subject.

Robin comes across as peculiarly passive. When she first appears, she is literally unconscious, and much of her story is a series of awakenings in which she appears never truly to awaken. As Felix courts her, he notices that she is unusually "silent" (*N*, p. 41); when she accepts his marriage proposal, the surprised Baron takes it as evidence that "Robin's life held no volition for refusal" (*N*, p. 43). Her capitulation to Felix's demands for a son is in keeping with this apparently volitionless nature. Yet Robin does offer a quiet, passive resistance to Felix's scheme that partakes of "a stubborn cataleptic calm" (*N*, p. 45). Thus, when the novel's second scene of childbirth arrives it recalls the first in its refusal to offer the slightest note of joy or consolation:

Amid loud and frantic cries of affirmation and despair Robin was delivered. Shuddering in the double pains of birth and fury, cursing like a sailor, she rose up on her elbow in her bloody gown, looking about her in the bed as if she had lost something. "Oh, for Christ's sake, for Christ's sake!" she kept crying like a child who has walked into the commencement of a horror. (*N*, p. 48)

The passage describes not Robin's thoughts but her behavior – or, rather, it describes her behavior by describing *hypothetical* thoughts: "*as if* she had lost something," "*like* a child." Described with a Lewisian attention to externals, Robin seems a mere witness to the "horror" that is her own experience. Yet even after this abrupt "entrance" into her own consciousness, it is a week before Robin fully rejects Felix's plan: "A week out of bed she was lost, as if she had done something irreparable, as if this act had caught her attention for the first time" (*N*, p. 48). Here the "as if" occurs twice more, and seems extraneous: how could the act *not* be irreparable? The phrase, however, is a signifier of exteriority, a marker of the refusal to venture any psychological interpretation of Robin's behavior that would mitigate its strangeness. Barnes uses the device again when Robin finally leaves Felix: "She looked about her, about the room, as if she were seeing it for the first time" (*N*, p. 49). Robin remains viewed from without.

Yet this external representation is not primarily comic. The gesture with which Robin attempts to cancel out the "horror" of motherhood assumes a form that is itself dreamlike and horrific: "One night, Felix, having come in unheard, found her standing in the centre of the floor holding the child high in her hand as if she were about to dash it down, but she brought it down gently" (*N*, p. 48). While Robin's gesture can be understood as a step in the forging of a less constrictive sexual identity, its violence cannot be subsumed by a progressive politics.[24] The threatened violence replays Hedvig's "thrusting" away of the newborn Felix and dramatizes an underlying suspicion about perpetuation. Thus Robin's relationship with Nora parallels in many ways her marriage to Felix. The parallels become most striking when Robin destroys the doll that the women share as "their child" (*N*, p. 142). As Nora tells O'Connor:

I would find her standing in the middle of the room in boy's clothes, rocking from foot to foot, holding the doll she had given us – "our child" – high above her head, as if she would cast it down, a look of fury on her face. And one time, about three in the morning when she came in, she was angry because for once I had not been there all the time, waiting. She picked up the doll and hurled it to the floor and put her foot on it, crushing her heel into it; and then, as I came crying behind her, she kicked it, its china head all in dust, its skirt shivering and stiff, whirling over and over across the floor. (*N*, pp. 147–48)

The doll, as Nora has explained, is "the life they cannot have" (*N*, p. 142). Robin's brutalizing of the doll-child is thus doubly "anti-procreative" in that it destroys a "child" which itself exists in place of a life never born.

For O'Connor, the doll also signifies sexlessness because of its strange symmetrical perfection – "the conjunction of the identical cleaved halves of sexless misgiving" (*N*, p. 148), and this same image of the sexless doll surfaces in the description of the trapeze artist Frau Mann: "The span of the tightly stitched crotch was so much her own flesh that she was as unsexed as a doll ... The needle that had made one the property of the child made the other the property of no man" (*N*, p. 13). According to

the *Oxford English Dictionary*, the word "unsex" means "to deprive or
divest of sex, or of the typical qualities of one or the other (*esp.* the female)
sex," and Barnes exploits the ambiguity of the word in her description of
the mannish woman who is both *deprived* of sex, stitched up as she is, and
literally *divested* (undressed) of the "typical qualities" of femininity. The
unusual word, moreover, inevitably alludes to its inaugural usage:

> Come, you spirits
> That tend on mortal thoughts, unsex me here,
> And fill me from the crown to the toe top full
> Of direst cruelty! Make thick my blood,
> Stop up th' access and passage to remorse,
> That no compunctious visitings of nature
> Shake my fell purpose, nor keep peace between
> Th' effect and it! Come to my woman's breasts,
> And take my milk for gall, you murth'ring ministers. (*Macbeth*, I. v. 40–48)

Lady Macbeth's words refer to her earlier worry that her husband's
"nature" might be "too full o' th' milk of human kindness" to carry out
Duncan's murder; unsexing means replacing that milk of human kindness
with the "gall" of "cruelty" – withdrawing nourishment in order to
obstruct inheritance.

The entire play *Macbeth*, itself a nocturnal and wooded tragedy, is
concerned with issues of lineage and procreation that overlap substantially
with Barnes's novel. In understanding Robin, therefore, one can hardly
ignore Barnes's description of her as "the born somnambule" (*N*, p. 35).
Even though Jane Marcus argues that the term alludes to Bellini's *La
sonnambula*,[25] it is hard not to heed O'Connor's advice to Nora: "remember Lady Macbeth" (*N*, p. 129). For Robin's gesture of "holding the child
high in her hand as if she were about to dash it down" strongly echoes
Shakespeare's play:

> I have given suck, and know
> How tender 'tis to love the babe that milks me;
> I would, while it was smiling in my face,
> Have pluck'd my nipple from his boneless gums,
> And dash'd the brains out, had I so sworn as you
> Have done to this. (*Macbeth*, I. vii. 54–59)

Shakespeare's third reference to the milk of human kindness entails yet
another image of thwarted procreation: infanticide.

Robin too, like Frau Mann, is doll-like, lacking "human kindness" not
only in the sense of a nourishing gentleness but also in the sense of

belonging to the human kind; O'Connor deems her "outside the human type" (*N*, p. 146). He describes to Nora a similarity between her love for the boyish Robin and the attachment a child feels for a doll: "The doll and the immature have something right about them, the doll because it resembles but does not contain life, and the third sex because it contains life but resembles a doll" (*N*, p. 148). Felix also thinks of Robin as doll-like; she reminds him of "an old statue in a garden" (*N*, p. 41) and a ship's "figurehead in a museum" (*N*, p. 38) whose fearful symmetry implies the same sexlessness as the "identical cleaved halves" of the doll O'Connor describes. This pattern of imagery surrounding Robin, like the animal imagery that also surrounds her, positions her on the fringes of the human – or, as Kaivola says, "antithetical to culture."[26]

As noted already, dolls are an old uncanny motif. Freud recognizes the uncanniness of "the impression made by waxwork figures, ingeniously constructed dolls and automata," and discusses the tendency in children for "treating their dolls like live people."[27] The animating fantasies of the child, he argues, illustrate "the subject's narcissistic overvaluation of his own mental powers."[28] Adults, however, find the animate doll uncanny because it betokens the *return* of repressed "residues of animistic mental activity."[29] In the somnambulistic Robin, then, it is her proximity to the inanimate – the fact that she "contains life but resembles a doll" – that evokes uncanny feelings. Like "the living statues" (*N*, p. 13) on display at Count Altamonte's party, Robin hovers between the animate and the inanimate.[30] In combining the two meanings of unsex – assuming an "unfeminine" murderousness and an asexual innocence, Robin displays both a dollishness and a capacity to destroy the doll. She is, as O'Connor notes, innocent and fearsome at once.

Robin's doll-like nature is also linked to her hands. Gazing at her as she sleeps in a chair, Felix notes her "one arm fallen over the chair's side, the hand somehow older and wiser than her body" (*N*, p. 44). His attention to this unconscious bodily wisdom recalls his father Guido's perception of Hedvig's "condensed power of the hand, patterned on seizure ... as sinister in its reduction as a doll's house" (*N*, p. 4). When Felix watches Robin handle objects, "he experienced an unaccountable apprehension. The sensuality in her hands frightened him" (*N*, p. 42). Robin herself is likened to an uncanny amputated hand when she leaves Nora to roam the cafes of Paris: "Robin was an amputation that Nora could not renounce. As the wrist longs, so her heart longed" (*N*, p. 59). The amputated hand – the hand possessed of its own volition – is of course another well-established locus of the uncanny, seen in West's Homer Simpson and Anderson's Wing Biddlebaum.[31] A cluster of interconnected images (dolls, hands, symmetries, unsexing) thus surrounds Robin and renders her uncanny. As we have seen, however, the same doll-like, inhuman quality can also describe the technique of satire. And, as Freud observes, the comic element of satire mitigates uncanny effects by emotionally disengaging the reader from the text. Yet Robin seems to defy satirizing. That Robin's uncanniness proves immune to satiric treatment, then, suggests that satire requires a residual notion of the human in order to reduce its characters to caricature. Robin, outside the human type, cannot be accused of vice. Just as the satiric can temper the effects of the uncanny, so the uncanny can prevent the emergence of the satiric.

Robin's uncanny aura becomes the focus of the novel's conclusion, in which Robin "go[es] down" (*N*, p. 169) on all fours, laughing, barking, and baring her teeth in erotic play with Nora's dog – a regression that provokes fear in others. Jenny "accuse[s] [her] of a 'sensuous communion with unclean spirits'" (*N*, p. 168), and the chapter itself is entitled "The Possessed," punning on the demonic and erotic senses of the word. The dog too seems frightened, backing away and whimpering. But from this disquieting moment of uncanny reduction Barnes again salvages something like sympathy:

Then she began to bark also, crawling after him – barking in a fit of laughter, obscene and touching. The dog began to cry then, running with her, head-on with her head, as if to circumvent her; soft and slow his feet went padding. He ran this way and that, low down in his throat crying, and she grinning and crying with him; crying in shorter and shorter spaces, moving head to head, until she gave up, lying out, her hands beside her, her face turned and weeping; and the dog too gave up then, and lay down, his eyes bloodshot, his head flat along her knees. (*N*, p. 170)

The paragraph begins with Robin reduced to a mechanistic "fit of laughter" (*N*, p. 170) and recalls other moments in *Nightwood* of laughter as corporeal automatism. Yet as the passage surrenders its Latinate diction and present participles, the motion and energy of the scene give way to the stasis of the unadorned past tense. The initially profligate doubling of language – "head-on with her head," "this way and that," "grinning and crying," "shorter and shorter," "head to head" – is dissipated as grammatical inversion ("soft and slow his feet went padding"; "low down in his throat crying") and increasingly monosyllabic language slow the reader's pace. The dog now takes on the affect that Robin never herself expresses. While her behavior appears mechanistic, its actions look increasingly human. The dog almost speaks for Robin, its inarticulate, animal crying being the most authentic form that an expression of suffering can take in *Nightwood*.

SECOND-HAND DEALINGS WITH LIFE

To review: while Robin's *function* in the novel might be seen as satiric to the extent that she serves as an unconscious agent of, or metaphor for, forces that block inheritance, the novel's *representation of* Robin never becomes satiric, never feels laden with caricature, precisely because it adheres to the aesthetic protocols of the uncanny. In the same fashion, *Nightwood* never satirizes Nora's love for Robin or questions its authenticity. Even if the novel hints at an element of narcissism in the way that Nora treats Robin as a fantasy object, or of melancholia (as Victoria Smith has suggested) in the way she fails to recover from her loss, to ridicule Nora's expressions of love would be to diminish the uncanny power of Robin's hold over her. Instead, the novel suggests that Nora's passion for Robin sets a standard by which other loves can be measured. Significantly, it invokes the force of Nora's passion during its introduction of Jenny Petherbridge, the woman for whom Robin deserts Nora, and it does so deliberately in order to discredit the value of Jenny's feelings: "As, from the solid archives of usage, she had stolen or appropriated the dignity of speech, so she appropriated the most passionate love that she knew, Nora's for Robin. She was a 'squatter' by instinct" (*N*, p. 68). It is by way of juxtaposition to Jenny's stolen feelings that Nora's passion appears authentic, the original of which Jenny's is the copy.

In contrast to the uncanny power of love that Barnes displays in Nora's attachment to Robin, her treatment of Jenny is ruthlessly and unabatingly satiric. Indeed, my claim that *Nightwood* never fully exercises a satiric treatment of human character must allow for the significant exception of Jenny. For the most unequivocally satiric passage of the novel is undoubtedly the beginning of "The Squatter":

The words that fell from her mouth seemed to have been lent to her; had she been forced to invent a vocabulary for herself it would have been a vocabulary of two words, "ah" and "oh." (*N*, p. 66)

To men she sent books by the dozen; the general feeling was that she was a well-read woman, though she had read perhaps ten books in her life. (*N*, p. 67)

She had the fluency of tongue and action meted out by divine providence to those who cannot think for themselves. She was master of the over-sweet phrase, the over-tight embrace. (*N*, p. 68)

One inevitably thought of her in the act of love emitting florid *commedia dell'arte* ejaculations; one should not have thought of her in the act of love at all. (*N*, p. 68)

All of these insults, and many others, share a logic of appropriation: "Her walls, her cupboards, her bureaux, were teeming with second-hand dealings with life" (*N*, p. 66).

This second-hand quality notably extends to Jenny's emotions: "Since her emotional reactions were without distinction, she had to fall back upon the emotions of the past, great loves already lived and related, and over those she seemed to suffer and grow glad" (*N*, p. 68). She *seemed* to suffer and grow glad, the narrator tells us, because after this indictment one must question what "real" suffering and gladness are. Hence when Barnes describes Jenny's "appropriation" of Nora's love, the borrowed nature of this love renders it "dishonest": "When she fell in love it was with a perfect fury of accumulated dishonesty; she became instantly a dealer in second-hand and therefore incalculable emotions" (*N*, p. 68). A second-hand emotion is, we must assume, something more subtle than mere fakery. The peculiar suggestion is that there can be an emotional state that would feel just like a real emotion yet lack its reality. But this possibility is summoned only through explicit narratorial intervention; the narrator's assertion of knowledge – exposing to the reader the "real" Jenny behind the false public perception of her – is necessary to make Jenny a figure of ridicule. This access to a special plane of knowledge about Jenny is, furthermore, only possible through the heightened epistemological authority that a heterodiegetic narrator possesses over her fictional subjects. Barnes is playing her narratorial trump card – omniscience – in order to guarantee Jenny's secondariness.

Recent critics who have addressed the function of laughter in *Nightwood* have recognized Jenny's peculiar emptiness. Tyrus Miller remarks that Jenny's character "embodies secondariness and compulsive repetition," while Justus Nieland describes her as "primarily *secondary* in her emotional life, all bourgeois characteristicness but absent the interior vitality of modernist character."[32] Both critics take the function of laughter in Barnes's text as closer to a Lewisian program of signalling inhuman automatism than to a Bergsonian agenda that would restore human sociability. Yet in both of these otherwise compelling readings the actual *satire* of Barnes's representation of Jenny subtly escapes. Miller remarks that "the savagery of Barnes's depiction ... requires little comment" and instead views Jenny metafictionally, as a belated reader of the text of Nora's love. Nieland, in contrast, takes Jenny as representative of the way that the category of personality – of personhood – fails to account for affect in *all* of the novel's characters; for him Jenny's "comic gestures, like the protocols of her emotional life, epitomize how laughter in *Nightwood* ... contraindicates the human."[33] For Miller, Barnes's treatment of Jenny requires little interpretation, while for Nieland it is an interpretive key that extends to the novel as a whole.

Satire escapes in these readings perhaps because the distinction between Barnes's characterization of Jenny and her characterization of Robin is not fully attended to. This distinction is especially elusive because the metaphors and techniques with which Barnes derides Jenny are often remarkably similar to those she uses to establish Robin's uncanny strangeness. For example, while Robin is likened to "a beast turning human" (*N*, p. 37) and "a wild thing caught in a woman's skin" (*N*, p. 146), Jenny too hovers on the borders of the human: "somewhere about her was the tension of the accident that made the beast the human endeavour" (*N*, p. 67). Likewise, the motif of the severed body part, which Barnes uses to communicate the uncanny power of the bond between Nora and Robin, resurfaces in the picture of Jenny: "She had a beaked head and the body, small, feeble, and ferocious, that somehow made one associate her with Judy; they did not go together. Only severed could any part of her have been called 'right'" (*N*, p. 65). But the device that endows Robin with a frightful primitivism renders Jenny a caricature, and she proves to be the only person O'Connor has seen whom he deems to be uglier than himself (*N*, p. 98). Her pattern of appropriating the objects of others and assembling them haphazardly extends to her appearance, so she becomes no more than an incoherent compilation of parts, a visual definition of the grotesque.

Barnes's scathing portrait of Jenny redeploys for its satiric ends not only the particular uncanny trope of the severed body part but also the more general pattern of unconscious bodily knowledge that permeates the depiction of Robin. But while in Robin the unconsciousness of the body seems atavistic, provoking apprehension in characters and reader alike, in Jenny, it provokes amusement. The way Jenny tells a humorous story resembles the action of a mechanical toy:

Hovering, trembling, tip-toeing, she would unwind anecdote after anecdote in a light rapid lisping voice which one always expected to change, to drop and become the "every day" voice; but it never did. The stories were humorous, well-told. She would smile, toss her hands up, widen her eyes; immediately everyone in the room had a certain feeling of something lost, sensing that there was one person who was missing the importance of the moment, who had not heard the story; the teller herself. (*N*, p. 66–67)

Barnes's description is similar to West's account of Faye Greener enchant-
ing her suitors in Hollywood, yet West's passage does not achieve the
ruthlessness of Barnes's, since West's narratorial voice gradually occupies
the space of male sexual excitement and suspends critical judgment.
Jenny's stories, however, excite neither lust nor sympathy, as Barnes builds
to a withering punchline.

Thus, while Jenny resembles Robin in certain ways, in others she is
Robin's diametrical opposite. To Robin's "stubborn cataleptic calm" is
opposed Jenny's "panicky" nervous energy (*N*, p. 65). Robin's affinity
with prehistory and nature lends her an air of authenticity, but Jenny
suffers from an excess of culture. Robin's animality is metonymic (she is
kin to lionesses and dogs), whereas Jenny's is metaphoric (her beaked head
suggests a human-animal analogy). Moreover, even though Robin is
outside the human type, it is Jenny alone who "defile[s] the very meaning
of personality in her passion to be a person" (*N*, p. 66). The verb to defile
(originally to *defoul*) sounds a scatological note and consequently a moral
judgment, and thus, while Robin is nicknamed "La Somnambule,"
Jenny is "The Squatter," an epithet in which Kenneth Burke sees not
only a reference to her rapacity but also to the posture of excretion.[34]
Finally, whereas Robin is excluded by her "primitive innocence" from
O'Connor's moral condemnation, Jenny receives his unqualified scorn:
"That woman ... would use the third-rising of a corpse for her [own]
ends" (*N*, p. 116).

It is in the depiction of Jenny, then, that Barnes displays not only the
wit and malice that characterize satire, but also the moral condemnation
that it so often carries. This short chapter is also, not coincidentally, the
point in the novel where the exceptional *anger* of the narratorial voice may
be likely to tempt the interpreter with the allure of psychobiography. It is
the point where *Nightwood* approaches "nigh T. Wood" – near to Thelma
Wood, the prototype for Robin, whose name, as Barnes claimed to have
realized only after the fact, is encoded in the book's title.[35] But just as
Waugh, in *A Handful of Dust*, saves his bitterest insults not for the fickle
Brenda (based on his ex-wife) but for her lover John Beaver (based on her
lover John Heygate), so it is not Thelma but Henriette McCrea Metcalf,
the model for Jenny, who gets the worst of the author's bile.[36] The
recourse to biography is tempting because the text here chooses sides
quite openly; this is where the narrator puts her thumb on the scale in
order to make sure the reader comes away with the desired moral judgment on Jenny. And the simplest explanation for the narrator's uncharacteristic anger is to psychologize the narrator by conflating her with the

scorned lover who wrote the book. Biography enters interpretation because (satiric) narratorial affect appears gratuitous.[37]

Now I am not actually claiming validity for such a biographical reading, which would require a detailed engagement with Barnes's life and close reading of her correspondence. The point is that the malice in Jenny's depiction stabilizes the moral frame of the text, reasserting an interpretive order in pronounced contrast to the novel's ubiquitous dissolution of norms. The ridicule of Jenny is not merely an *expression* of anger at the character on the part of an author or narrator. On the contrary, the narrator's portrait of Jenny as a fake actually *sanctions* her anger at the woman. Barnes constructs Jenny as morally debased and then mocks her for being drawn that way.

This is not to say that Nora herself wholly escapes from authorial (self-) satire, that she is never ridiculed for her narcissism or possessiveness. But it *is* to say that the authenticity of her love is guaranteed within the text by the satiric treatment of Jenny's emotions. Nora gains the moral high ground through the narrator's abasement of Jenny. This moral polarization of Nora and Jenny may itself be seen as a reaction-formation, a protesting-too-much against the threat that Nora's own love too is ultimately inauthentic. After all, Nora's love itself has been preceded in any number of ways: within the text (by Felix), intertextually (by Catherine and Heathcliff), biographically (by grandmother Zadel).[38] But even such an interpretation of the novel's stark moral judgments would still accept the premise that the text carefully calibrates the authenticity of the characters' love with their moral standing.

In short, satire surfaces in the text to make clear the author's moral arrangement of the characters. By establishing Jenny as a creature whose "present is always someone else's past" (*N*, 98), as a woman unable to connect with the past in any way other than imitation, the novel dooms her to presentness. Jenny's imitation produces only an ironic or secondary relation to the past. She thus represents the underside of the modernist equation of originality and authenticity: making it new is impossible for her. Because she degrades things by appropriating them and imitating them, she herself is degraded by the author. Or, better put, she is degraded *by being represented as* an agent of degradation; she is satirized by being rendered as a force that mocks the emotions of the past in its uncritical reproduction of them.

In contrast, Robin's uncanniness retains implicit authorial approval, made all the stronger by the degradation of Jenny's imitative existence. If we return to O'Connor's analogy, in which Robin offers the sort of contact with the primitive that the modern reader gains by reading of violence in the newspaper, the function of this uncanniness becomes clearer. O'Connor's recognition of newspaper reading as vicarious thrill-seeking might recall Waugh's Brenda Last cavalierly skimming through an account of a little girl's strangulation, or West's "starers" who crave their daily dose of murders and sex crimes. Yet, for Waugh, the reader's participation in the thrilling affect of sadism is clearly a moral failing. In West, the vicariation, attributed to anonymous masses, is presented first of all as a social symptom. For Barnes, however, it is not even clear that this vicariousness is condemned. For such vicarious access to the primitive is, after all, something that not only the newspapers provide; it is also supplied by modernist fiction itself, through works such as *Nightwood*.

Thus, while the trend of finding in *Nightwood* a democratic embrace of anti-essentialism is laudable enough, this novel retains a heavy investment in authenticity. Incontestably, *Nightwood* repeatedly shows history, tradition, and aristocracy – not to mention gender, sexuality, and race – to be "splendid and reeking falsification[s]" (*N*, p. 11); it recognizes performances behind the confining, often tyrannical reduction of people to racial or sexual types. Yet if things like Jewishness, femininity, even personality are shown to be inauthentic, this exposure actually serves to guarantee a more fundamental authenticity on the level of the uncanny, the nonlinguistic, or the creaturely. It may be that ultimately Barnes's uncanny is itself a ruse, since every bid for authenticity can be redescribed as sentimentality, and literary history is full of aspiring prophets who sound to more modern ears like overheated adolescents. But that is only to say that any literary strategy has risks. It should not prevent us from discerning how *Nightwood* uses satiric unmasking to secure the uncanny as authentic. Like her creation Dr. O'Connor, the satirist Barnes makes the movements common to the dumbfounder, offering a series of "honesties" that allow her to prepare the most flagrant part of her hoax.

CHAPTER 8

Beckett's authoritarian personalities

Samuel Beckett, long discussed as a, if not the, final figure in the great procession of modernist writers, is a natural if not unavoidable figure in any investigation of late modernist satire. Yet while *Murphy* (1938) might seem the obvious choice for the completion of a study that has focused on the 1930s, I here choose to read a later novel, 1951's *Molloy*, sacrificing a bit of chronological unity in order to adumbrate how the idea of late modernist satire can be extended into the post-war years. In doing so, I aim to avoid a simplistic historicism by acknowledging the ways in which some of the post-war themes that emerge in this reading – Beckett's treatment of authority and compulsion – can, despite the undeniable impact of the war and the Holocaust, yet be seen as the fulfillment of emerging pre-war tendencies.

Chronologically, *Molloy* serves as an optimal text for reading Beckett as a late modernist. If any theorization of late modernism must rest in part upon discerning a skepticism toward or revision of earlier modernist practices, then the post-war moment would seem to solidify what was already emergent in the 1930s: the exhaustion of modernist romantic, revolutionary, or utopian energies. In describing late modernism, Fredric Jameson argues that "the Cold War spelled the end of a whole era of social transformations and indeed of Utopian desires and anticipations"[1] – and in a different sense the Holocaust too put an end to such utopianism. At the same time, the major trends (and resurgent utopianisms) most frequently identified with postmodernism had yet to attain cultural centrality, so that the immediate post-war years present a lacuna in standard periodizations of the century.

Formally, too, *Molloy* might be called late modernist. While it continues the modernist breaking of realist conventions, it also effects a second break, a break from Beckett's own modernist masters that is frequently signaled through allusion. Take, for example, this funereal double reference to Joyce:

I who had loved the image of old Geulincx, dead young, who left me free, on the black boat of Ulysses, to crawl towards the East, along the deck. That is a great measure of freedom, for him who has not the pioneering spirit. And from the poop, poring upon the wave, a sadly rejoicing slave, I follow with my eyes the proud and futile wake. (*M*, p. 51)[2]

If Beckett here implies that Joyce's *Wake* is futile, he elsewhere disdains Proust's faith memory, a rejection he signals through satiric reference to Marcel's adored blossom: "The white hawthorn stooped towards me, unfortunately I don't like the smell of hawthorn" (*M*, p. 27). And for good measure, Beckett redescribes Yeats's Irish heroine as a cloacal mother: "for me the question did not arise whether to call her Ma, Mag or the Countess Caca" (*M*, p. 17).[3] The post-war trilogy, then, and *Molloy* in particular, might be seen as a linchpin between a modernist Beckett sloughing off the influence of his precursors, and a postmodernist Beckett who makes possible the *nouveau roman* and large portions of poststructuralism.[4]

But since (I am arguing) satire is a dominant sensibility in late modernism, it should be noted that the function of laughter in Beckett's fiction has become linked to his status as a modernist. Beckett of course has long been recognized as a comic writer, and his debts to vaudeville, silent films, and circuses do not need further tallying. In his fiction and his plays, bodies break down and decay; language drifts into paradox or nonsense; philosophy dead-ends.[5] Still, the interpretation of this comedy has become highly contested. Paul Sheehan has decried the "glib caricature" of an existentialist Beckett as a heroic artist working to salvage value from nihilism, an artist whose humor performs a "cathartic, therapeutic, and heroic" function in enabling the individual to transcend the meaninglessness of existence.[6] Sheehan calls this outdated stereotype the "humanist Beckett," but it is also, for Tyrus Miller, a modernist Beckett in whom critics have found a testament to the redemptive powers of art. Miller reads Beckett's work not as a high modernist glorification of art, but as a late modernist revelation of "social and semantic contingency": the discourse of *Watt*, for example, "has little to do with artistic intentionality or self-conscious purification of the language of the tribe," but rather "testifies to Watt's loss of autonomy, his increasing subjection to an impersonal language-machine," while in *Murphy*, Beckettian laughter serves to provide "the comic face of social domination."[7]

Yet as salutary as it is to jettison the easy clichés of (modernist, humanist) laughter in the face of despair, Miller's move to elucidate the subjection of Beckett's characters to sociopolitical and linguistic structures gives us instead an equally familiar image – a postmodern Beckett that is already visible in Jameson's 1979 description of "the openly schizophrenic discontinuities of such postmodernist 'texts' or *écriture* as Beckett's *Watt*," and which Jameson identifies as paradigmatic of the postmodern condition.[8] (I will leave aside the further objection that the vilified "modernist" Beckett is in a chronological sense not properly "modernist" at all, but *itself* late modernist, the product of post-war existentialism.) As Miller revises the narrative of Beckettian comedy from a modernist story of liberation to a Foucauldian parable of domination, laughter becomes merely the most ingenious weapon in the arsenal of power. In this quick reversal, it is easy to see an unintended consequence of Foucauldian thought, one against which Eve Sedgwick has warned: "his analysis of the pseudodichotomy between repression and liberation has led, in many cases, to its conceptual reimposition in the even more abstractly reified form of the hegemonic and the subversive."[9] Recognizing as hegemonic what had first appeared subversive merely shifts the cachet of liberatory critique from the author to the critic, who thereby achieves the standing to free us from our false faith in the redemptive powers of art.

What's wrong here, then, is not the possibility that Beckett might in certain accounts look like a cliché of a modernist and in others look like a cliché of a postmodernist. That hazard is probably inevitable. What is wrong is the choice itself, which imposes a rigid binary that Sedgwick aptly calls moralistic, and erases "the middle ranges of agency"[10] – the eastward movement of the slave on the deck of the westward sailing boat, to use Beckett's metaphor. The debate over whether laughter is transgressive or normative beats a hasty retreat from the bewildering affective encounter with Beckett's writing to the safety of one of two stable, fortified, and unexciting positions. In contrast, Shane Weller has argued that Beckett's comedy might best be seen as *anethical*, while Ruby Cohn has noted simply: "So ambiguous are Beckett's comic heroes that we scarcely know ... whether we laugh *at* or *with*."[11] Indeed the very problem of how to read laughter is foregrounded in *Molloy*, when Lousse buries her dog: "I thought she was going to cry, it was the thing to do, but on the contrary she laughed. It was perhaps her way of crying. Or perhaps I was mistaken and she was really crying, with the noise of laughter. Tears and laughter, they are so much Gaelic to me" (*M*, p. 37). As Weller notes, Beckett defeats before it is raised the notion that laughter will be unitary, easily explicable, or even distinguishable from its opposite.

I want to revisit the question of laughter in Beckett by recognizing that the pleasurable affects usually associated with the comic emerge in our reading of Beckett from an interplay of other feelings that include irritation, boredom, frustration, anxiety, and surprise. While I think Beckettian laughter is a good thing to the extent that it gives me pleasure, I still find it duplicitous: liberating in its capacity to free us, however temporarily, from oppressive emotional identifications, but malicious and even sadistic in the way it lifts inhibitions that can possess legitimate social or ethical value. Recognizing this duplicity would at the least reveal the limits of reading Beckett within the moralistic binary of hegemony versus subversion. (Might every act of subversion cast the shadow of a nascent hegemony?) It would also illumine Beckett's mode as a kind of satire. Although Beckett's satire is not the English comedy of manners we see in Waugh and Gibbons, nor the symbol-heavy American grotesquerie of Barnes and West, it shares with those works a tendentiousness that cannot easily be sentimentalized as benign or reparative.

Initially, my reading of *Molloy* will examine how Beckett's satire takes as a target the exercise of paternal authority within the modern state marked by the threat of fascism; it will do so with reference to two key texts, Coleridge's "Frost at Midnight" and Adorno's *The Authoritarian Personality*. Beckett's representation of fatherhood undermines sentimentalized ideals of the bourgeois family, and reveals sadomasochistic dynamics at work in the exercise of modern social, political, and religious authority. It implicates the reader in its sadistic structures, yet exposes the operations of that sadism. Turning from the character of Moran to Molloy himself, I then extend this reading of authority to a broader reading of compulsion, in which Beckett's laughter can be seen as occurring on the border between compulsion and freedom. The modulations of affect in Beckett prove irreducible to a humanist or antihumanist position, since they exist in the interspace that constitutes those positions in the first place.

MORAN AS BUREAUCRAT AND FATHER

Molloy is divided into two parts. In the first, the lame and dying Molloy sits in his "mother's room" and writes pages for vaguely identified men; these pages, which presumably constitute the first part of the novel, tell of Molloy's journey through an unnamed town and its surrounding country – on his bicycle, on crutches, crawling on his back – to his mother. The second half of the novel introduces a new narrator, one Jacques Moran, whose narrative is a report of his mission to find Molloy, undertaken at the command of the enigmatic, Godot-like Youdi. Moran embarks on the mission with his son Jacques, Jr., who is "thirteen or fourteen" (*M*, p. 94); as the search goes on, Moran comes increasingly to resemble Molloy, in the nature of his adventures, in the physical infirmities that overcome him, in the aimlessness of his journey and of his discourse.[12] On returning home, he concludes by declaring that the first words of his report are false.

In perhaps Beckettian fashion, I begin my reading of *Molloy* in the middle, with the priggish and moralistic Moran. Despite Moran's obnoxious qualities, the first encounter with him is likely to bring some measure of comfort. For Moran craves precision. "Vagueness I abhor" (*M*, p. 99), he declares, and this abhorrence functions as a surrogate for or extension of the reader's own antipathy – an antipathy that has been provoked by the reading of the first half of the novel. Molloy's narrative, after all, is full of maddening vagueness and vagaries, offered to the reader in an almost continuous ninety-page block of unparagraphed type; turning the page to discover a new, apparently more precise voice, the reader finds in Moran's report reassuring certainties. Moran provides proper names,[13] paragraphs, days of the week, months of the year. He owns a house, knows his neighbors, attends a local church, and even refers to Flaubert and Goering – linking us, however tenuously, to a world we think we know. Religious, propertied, employed, widowed, Moran holds an identifiable and (initially) stable position within familiar social structures.

Moreover, while the exact the nature of Moran's employment (taking orders from the messenger Gaber on behalf of Youdi) is vague, even here his task is one of restoring legibility, working on behalf of the reader's desire to re-establish the comforts (setting, character, motive) of realist narrative. As H. Porter Abbott has pointed out, Moran is a writer of an administrative "report," and "Beckett's use of the report as a narrative device" exerts a steady "control over our response."[14] John Guillory has recently described the report, with its cognates, the form, and the memo, as the quintessential modern genre of writing, one that is produced far more regularly than poems or scientific papers. The report, Guillory observes, is "linked to the theme of bureaucracy"; born from the needs of twentieth-century administration, it is "founded on the deliberate suppression of rhetorical techniques" including the inefficient social niceties of the nineteenth-century business letter.[15] The report, in sum, aspires to a certain affective quality, the no-nonsense manner of the bureaucrat. Thus Moran emerges as an anti-rhetorical, even anti-literary voice: "It is not at this late stage of my relation that I intend to give way to literature" (*M*, p. 151). Promising to ascertain the facts, names, and dates that are inexact, contradictory, or missing in Molloy's narrative, his report is a "paltry scrivening" (*M*, p. 132), an administrative and supplementary text that will classify and clarify the first. Moran thus also serves as a surrogate reader, and works in alliance with the actual reader seeking clarification of Molloy's cryptic text. In addition to promising a less literary mode of language, then, the report form intimates the presence of what Abbott calls "an elaborate bureaucracy."[16] (Beckett's attention to the language of bureaucrats is preceded by Melville, Conrad, and Kafka, and anticipates the underworld networks of Pynchon and DeLillo.[17]) Of course, the increasingly Molloy-like Moran is both funny and interesting to the extent that his discourse fails to conform to the protocols of its bureaucratic genre. Yet the conditions under which he is compelled to write are crucial to understanding his role in the novel.

To make sense of the elusive "Molloy affair" (*M*, p. 98), Moran needs to gather information like a detective or spy: "Peeping and prying were part of my profession" (*M*, p. 94). Beckett's evocation of the detective genre allows him to invoke the professionalization of both labor and feeling covertly celebrated by that genre – the modern professional detective's "ethical" code of executing his task while bracketing any "personal" interest or emotion. Beckett thus registers the pressures of an administrative modernity in both the genre of his text and the tone of his narrative. Moran's role as an agent of meaning – working on behalf of a bureaucratic authority, returning to familiar protocols of communicative language, promising classification and knowledge-production – occurs within a specifically modern (or late modern) social formation.

Throughout the report, Moran's role as a restorer of meaning and authority overlaps substantially with his role as a father. (Moran's narrative of fathers and sons, with its oedipal dynamics, complements Molloy's mother-centered quest, marked by pre-oedipal themes.[18]) His opening paragraph introduces this theme:

It is midnight. The rain is beating on the windows. I am calm. All is sleeping. Nevertheless I get up and go to my desk. I can't sleep. My lamp sheds a soft and steady light. I have trimmed it. It will last till morning. I hear the eagle-owl. What a terrible battle-cry! Once I listened to it unmoved. My son is sleeping. Let him sleep. The night will come when he too, unable to sleep, will get up and go to his desk. I shall be forgotten. (*M*, p. 92)

A scene of nocturnal stillness, an agitated father guarding a peacefully sleeping son, harsh outdoor weather contrasted with a flame-lit sheltered interior – Beckett's "It is midnight" indubitably references Coleridge's "Frost at Midnight," *locus classicus* of paternal tenderness, where, with his infant Hartley sleeping "cradled by [his] side," Coleridge, like Moran, finds vexation in calmness itself:

> 'Tis calm indeed! so calm, that it disturbs
> And vexes meditation with its strange
> And extreme silentness.[19]

Even Moran's eagle-owl, the objective correlative of the agitation that disturbs his mind, alludes to Coleridge's opening lines: "The owlet's cry / Came loud – and hark, again! loud as before."[20] But Beckett replaces the rich images and rhythms of the lyric monologist with the clipped and methodical cadences of a diarist, the adored infant with a repulsive adolescent, and the exuberant hopes of a father for his child with a bitter prediction that the son's life will only repeat, blindly and mechanically, the father's disappointed course. Most importantly, the idealized loving relation between father and son in Coleridge's lyric will be revealed in Beckett's text as fraught with sadism and violence. And so the novel's conclusion – "Then I went back into the house and wrote, It is midnight. The rain is beating on the windows. It was not midnight. It was not raining" (*M*, p. 176) – is not merely an early postmodern acknowledgement of the rhetoricity or fictionality of historical discourse, but a confession of literary artistry that specifically disavows the false paternal sentiment in which the narrative originates.

As I have noted, even such works as Waugh's *A Handful of Dust* and Barnes's *Nightwood* – hardly warm and fuzzy tales of spiritual uplift – seek out their rare moments of poignancy in father–son relationships: Tony taking John Andrew's small hand in his own as they walk to church, Felix Volkbein rubbing oil into the chapped hands of the simple-minded Guido. Such feelings are also one of the key emotional touchstones of *Ulysses*, where paternity may be a legal fiction but Leopold Bloom's repeated imagination of his dead son Rudy still alive at age eleven and memories of his suicide father stimulate a reader's compassion for the doubly bereaved hero. But Moran's few moments of paternal affection hardly summon such sympathy. They rarely last long before degenerating into suspicion and anger in sudden affective reversal: "I drew him to me. What do you say to that? I said. Did he love me then as much as I loved him? You could never be sure with that little hypocrite" (*M*, pp. 119–20). (Maria DiBattista has in fact characterized Beckett as "the master of the emotional upheaval and affective reversal."[21]) The Moran–Jacques relationship offers a comic-satiric debunking of Coleridgean paternal affection, favoring a view of fatherhood steeped in sadomasochism and rivalry.[22] At one point Moran even fantasizes that "I could chain my son to me in such a way as to prevent him from ever shaking me off again" (*M*, p. 129): the master–slave relationship of *Godot*'s Lucky and Pozzo is in the wings.

While this sadomasochistic relationship functions as an ironic redescription of the Coleridgean exaltation of the bourgeois family, it also carries a political charge in post-war Europe. For *Molloy* is contemporaneous with a movement in political theory and social science that sought to understand, in the wake of totalitarianism and genocide, the psychological dimensions of fascist and anti-Semitic thinking. Hannah Arendt's *The Origins of Totalitarianism* (1951) may be the most famous text of this moment, and in France a signal work was Sartre's *Reflections on the Jewish Question* (1946), while in the United States, Richard Hofstadter's slightly later "The Paranoid Style in American Politics" (1964), sought to fuse social history with psychoanalysis in order to understand racism and McCarthyism. However, at least according to the commentator Irwin Katz, "the dominant influence on thinking about the causes of ethnic prejudice" during this time "was Adorno *et al.*'s (1950) psychoanalytically inspired study, *The Authoritarian Personality*."[23] The study, written by Theodor Adorno and several colleagues at the Institute for Social Research in conjunction with the Berkeley Public Opinion Study, funded by the American Jewish Committee, and published by Harper and Row, "proposed that bigotry was a component of a more general antidemocratic ideology commonly found in personalities marked by cognitive rigidity, repressed affect, and self-alienation."[24] Drawing on theoretical work dating back before the war (particularly that of erstwhile member Erich Fromm), *The Authoritarian Personality* aimed, in Richard Sennett's words, "to be much more historical and specific than was Freud about the ways culture plays a role" in shaping such personalities; Adorno's "concept refers to an intersection" of psychological and social forces.[25]

Specifically, Adorno posits an "authoritarian syndrome" that "follows the 'classic' psychoanalytic pattern involving a sadomasochistic resolution of the Oedipus complex" whereby the superego "assumes an irrational aspect."[26] Adorno elaborates: "The subject achieves his own social adjustment only by taking pleasure in obedience and subordination. This brings into play the sadomasochistic impulse structure both as a condition and a result of social adjustment."[27] Such an "adjustment," which allows for the "gratification" of "sadistic as well as masochistic tendencies,"[28] results from the particular way in which oedipal rivalries are "resolved" after love for the mother is forbidden:

The resulting hatred for the father is transformed by reaction-formation into love. This transformation leads to a particular kind of superego. The transform-ation of hatred into love, the most difficult task the individual has to perform in his early development, never succeeds completely. In the psychodynamics of the "authoritarian character," part of the preceding aggressiveness is absorbed and turned into masochism, while another part is left over as sadism, which seeks an outlet in those with whom the subject does not identify himself: ultimately the outgroup.[29]

This developmental conflict ultimately has ramifications in the realm of the sociopolitical: "The Jew frequently becomes a substitute for the hated father."[30]

The centrality of Beckett's writing to Adorno's larger defense of literary modernism is well known: Beckett's works through their very forms offer a critique from within of social conditions that the polemical art of Brecht or Sartre can only emptily proclaim.[31] But my point here is not to rehearse, challenge, or untangle Adorno's argument, only to indicate the immediacy of the connection between Adorno's analysis of authoritarian-ism and his championing of modernism. In the 1962 essay "Commit-ment," Adorno reviews the "insights of social psychology into the authoritarian personality" – his own insights, that is – and remarks: "[The authoritarian personality's] hostility to anything alien or alienating can accommodate itself much more easily to literary realism of any provenance, even if it proclaims itself critical or socialist, than to works which swear allegiance to no political slogans."[32] The political charge of committed art can easily be reversed because of its failure to offer any formal resistance to right-wing authoritarianism (indeed, it may formally reduplicate authoritarianism), whereas, in the works of Beckett and Kafka, the "mere guise is enough to disrupt the whole system of rigid coordinates that governs authoritarian personalities."[33] Here, however, I want to offer a different deployment of Adorno's insight: Beckett's novel is relevant to an analysis of authoritarian structures simply because it constitutes a portrait of precisely those proto-fascist or authoritarian personality traits that, as Adorno claims in a contemporaneous essay, emerge in modernity as "not simply the reoccurrence of the archaic but [as] its reproduction in and by civilization itself."[34]

The above excursus will be forgiven, I hope, if we can now see the benefits of regarding Moran as an Adornian authoritarian personality. Such a type, despite the conceptual objections psychoanalysts and social scientists have raised about it, neatly brings together Moran's role as a bureaucratic professional hunting down the wayward Molloy with his role as a non-Coleridgean father. Moran's narrative enacts the intertwining of familial power relations with wider social structures that Adorno remarks upon; the oedipal relationship between Moran and his son parallels and reproduces his professional relationship with Youdi. When Moran forbids his son to bring his stamp collection, he explicitly mimics Youdi's bureaucratic edict: "You leave both your albums at home, I said, the small one as well as the large one. Not a word of reproach, a simple prophetic present, on the model of those employed by Youdi. Your son goes with you" (*M*, p. 109). Borrowing Youdi's grammatical forms of command as well as obeying their content, Moran extends into the family the relationship of domination which governs his professional life.

It is worth noting here, with Richard Sennett, that no less an authoritarian personality than Stalin pronounced, "The state is a family, and I am your father."[35] According to Sennett, the totalitarian authority deliberately aims to revive the linkage between the head of family and the head of state that had been dissolved with Locke. Adorno too claims that "the psychological image of the leader is apt to reanimate the idea of the all-powerful and threatening primal father."[36] If we then observe with Alan Astro that the name Youdi not only suggests God (reversing the syllables of *dieu*) but is also an old French slur for Jew, derived from the Hebrew *yehudi*,[37] then Adorno's claim that "the Jew frequently becomes a substitute for the hated father" takes on new specificity in reading Moran's report. When we observe as well, with Anthony Uhlman, Moran's offhand mention of Goering – "Who is this bicycle for, I said, Goering?" (*M*, p. 141) – and we note that the bicycle is actually for the Goering-like Moran,[38] then Beckett's text begins to appear at least somewhat rooted in its historical location. Moran's obedience to the idealized yet hated Youdi suggests an identification with an ego-ideal in the form of leader of the sort that had been recently demonstrated all too vividly in Europe: "the leader's image immediately gratifies the follower's twofold wish to submit to authority and to be the authority himself."[39] Beckett's representation of Moran as both dictatorial father and subordinate functionary thus displays not only Adorno's insights into the authoritarian character type but also Sennett's further discernment of a crucial attribute of the relationship to authority under modernity – that it is characterized by "a split between authority and legitimacy,"[40] in which authorities are resented and discredited in defensive compensation for the subordinate's sense of shame at his own subordination.

MORAN'S COMIC LAW

The historical proximity of Adorno's writing on authority and Beckett's novel thus open a vantage from which Beckett's own analysis of authority can be profitably placed in a specific post-Holocaust context. Yet there remains an important difference between *The Authoritarian Personality* and *Molloy* that few will deny: *Adorno's text is not nearly as funny as Beckett's*. It could be conceded of course that certain interviews with racists and anti-Semites in Adorno's volume might raise a chuckle if we imagine them spoken by Moran: "Actually there is more underhandedness amongst Armenians than there is amongst Jews, but the Armenians aren't nearly as conspicuous and noisy."[41] But such an amusing thought-experiment only testifies to the imaginative accomplishment of Beckett's text, which delicately balances the absurdity and the horror of Moran's fascistic thought. That the mind of a rigid and rageful functionary who is "still obeying orders" (*M*, p. 132) should interest Beckett in the aftermath of the Second World War is not surprising: the churchgoing Moran is in many ways a representative citizen of Vichy France. But more curious is the degree to which Moran's sadistic personality should become the site of so much laughter. Simon Critchley seems correct in noting that Adorno tends to misread or ignore Beckett's humor, and Adorno's own moralistic streak may make him somewhat tone-deaf to Beckett's comedy.[42] But the laughter that accompanies Moran's sado-masochistic interactions with his son and others suggests the double movement of satire that I have tried to show throughout this book. Beckett finds a form in which he can ridicule Moran's authoritarian thinking but also, at the same time, inhabit that thought, and inhabit it joyfully.

By no means should such a claim be taken to suggest the crude psychobiographical position that either Beckett or his father possessed an authoritarian personality. (Nor do I want to suggest that Adorno's concept itself has diagnostic value outside the generalized sense in which I am invoking it.) While James Knowlson reports that Beckett did have a violent temper, and even as a boy "display[ed] the meticulousness that was to be one his most striking characteristics as an adult,"[43] he also reminds us that Beckett risked his life in the fight against fascism (where he, like Moran, often awaited orders from vague sources) and throughout his life showed sensitivity to even small acts of cruelty. Still, Knowlson points out, "*Molloy* is full of . . . echoes of [Beckett's] childhood,"[44] including key details from Moran's narrative, such as Jacques, Jr.'s stamp collection and his teddy bear, Baby Jack, whose real-life prototype the prepubescent Sam could not sleep without.[45] Such poignant affect – sentimental value – invested in Winnicottian transitional objects might then suggest a tension between Beckett's own exacting (sadistic) meticulousness and his own childlike (masochistic) vulnerability; Beckett might be said to use Moran's narrative to scrutinize tender childhood memories as a way to question nostalgic or sentimental treatments of childhood that would deny the force of the sadomasochistic aspect of familial relations.

In turning to an appreciation of the comic side of Moran's fascist tendencies then, it will be useful to bring in not only Adorno but also Gilles Deleuze, who specifically relates sadism and masochism to the comic: "The comic is the only possible mode of conceiving the law, in a peculiar combination of irony and humor."[46] Deleuze sees irony and humor as strategies for "subversion of the law"; irony is tied to sadism, which posits a "primary nature" anterior to the end of the law, while humor is tied (very tightly) to masochism, which defeats the law by making it malfunction, turning punishment into pleasure, and hence cause for reward.[47] Moran's sadism, even as it claims the law as its justification, thus "ironically" reveals itself as a "primary nature," and an end to itself.[48] Thus Moran – consistent with the double movement of satire – savors both his enforcement of the law and his own subjection to it. A "pompous, orthodox bourgeois,"[49] he claims to be "meticulous and calm in the main" (*M*, p. 114) and to have a "methodical mind" (*M*, p. 98); he even remarks, "I rather enjoyed dotting my i's" (*M*, p. 117). At the end of his journey, when he is limping home in torn clothing, filthy from his own incontinence, he still wears his tie knotted, "out of sheer bravado, I suppose" (*M*, p. 171) – bravado signaling his pride in (masochistic) submission to social strictures that have become wholly formal. Nowhere does Moran better illustrate what Deleuze calls the pure formalism of the law than when he enforces it, in true Kantian fashion, despite his dislike of its consequences: "I finally decided that to go back on my decision ... would deal a blow to my authority that it was in no condition to sustain. I did so with sorrow" (*M*, 121). Here the law reveals itself, in Deleuze's phrase, as "self-grounded and valid solely by virtue of its own form."[50] Moran's "sorrow" – "this hurts me more than it hurts you," as the cliché goes – is a residual pathos that survives the renunciation of human sympathy and indicates the gap between the demands of the law and the claims of personal sentiment. The law must be formal, inhuman, cold – like the satiric impulse itself, which loses its force as soon as it shows any signs of mercy or compassion.[51]

The moral Moran in fact has internalized the law to such a degree that he no longer associates it with Youdi himself, and certainly not with the messenger Gaber, whom he views as an utterly illegitimate rival. By the end of his narrative, Moran confesses that he only fears Youdi "from the force of habit":

And the voice I listen to needs no Gaber to make it heard. For it is within me and exhorts me to continue to the end the faithful servant I have always been, of a cause that is not mine, and patiently fulfil in all its bitterness my calamitous part, as it was with my will, when I had a will, that others should. (*M*, pp. 131–32)

Moran's very will has been subsumed by the internalized edict, which he obeys even as he denies that it is his own. In fact it is precisely because the cause is not his own that he enjoys serving it. And so, neatly illustrating the authoritarian personality's ambivalent relation to the loved and hated leader-imago, Moran adds: "And this with hatred in my heart, and scorn, of my master and his designs" (*M*, p. 132).

The sadism of Moran's adherence to moral principle is most visible in the gratuitous physical violence that he inflicts on his son: "I was sometimes inclined to go too far when I reprimanded my son, who was consequently a little afraid of me" (*M*, p. 95). Deleuze notes that "when the superego runs wild, expelling the ego ... then its fundamental immorality exhibits itself as sadism,"[52] and Moran's fear-inspiring reprimands reveal the paradoxical condition of the superego as fundamentally immoral. Moran's cruelty, furthermore, entails a displacement of the proper object of his sadism, which is himself:

I myself had never been sufficiently chastened. Oh I had not been spoiled either, merely neglected. Whence bad habits ingrained beyond remedy and of which even the most meticulous piety has never been able to break me. I hoped to spare my son this misfortune, by giving him a good clout from time to time, together with my reasons for doing so. (*M*, p. 95)

Moran's pedagogical justification for his violence – "together with my reasons for doing so" – of course rings hollow; it is emotionally tacked onto the "good clout" just as the phrase is grammatically tacked onto the sentence.

Yet it is not merely sadism that renders Moran a comic figure. Rather, the comedy stems from *fluctuations* in affect, particularly the escalation of intensity that occurs when the world fails to conform to Moran's authoritarian schemes: "The more things resist me, the more rabid I get" (*M*, p. 156). His violence derives from a need for obedience, and when a recalcitrant world fails to obey him, his rabidity increases. This rising violence provides many of the novel's biggest laughs, including a wonderful slapstick scene when Moran tries to rouse Jacques from bed:

Desperately he clung to his sleep. That was natural. A few hours sleep however deep are not enough for an organism in the first stages of puberty suffering from stomach trouble. And when I began to shake him and help him out of bed pulling him first by the arms, then by the hair, he turned away from me in fury, to the wall, and dug his nails into the mattress. I had to muster all my strength to overcome his resistance. But I had hardly freed him from the bed when he broke from my hold, threw himself down on the floor and rolled about, screaming with anger and defiance. The fun was beginning already. This disgusting exhibition left me with no choice but to use my umbrella, holding it by the end with both hands. ... Shame on you, I cried, you ill-bred little pig! I would get angry if I were not careful. And anger is a luxury I cannot afford. (*M*, pp. 126–27)

Despite Moran's cruelty here, the reader is likely to experience amusement or even delight. Moran's matter-of-fact reporting of his methods, his transparent self-justifications, his clinical diction, and above all his ability to reflect on the struggle with understated ironic detachment – all shift attention from Jacques' suffering to Moran's own pronounced emotional deficiencies, which enable him to inflict extreme pain and prevent him from expressing remorse afterwards. At the same time, the subdued affect of Moran's narrative tone does nothing to conceal Moran's own *heightened* affect during the struggle itself. Moran's irony aside, the struggle *is* fun. Indeed, Beckett's technique is particularly remarkable for the way in which it allows Moran to maintain two affective levels at once: a calmness in tone characterizes the level of narration, while on the level of the narrated events the states described possess enormous intensity. The suppression of affect is, moreover, essential to Moran's image of himself as a good servant of the law, and he can no more allow anger to unsettle him than he can his occasional pang of compassion. Thus when Moran feels his anger rising he seeks to restore his calm and meticulous surface: "Quiet, Moran, quiet. No emotion, please" (*M*, p. 132).

In this suppression of emotion, Moran bears a curious resemblance to Gibbons's Flora Poste, who exerts her own authority over her relations at Cold Comfort Farm in as cool and professional a manner as she can muster. Flora's much greater success at her affective regulation, however, allows the reader to retain a view of that task as salutary, and Gibbons's novel consequently describes satire as a benevolent kind of regulation that makes happiness possible. In *Molloy*, on the other hand, satire itself is an uncontrollable force, a superego run wild. Moran is anything but blasé, while Flora's affective pattern is predicated on the very flexibility that Moran lacks. Moran simply cannot attain Flora's modern ironic cool – or he can only attain it when he occupies his narratorial role, from which he can recollect his emotion in tranquility. Thus the narrative produces a steady tension between control and its loss, evident in the device of euphemism or understatement, which stifles emerging narratorial affect: "[I] took the iodex and rubbed it into my knee . . . Let it soak well in, said my son. He would pay for that later on" (*M*, p. 119). Or later: "I looked at my son. He began to protest. I soon put a stop to that" (*M*, p. 156). True indifference can only be achieved in retrospection, as when Moran tries to recall why his son abandoned him: "That night I had a violent scene with my son. I do not remember about what . . . I have had so many scenes with my son" (*M*, p. 160).

Despite his efforts to quell emotion, to administer the law in a professional way, Moran is always simmering, just on the verge of boiling over. Beneath his "meticulous and calm" surface is an overwhelming quantity of explosive tension. Thus, like many a familiar sitcom character, Moran's temper erupts in rage with pleasing regularity. The affect that is central to Moran's character, then, is not blasé indifference, but *irritation*. Irritation, Sianne Ngai notes, is more a mood than an emotion; she quotes Annette Baier's claim that "moods are either objectless, or have near all-inclusive and undifferentiated objects."[53] Unlike anger, irritation suggests both "hyperresponsiveness"[54] and underresponsiveness; the irritated person gets irritated at everything, even though the removal of any specific provocation will fail to relieve the predominant feeling.[55] Moran is a figure of irritation *par excellence*, with a litany of arbitrary dislikes:

Now if there is one thing I abhor, it is someone coming into my room, without knocking. (*M*, p. 102)
If there is one thing that gets on my nerves it is music. (*M*, p. 105)
I don't like animals. It's a strange thing, I don't like men and I don't like animals. As for God, he is beginning to disgust me. (*M*, p. 105)
The sight of my moustache, as always, annoyed me. (*M*, p. 119)
There is something about this strict sit of hats and caps that never fails to exasperate me. (*M*, p. 130)
Hurrah! cried my son. How I loathe that exclamation! I can hardly set it down. (*M*, p. 157)

Irritation proves to be a supremely comic affect in part because – unlike a morally justified anger – it is inexhaustible, always promising another predictable funny explosion. While anger might expend itself, irritation, despite the low level of affect that it suggests, is actually closer to sadism, because it needs no spur beyond itself. Both the proliferation and the triviality of objects of Moran's annoyance therefore suggest a temperament already on the lookout for a cause for rage, a law always anticipating its own violation and preparing its punitive, violent apparatus of "enforcement." And of course this enforcement will accomplish little, since the next idiosyncratic object of irritation has yet to be announced or even determined. For Moran, irritability, manifested in the multiplicity of his pet peeves, thus reveals the law as arbitrary in its object. As Deleuze notes, "The law cannot specify its object without contradiction."[56]

Thus the very qualities that make Moran terrifying to his son also make him, to the reader, thoroughly comic. His violent impulses exist in a state of constant tension, simply waiting for some tiny violation to provoke them into rage. His reverence for and obedience to the law are a desire to subject a recalcitrant world to his own whims, whims which merely serve as a pretext for finding the world unsatisfactory and exerting control over it. Moran's affective pattern is one of a constant movement between control, irritation, and explosion, a simmering of annoyance that erupts in rabid violence but offers only the most temporary of catharses before arising again.

FOLLOW ME CAREFULLY: MOLLOY'S OBSESSIONS

In turning to the first half of the novel, Molloy's narrative, I want to suggest that Moran's fascistic tendencies can be seen as a special case of a larger phenomenon, and that his characteristic affective pattern – building tension or irritation leading to sudden and violent, if comic, explosions of rage – is typical of Molloy as well, who in so many other ways seems Moran's opposite. This sort of obsessive-compulsive fussiness is a much-discussed feature of Beckett's pre-war fiction, and characters such as Murphy and Belacqua struggle with a world that resists their demands for order. These characters of course pre-date Beckett's experience in France under German occupation, and the comedy generated by their obsessive rigidity and sudden explosions might argue that Beckett's engagement with European fascism (which he witnessed rising during his time in Germany during the 1930s) is only part of a larger interest in the nature of compulsion and anger. Still, what Adorno says of Freud could equally be applied to Beckett, that the "intuitions" of the analyst might be "capable of anticipating [sociopolitical] tendencies still latent on a rational level."[57] Freud, writes Adorno, "developed within the monadological confines of the individual the traces of its profound crisis and willingness to yield unquestioningly to powerful outside, collective agencies."[58] Similarly, Beckett's pre-war attention to compulsive and authoritarian types might bespeak a latent political intuition about the way the human personality gets squeezed in modernity.

Although Molloy shares with Moran an exacting relation to the world, he rejects the apparatuses of the law that Moran loves to enforce: "To apply the letter of the law to me is not an easy matter" (*M*, p. 24). Molloy confounds the law with his literalness; when asked by a policeman for his "papers," Molloy produces only the old "bits of newspaper to wipe [him]self ... when [he has] a stool" (*M*, p. 20). Yet the lawless Molloy also confesses to "a mania for symmetry" (*M*, p. 85), a mania with which he justifies the sadistic violence he inflicts on a hermit whom he meets in the forest. Having kicked the old man in the ribs on one side, Molloy notes, "I rested a moment, then got up, picked up my crutches, took up my position on the other side of the body, and applied myself with method to the same exercise" (*M*, p. 84). While Moran covers his sadism with the bourgeois demands for filial obedience and moral education, Molloy invokes as his rationale a purely mathematical concept of symmetry. It makes perfect sense then that Molloy considers himself a good citizen despite his lawlessness: "I have only to be told what good behaviour is and I am well-behaved, within the limits of my physical possibilities" (*M*, pp. 24–25). He makes the very possibility of "good behaviour" dependent upon rationality – upon the determination of clear "principles":

And if I have always behaved like a pig, the fault lies not with me but with my superiors, who corrected me only on points of detail instead of showing me the essence of the system, in the manner of the great English schools, and the guiding principles of good manners ... For that would have allowed me, before parading in public certain habits such as the finger in the nose, the scratching of the balls, digital emunction and the peripatetic piss, to refer them to the first rules of a reasoned theory. (*M*, p. 25)

Molloy's failure to obey the law, he maintains, results not from a lack of respect for it, but from the failure of his education to provide him with a coherent justification for various prohibitions. A philosopher of the bodily function, Molloy seeks "the first rules of a reasoned theory."

Molloy's mania for symmetry also resembles Moran's meticulousness in its obsessive quality, and to enter into Beckett's writing means to enter into Molloy's obsessions. "Follow me carefully" (*M*, p. 77), he enjoins the reader as he sets out to describe in meticulous detail the differences between the "old" pain in one leg and the "new" pain in the other. This description, which rehearses several pages of arguments and counter-arguments, is merely one of an abundance of examples of what Deleuze calls "the exhaustive *and* the exhausted" in Beckett, where an attempt at the systematic intellectual consideration of possibilities accompanies "a certain physiological exhaustion."[59] Crucially, Molloy's exhaustive rehearsals are, like Moran's, counter-balanced by a characteristic gesture of sudden outburst. Molloy describes his encounter with a social worker who tries to feed him some toast and tea:

Against the charitable gesture there is no defence, that I know of. You sink your head, you put out your hands all trembling and twined together and you say, Thank you, thank you lady, thank you kind lady. To him who has nothing it is forbidden not to relish filth. The liquid overflowed, the mug rocked with a noise of chattering teeth, not mine, I had none, and the sodden bread sagged more and more. Until, panic-stricken, I flung it all far from me. I did not let it fall, no, but with a convulsive thrust of both my hands I threw it to the ground, where it smashed to smithereens, or against the wall, far from me, with all my strength. (*M*, p. 24)

Deriding the mnemonic powers of the Proustian tea, Molloy here unmasks the social worker's compassion as a guise of the coercive law, redescribing the sentimental gesture of charity as a ruse of power. Yet his resistance to the law manifests an affective pattern just like Moran's enforcement of it: the accretion of tension through a careful examination of a situation – typical here is the repetition with variation of the phrase "thank you lady," and the present-tense philosophical aside – which culminates in a violent gesture of defiance.

Molloy notes, while discussing his sucking stones, "I would sometimes throw away all I had about me, in a burst of irritation" (*M*, p. 45), and this "burst of irritation" is his signature comic device. Repeatedly, irritation or anxiety, throbbing along at an affective level well below rage or panic, builds incrementally until a breaking point is reached and tension is released through a sudden, violent flinging-away. This flinging-away or burst of irritation is characteristic not only of Molloy's physical behavior but also of his thought and his language. For example, he painstakingly reasons through the relationship between words and objects but then suddenly discards the whole issue: "To hell with it anyway. Where was I?" (*M*, p. 32). Equally illustrative is his slapstick account of how he communicates with his deaf (and presumably blind) mother: "I got into communication with her by knocking on the skull. One knock meant yes, two no, three I don't know, four money, five goodbye" (*M*, p. 18). Yet because his aged mother cannot count past two, the code fails:

It was too far for her, yes, the distance was too great, from one to four. By the time she came to the fourth knock, she imagined she was only at the second, the first two having been erased from her memory as completely as if they had never been felt, though I don't quite see how something never felt can be erased from the memory, and yet it is a common occurrence. She must have thought I was saying no to her all the time, whereas nothing was further from my purpose. (*M*, p. 18)

Beyond the familiar Beckettian themes of fallible memory and physical decay, we see here a meticulous i-dotting like Moran's – an exploration of the consequences of every phrase, in a language that enacts the process of thinking through the problem. Yet such meticulousness gives way to sudden violence:

Enlightened by these considerations I looked for and finally found a more effective means of putting the idea of money into her head. This consisted in replacing the four knocks of my index-knuckle by one or more (according to my needs) thumps of the fist, on her skull. That she understood. (*M*, p. 18)

Molloy's thought here picks up the detached tone of his previous ruminations with a technical description of the problems in implementing the code. But the calm way in which the violence is narrated vanishes, and the affect of his language intensifies with the sadistic thumps on the head ("That she understood"). And no sooner does Molloy succeed in establishing communication than he flings away the entire undertaking: "In any case I didn't come for money" (*M*, p. 18).

This pattern of total immersion in obsession followed by a violent renunciation of the affective investment in the object of the obsession might usefully supplement Ngai's discussion of Deleuzean exhaustion in Beckett, an affective state she calls *stuplimity*. Ngai coins this portmanteau, fusing stupor and sublimity, to capture the quality Beckett has of appearing as "simultaneously astonishing and deliberately fatiguing,"[60] inspiring through the sheer agglutination of prose, or through the exhaustive rehearsal of combinatorial possibilities, a mix of awe and tedium. For Ngai, stuplimity offers neither the transcendence of the sublime proper, nor the cynical, critical distance typical of a glossy postmodernism. Instead, it achieves a cognitive and affective paralysis that wears away the reader's defenses and produces "a condition of utter receptivity in which difference is perceived (and perhaps even 'felt') prior to its qualification or conceptualization."[61] While Ngai focuses largely on

Beckett's later writings, she does cite *Molloy* as an example where Beckett's "fatigues can be darkly funny."[62] Grouping *Molloy* with the stubborn comic mechanical performances of slapstick comedians such as Keaton and Chaplin, Ngai invokes Deleuze's theorization of humor as a masochistic subversion of the law to account for a slapstick "going limp or falling down" that enables "small subjects" moments of resistance "in their confrontation with larger systems."[63] The quasi-fascist agency hunting down Molloy would be one such system, but that agency itself might only be a special, extreme case of the increasing bureaucratic control impinging on modern life.

Yet the extension of Ngai's concept of stuplimity to account for the repetitiveness of slapstick is only partially convincing. For slapstick, despite its repetitiveness, never inspires tedium or awe – that is, unless it *ceases* to be funny.[64] While laughter in Beckett indeed derives from obsessive-compulsive repetition or tedious-awesome exhaustion, it also signals the *break* from the tedium of obsession. Like a piece of driftwood happily discovered, laughter is something the reader can cling to in the oceans of possibilities in which Beckett's prose immerses her. Or, to change metaphors, laughter not only accompanies but enacts the gesture of flinging away, reversing the tense and obsessive enumeration of possibilities. For Beckett's reader, laughter brings about a release akin to what the rageful flinging away accomplishes for the character. Laughter is kin to Moran's beating of his recalcitrant son with an umbrella, or Molloy's unprovoked pummeling of the charcoal-burner.

The process is perhaps best illustrated through Molloy's famous sucking-stone episode – an approximately 2,500-word account of Molloy's efforts to distribute among his four pockets sixteen stones that he can suck one at a time, while in the long run sucking them all equally. The problem of how to distribute and choose the stones, of course, is entirely Molloy's own construction, "a goal I had set myself" (*M*, p. 70); like Youdi's orders, the imperative is wholly arbitrary. Yet like most unconsciously imposed obsessions, its arbitrary nature does not mitigate the unpleasure it causes, and Molloy experiences feelings of "anger and perplexity" (*M*, p. 71), along with "anxiety" (*M*, p. 74).

Temporary relief from this steady pulsation of unpleasure arrives when Molloy is struck by the possibility that he might "sacrific[e] the principle of trim" (*M*, p. 71) – the principle of even distribution of stones among his pockets. Giving up the mania for symmetry promises a release from compulsion and brings an emotional surge: "the meaning of this illumination . . . began suddenly to sing within me, like a verse of Isaiah, or of

Jeremiah" (*M*, p. 71). Yet this sudden glory quickly dissipates as Molloy begins to examine his solution in detail: "All (all!) that was necessary was to put for example, to begin with, six stones in the right pocket of my greatcoat, or supply-pocket, five in the right pocket of my trousers, and five in the left pocket of my trousers, that makes the lot, twice five ten plus six sixteen . . ." (*M*, p. 72), and on and on for several more sentences. And so, once again, the reader is immersed in the mad and maddening rehearsal of the new method of distribution.

Eventually, Molloy recognizes that his obsessive desire to suck the stones "with method" (*M*, p. 74) is unimportant, even trivial – as obsessions generally are: "And deep down it was all the same to me whether I sucked a different stone each time or always the same stone" (*M*, p. 74). Just as the mania for symmetrical distribution has been discarded, so now is the need to suck stones in the first place: "But deep down I didn't give a fiddler's curse about being without [any stones]" (*M*, p. 74). Thus, after days on the beach puzzling over the problem, and pages of the reader's immersion in the reversals of his attempt to solve the impossible problem, the whole obsession is blithely dropped, in another abrupt and astonishing gesture of flinging-away: "And the solution to which I rallied in the end was to throw away all the stones but one, which I kept now in one pocket, now in another, and which of course I soon lost, or threw away, or gave away, or swallowed" (*M*, p. 74).

The sucking-stones episode, then, is merely the most elaborate example of a pattern in Molloy's narrative between an immersion in obsession and a release from it, a release which is invariably accompanied by sudden change in affect. The overcoming of obsession, which the reader generally experiences as comic, registers a shift in scale whereby the all-consuming, massive obsession that offers only tedium and awe is suddenly recognized as small or unimportant. Surely this pattern fits Freud's analysis of the comic whereby an "inhibitory expenditure" of energy "suddenly becomes unutilizable" and "is discharged by laughter."[65] It also fits Critchley's suggestion that Beckett's texts parody philosophy rather than philosophize;[66] they produce laughter, we might add, not merely from the failure of philosophy but from the failure of the obsessive tendency of intellection itself.

As I have noted probably too many times already, the recognition of this mechanical, compulsive quality is also the essence of Bergson's notion of the comic, which restores human sociality by supplying the flexibility that the obsessive-compulsive lacks. Father Ambrose remarks to Moran the old Aristotelian observation, crucial to Bergson, that laughter "is peculiar to man": "Animals never laugh, he said. It takes us to find that funny ... Christ never laughed either, he said, so far as we know" (*M*, p. 101). (Baudelaire, who remarks on the absence of divine laughter, is alluded to here as well.) And while any reader of Beckett should remain wary of wisdom coming from such a source, there is something salutary in a Bergsonian reading of *Molloy* that lets us see the sociable side of a writer who is commonly made out to be the least sociable of artists. Molloy's professed aim is, after all, the fundamentally polite gesture of "say[ing] my goodbyes" (*M*, p. 7). His deathbed farewell, idiosyncratic as it is, partakes of the rich novelistic tradition of teary, sentimental scenes of dying.

A Bergsonian reading of Beckettian laughter no doubt overplays Beckett's sociality and underplays the fact that in all this repetition, obedience, and sadism there remains something uncanny and inhuman. Paul Sheehan has noted the centrality of compulsion in Beckett, seeing it as an inhuman reworking of an ethical notion of obligation.[67] Indeed, the entire novel *Molloy* is an exploration of compulsion, whether that exploration proceeds through Moran's moralistic, sadistic authoritarianism, or through Molloy's abstract mania for symmetry. This compulsion is, of course, the very situation of writing in Beckett: the need to write is famously in his work an exacting, sadistic, unconscious injunction, one that demands a ruthless and impossible precision.[68]

Thus Molloy obsesses, but he also desires to get to the end of his obsession:

And if I failed to mention this detail in its proper place, it is because you cannot mention everything in its proper place, you must choose, between the things not worth mentioning and those even less so. For if you set out to mention everything you would never be done, and that's what counts, to be done, to have done. (*M*, p. 41)

To have done, to be done, to rest: as Freud frames the idea in *Beyond the Pleasure Principle*, life is but a way of the creature dying on its own terms. *Molloy* continues: "Oh I know, even when you mention only a few of the things there are, you do not get done either, I know, I know. But it's a change of muck. And if all muck is the same muck that doesn't matter, it's good to have a change of muck, to move from one heap to another a little further on" (*M*, p. 41). What initially looks like a death drive, the wish to be done, shades into a desire for change, for new muck rather than old. Beckett thus places thanatos and eros side by side, another set of doubles, another pair of clowns – or, as he calls them in *The Unnamable*, another pseudocouple:[69] "For in me there have always been two fools, among others, one asking nothing better than to stay where he is and the other imagining that life might be slightly less horrible a little further on" (*M*, p. 48).

The whole process of determining whether Beckett's satire critiques or affirms "the human" is, to use Beckett's own phrase, a mug's game. Rather, what Beckett and our critical struggles with him reveal is the proximity of these affects, the close cohabitation of compulsive subjection, and sudden, surprising freedom. Registering the pressures of modernity's power arrangements, *Molloy* indicates the interdependence of two sides of authoritarian behavior. For if totalitarian structures deform the personality into a docile machine for the execution of a repressive will and persecution of what Adorno called the social outgroup, they also stand revealed in Beckett's fiction as susceptible to satiric derision. While Beckett's life would seem to suggest that he believed action not writing must be the first response to such violence, his literature may still give us some understanding of the conditions under which such violence is produced. In this sense Beckett as well as any writer lays bare the impossible bind of late modernist satire. Unable to accept the clichés and deceptions of sentimentality, uneasy with the sadism of his own satiric negations, Beckett, like the other writers in this late modernist company, performs the impossible trick of making something out of nothing.

Notes

PREFACE

1 Iain Topliss discusses this cartoon in *The Comic Worlds of Peter Arno, William Steig, Charles Addams and Saul Steinberg* (Baltimore, Md.: Johns Hopkins University Press, 2005), pp. 166–68. See also my review in *Modernism/Modernity*, 13.2 (2006): 401–03.

2 William Empson, *Some Versions of Pastoral* (New York: New Directions, 1974), p. 68.

3 Sigmund Freud, "The Uncanny," *The Standard Edition of the Complete Psychological Works of Sigmund Freud*, vol. xvii, trans. and ed. James Strachey (London: Hogarth, 1961), p. 251.

4 Henri Bergson, "Laughter," in Wylie Sypher (ed.), *Comedy* (Garden City, NY: Doubleday, 1956), p. 64.

5 Lionel Trilling, *The Liberal Imagination: Essays on Society and Literature* (New York: Harcourt, 1978), p. 207.

1 SATIRE AND ITS DISCONTENTS

1 Raymond Williams, *Marxism and Literature* (Oxford University Press, 1977), p. 132.

2 *Ibid.*

3 *Ibid.*, pp. 131–32.

4 Sianne Ngai, *Ugly Feelings* (Cambridge, Mass.: Harvard University Press, 2005), p. 5.

5 Elizabeth S. Goodstein, *Experience Without Qualties: Boredom and Modernity* (Palo Alto, Calif.: Stanford University Press, 2005), pp. 3, 7.

6 Justus Nieland, *Feeling Modern: The Eccentricities of Public Life* (Champaign: University of Illinois Press, 2008).

7 Ezra Pound, "A Retrospect," in T. S. Eliot (ed.), *Literary Essays of Ezra Pound* (New York: New Directions, 1968), p. 11.

8 Harry Levin's judgment is characteristic: "It is generally agreed that English satire enjoyed its heyday during the first half of the eighteenth century; it declined as, with the emergence of mere sentimental and romantic touchstones, wit deserted malice and mellowed into humor." Harry Levin,

Playboys and Killjoys: An Essay on the Theory and Practice of Comedy (Oxford University Press, 1987), pp. 199–200.

9 Chris Baldick, *1910–1940: The Modern Movement*, The Oxford English Literary History, vol. x (Oxford University Press, 2004), p. 235.

10 Quoted *ibid.*, p. 234.

11 Tyrus Miller, *Late Modernism: Politics, Fiction, and the Arts Between the World Wars* (Berkeley: University of California Press, 1999). Although Miller does view satire as central to modernism, it should be noted that the Lewisian strain of modernism he discusses is in his analysis largely opposed to the old modernist canon of Conrad, Woolf, Joyce, Eliot, and the rest. I discuss Miller's book in depth in Chapter 2. Another recent study of modernist satire is Lisa Colletta, *Dark Humor and Social Satire in the Modern British Novel* (New York: Palgrave, 2003). Colletta observes a confluence of satiric and modernist themes, such as the estrangement of the individual from a wider social community, conditions of extreme violence or brutality, and a predominant mood of helplessness or despair.

12 English looks at the particular political contexts and valences of comic, ironic, and satiric texts to analyze how those texts construct and limit communities; North focuses on the representation of the machine and of the mechanical as a special site of laughter. James English, *Comic Transactions: Literature, Humor and the Politics of Community in Twentieth-Century Britain* (Ithaca, NY: Cornell University Press, 1994); Michael North, *Machine-Age Comedy* (Oxford University Press, 2009). Nieland's reading of comedy posits an eccentric, even dissident, vein of laughter that resists the coercive sociality implicit in Bergson's view. See Nieland, *Feeling Modern*.

13 A partial list would include Alvin Kernan, *The Plot of Satire* (New Haven, Conn.: Yale University Press, 1965); Ronald Paulson, *The Fictions of Satire* (Baltimore, Md.: Johns Hopkins University Press, 1967); Leon Guilhamet, *Satire and the Transformation of Genre* (Philadelphia: University of Pennsylvania Press, 1987); Dustin Griffin, *Satire: A Critical Reintroduction* (Lexington: University of Kentucky Press, 1994).

14 Guilhamet usefully distinguishes between satire as a genre and satire as a mode, echoing Paulson's distinction between the "form" and "tone" of satire. Guilhamet, *Transformation*, p. 7; Paulson, *Fictions*, p. 4. Within generic discussions of satire, a further distinction exists between formal verse satire and prose (or Menippean) satire. In Guilhamet's terms, my discussion focuses on the satiric *mode* in narrative fiction; I stress attitude and sensibility rather than specific generic attributes.

15 George Meredith, "An Essay on Comedy and the Uses of the Comic Sprit," in Sypher, *Comedy*, p. 44; Levin, *Playboys and Killjoys*, p. 197; Northrop Frye, *Anatomy of Criticism: Four Essays* (Princeton University Press, 1957), p. 224.

16 Guilhamet, *Transformation*, p. 7.

17 Wayne C. Booth, *A Rhetoric of Irony* (University of Chicago Press, 1974), p. 5. Booth's emphasis on the constructive (even benevolent) dimension of irony extends to the laughter elicited by satire.

18 Jay Martin, *Nathanael West: The Art of his Life* (New York: Carroll and Graf, 1970), p. 320.

19 See, for example, Italo Calvino, "Definitions of Territories: Comedy," *The Uses of Literature: Essays*, trans. Patrick Creagh (New York: Harcourt, 1986), p. 64.

20 Kernan, *Plot of Satire*, p. 9; Frye, *Anatomy of Criticism*, p. 224.

21 Robert F. Kiernan suggests that a purely playful dimension characterizes the tradition he calls the "camp novel." Robert F. Kiernan, *Frivolity Unbound: Six Masters of the Camp Novel: Thomas Love Peacock, Max Beerbohm, Ronald Firbank, E. F. Benson, P. G. Wodehouse, Ivy Compton-Burnett* (New York: Continuum, 1990).

22 Wyndham Lewis, *Men Without Art* (New York: Russell & Russell, 1964), p. 103.

23 *Ibid.*, p. 106.

24 *Ibid.*, p. 112.

25 Friedrich Nietzsche, *On the Genealogy of Morals*, trans. Walter Kaufmann and R. J. Hollingdale, ed. Walter Kaufmann (New York: Random House, 1967), pp. 66–67; Martin Puchner, *Poetry of the Revolution: Marx, Manifestos, and the Avant-gardes* (Princeton University Press, 2006), p. 130.

26 Nietzsche, *Genealogy of Morals*, p. 67.

27 Sigmund Freud, *Jokes and Their Relation to the Unconscious*, trans. and ed. James Strachey (New York: Norton, 1989), p. 115.

28 *Ibid.*, p. 162.

29 *Ibid.*, p. 160.

30 *Ibid.*, p. 161.

31 Freud at this point had not worked out the tripartite scheme of the id, ego, and superego.

32 Freud, *Jokes*, pp. 167, 68.

33 *Ibid.*, p. 214.

34 Cf. Norman Holland, *Dynamics of Literary Response* (New York: Columbia University Press, 1989). Griffin distinguishes between pleasure that "derive[s] from the wit" of satire and pleasure which stems "from the pain of the attack," and usefully catalogs varieties and theories of satiric pleasure. Griffin, *Critical Reintroduction*, p. 161.

35 Bergson, "Laughter," p. 84.

36 Wyndham Lewis, *The Complete Wild Body* (Santa Rosa, Calif.: Black Sparrow, 1982) p. 158.

37 Nieland, *Feeling Modern*, p. 51.

38 Wyndham Lewis, *Men Without Art*, p. 116.

39 *Ibid.*, p. 226.

40 *Ibid.*, pp. 228–29. Kenneth Burke's 1937 theory is similar: asserting that "the satirist attacks *in others* the weaknesses and temptations that are really *within himself*," he sees satire as founded on an act of projection in which the satirist shares and takes pleasure in the corrupt or grotesque nature of his target, but he hides this pleasure by projecting it onto a target whom he can punish. Kenneth Burke, *Attitudes Towards History* (Berkeley: University of California Press, 1987), p. 49.

41 Michael Seidel, *Satiric Inheritance: Rabelais to Sterne* (Princeton University Press, 1979), p. 3. Stephen Weisenburger deploys Seidel's theory in his book on postmodern "Black Humor," *Fables of Subversion: Satire and the American Novel, 1930–1980* (Athens: University of Georgia Press, 1995).

42 William Ian Miller, *The Anatomy of Disgust* (Cambridge, Mass.: Harvard University Press, 1997), p. 184.

43 *Ibid.*, p. 185.

44 Calvino, "Definitions of Territories: Comedy," pp. 62–63.

45 Evelyn Waugh, "Fan-Fare," *The Essays, Articles and Reviews of Evelyn Waugh*, ed. Donat Gallagher (London: Methuen, 1983), p. 304.

46 W. H. Auden, "Notes on the Comic," *The Dyer's Hand and Other Essays* (New York: Random House, 1962), p. 385.

47 T. W. Adorno, *Minima Moralia: Reflections from a Damaged Life*, trans. E. F. N. Jephcott (New York: Verso, 1974), pp. 211–12.

48 *Ibid.*, p. 212.

49 Seidel, *Satiric Inheritance*, p. 263.

50 Cf. Christian Thorne, "Thumbing Our Nose at the Public Sphere: Satire, the Market, and the Invention of Literature," *PMLA*, 16.3 (2001): 537.

51 Richard Rorty, *Contingency, Irony, and Solidarity* (Cambridge University Press, 1989), p. 73.

52 Geoffrey Galt Harpham describes the grotesque as a "species of confusion" that "call[s] ... into question our ways of organizing the world." Geoffrey Galt Harpham, *On the Grotesque: Strategies of Contradiction in Art and Literature* (Princeton University Press, 1982), pp. xxi, 3. Bernard McElroy emphasizes the grotesque within modernism as an encounter with the monstrous; its function is "to direct our attention to the undignified, perilous, even gross physicality of existence, and to emphasise it by exaggeration, distortion, or unexpected combination." Bernard McElroy, *Fiction of the Modern Grotesque* (New York: Macmillan, 1989), p. 11.

53 Mary Russo, *The Female Grotesque: Risk, Excess, Modernity* (New York: Routledge, 1994), p. 7.

54 John Ruskin, *The Stones of Venice* (London: Faber and Faber, 1981), p. 115.

55 For a Jungian approach, see Arthur Clayborough, *The Grotesque in English Literature* (Oxford University Press, 1967); Heideggerian: Deiter Meindl, *American Fiction and the Metaphysics of the Grotesque* (Columbia: University of Missouri Press, 1996); feminist: Russo, *Female Grotesque*; race theory: Leonard Cassuto, *The Inhuman Race: The Racial Grotesque in American Literature and Culture* (New York: Columbia University Press, 1993).

56 Several works offer models of the psychic mechanism by which feelings of anxiety and amusement are produced, for example: Ernst Kris, *Psychoanalytic Explorations in Art* (New York: International Universities, 1952); Holland, *Dynamics*; Michael Steig, "Defining the Grotesque: An Attempt at Synthesis," *Journal of Aesthetics and Art Criticism*, 29 (1970): 253–60.

57 Mikhail Bakhtin, *Rabelais and His World*, trans. Helene Iswolsky (Bloomington: Indiana University Press, 1984), p. 26.

58 Wolfgang Kayser, *The Grotesque in Art and Literature*, trans. Ulrich Weisstein (New York: Columbia University Press, 1957), p. 18.

59 Bakhtin, *Rabelais*, pp. 38, 37. Peter Stallybrass and Allon White view the grotesque as the resurfacing of cultural material that has been repressed in the constitution of class hierarchies and bourgeois norms. Peter Stallybrass and Allon White, *The Politics and Poetics of Transgression* (Ithaca, NY: Cornell University Press, 1986). In this vein see also Terry Castle, *The Female Thermometer: Eighteenth-Century Culture and the Invention of the Uncanny* (Oxford University Press, 1995).

60 Bakhtin, *Rabelais*, p. 48. Attempts to examine the grotesque within modernism include John R. Clark, *The Modern Satiric Grotesque* (Lexington: University Press of Kentucky, 1991); Mark Fearnow, *The American Stage and the Great Depression: A Cultural History of the Grotesque* (Cambridge University Press, 1997); Joseph R. Millichap, "Distorted Matter and Disjunctive Forms: The Grotesque as Modernist Genre," *Arizona Quarterly*, 33 (1977): 339–47.

61 Fredric Jameson, *Postmodernism: Or, the Cultural Logic of Late Capitalism* (Durham, NC: Duke University Press, 1991), pp. 11–12.

62 Kenneth Burke, "Version, Con-, Per-, and In- (Thoughts on Djuna Barnes's Novel *Nightwood*)," *Language as Symbolic Action: Essays on Life, Literature, and Method* (Berkeley: University of California Press, 1968), pp. 244, 246.

63 D. H. Lawrence, "The Crown" [1915], *Reflections on the Death of a Porcupine and Other Essays* (Bloomington: Indiana University Press, 1963), p. 60; James Baldwin, "Everybody's Protest Novel" [1949], *Collected Essays*, ed. Toni Morrison (New York: Library of America, 1998), p. 12.

64 Suzanne Clark, *Sentimental Modernism: Women Writers and the Revolution of the Word* (Bloomington: Indiana University Press, 1991), pp. 1, 4–5.

65 Andreas Huyssen, *After the Great Divide: Modernism, Mass Culture, Postmodernism* (Bloomington: Indiana University Press, 1986); Jane Tompkins, *Sensational Designs: The Cultural Work of American Fiction, 1790–1860* (Oxford University Press, 1985).

66 Michael Bell, *Sentimentalism, Ethics, and the Culture of Feeling* (New York: St. Martin's, 2000) p. 160.

67 T. S. Eliot, "Tradition and the Individual Talent," *Selected Essays* (New York: Harcourt, 1964), p. 10.

68 Lawrence Rainey, *Institutions of Modernism: Literary Elites and Public Culture* (New Haven, Conn.: Yale University Press, 1998), p. 2. See also Jessica Burstein, "A Few Words about Dubuque: Modernism, Sentimentalism, and the Blasé," *American Literary History*, 14.2 (2002): 227–54.

69 Milan Kundera, *The Unbearable Lightness of Being*, trans. Michael Henry Heim (New York: Harper and Row, 1984), pp. 250, 252.

70 English, *Comic Transactions*, p. 17. The term *multiaccented* English borrows from Valentin Voloshinov.

71 Charles Altieri, *The Particulars of Rapture: An Aesthetics of the Affects* (Ithaca, NY: Cornell University Press, 2004), p. 50.

72 *Ibid.*, p. 48.

73 *Ibid.*, p. 50.

74 Ngai, *Ugly Feelings*, pp. 207–08.

75 Martha Nussbaum, *Love's Knowledge: Essays on Philosophy and Literature* (Oxford University Press, 1990), pp. 287–88.

76 T. S. Eliot, "Reflections on Vers Libre" [1917], *To Criticize the Critic and Other Writings* (New York: Farrar, 1965), pp. 1, 89.

77 Thomas Mann, *Past Masters and Other Papers*, trans. Helen T. Lowe-Porter (New York: Books for Libraries, 1968), pp. 240–41; Flannery O'Connor, *Mystery and Manners: Occasional Prose*, ed. Sally Fitzgerald and Robert Fitzgerald (New York: Noonday, 1961), p. 162.

78 Two recent studies of American modernism understand grotesque representation as broadly satiric or antisentimental. Joseph Entin examines how left-leaning writers used "sensational" representation to question the sentimental pleasure of empathetic identification with the poor, while Susan Edmunds focuses on the grotesque as a way of representing the "domestic exterior" – the area in which an emerging welfare state extended the social and cultural work of sentimental female domesticity. Joseph Entin, *Sensational Modernism: Experimental Fiction and Photography in Thirties America* (Chapel Hill: University of North Carolina Press, 2007); Susan Edmunds, *Grotesque Relations: Modernist Domestic Fiction and the US Welfare State* (Oxford University Press, 2008).

79 Ford Madox Ford, *The Good Soldier* (New York: Random House, 1983), pp. 26–27; Virginia Woolf, *Mrs. Dalloway* (New York: Harcourt, 1981), p. 36.

80 E. M. Forster, *Howards End* (New York: Random House, 1989), p. 65.

81 Eve Kosofsky Sedgwick, *Epistemology of the Closet* (Berkeley: University of California Press, 1990), p. 150.

82 Jay Dickson, "Defining the Sentimentalist in *Ulysses*," *James Joyce Quarterly*, 44.1 (2006): 20–22.

83 S. Clark, *Sentimental Modernism*, p. 3.

84 Dickson, "Defining the Sentimentalist in *Ulysses*," 22.

85 *Ibid.*, 23.

86 James Joyce, *Ulysses*, ed. Hans Walter Gabler (New York: Random House, 1986), 9.550–51. In quoting from *Ulysses*, I follow convention in citing chapter and line number rather than page number.

87 O'Connor, *Mystery and Manners*, pp. 147–48.

88 Paul Ricoeur, *Freud and Philosophy: An Essay on Interpretation* (New Haven, Conn.: Yale University Press, 1977), p. 33.

89 M. Bell, *Sentimentalism*, p. 148.

90 Lionel Trilling, *Sincerity and Authenticity* (Cambridge, Mass.: Harvard University Press, 1971), pp. 2, 4.

91 *Ibid.*, p. 11. Authenticity may ultimately be an empty concept; still, it retained considerable value for many modernist writers.

92 *Ibid.*, p. 94.

93 *Ibid.*, p. 11.

94 "Undoubtedly, the modern shift from sincerity to authenticity is best represented discursively in Nietzsche." M. Bell, *Sentimentalism*, p. 167.

95 Fredric Jameson, *A Singular Modernity: Essay on the Ontology of the Present* (London: Verso, 2002), p. 126.

96 *Ibid.*, p. 127.

97 *Ibid.*

98 *Ibid.*

99 Nietzsche, *Genealogy*, p. 19.

100 James Joyce, *A Portrait of the Artist as a Young Man* (New York: Penguin, 1992), p. 233.

101 *Ibid.*, p. 222.

102 Eliot, "Tradition and the Individual Talent," pp. 7, 10. Eliot also addresses the topic in "The Metaphysical Poets," where he introduces his notion of a historical dissociation of sensibility; see Eliot, "The Metaphysical Poets," *Selected Essays*, p. 247.

103 Eliot, "Hamlet and His Problems," *Selected Essays*, pp. 124–25.

104 Maria DiBattista, *First Love: The Affections of Modern Fiction* (University of Chicago Press, 1991), p. 31.

105 Ella Zohar Ophir, "Towards a Pitiless Fiction: Abstraction, Comedy, and Modernist Antihumanism," *MFS: Modern Fiction Studies*, 52.1 (2006): 92–120.

2 MODERNISM'S STORY OF FEELING

1 The bible of postmodern architecture itself quotes Richard Poirier's description of Joyce and Eliot as a prototype for *postmodernism*. Robert Venturi and Denise Scott Brown, *Learning from Las Vegas* (Cambridge, Mass.: MIT Press, 1972), p. 72.

2 Pericles Lewis, *The Cambridge Introduction to Modernism* (Cambridge University Press, 2007), p. xvii.

3 Lawrence Rainey, Introduction to *Modernism: An Anthology* (Malden, Mass.: Blackwell, 2005), p. xxiv; Peter Nicholls, *Modernisms: A Literary Guide* (Berkeley: University of California Press, 1995).

4 Fredric Jameson, *A Singular Modernity: Essay on the Ontology of the Present* (London: Verso, 2002), p. 150.

5 Lionel Trilling, *Sincerity and Authenticity* (Cambridge, Mass.: Harvard University Press, 1971), p. 119.

6 *Ibid.*

7 Oscar Wilde, Preface to *The Picture of Dorian Gray and Other Writings* (New York: Bantam, 1982), p. 3.

8 Oscar Wilde, "The Critic as Artist," *Literary Criticism of Oscar Wilde*, ed. Stanley Weintraub (Lincoln: University of Nebraska Press, 1968), p. 221.

9 Trilling, *Sincerity and Authenticity*, p. 120. Steven Jones maintains that the values of sympathy and sincerity themselves emerged as a Romantic reaction against Popean wit and satire: "Romantic or sentimental modes

come to be defined negatively, as meaning something very close to 'unsatiric'." Steven Jones, *Satire and Romanticism* (New York: Palgrave, 2000), p. 8.

10 Wilde, "The Critic as Artist," p. 217.

11 Sigmund Freud, *Jokes and Their Relation to the Unconscious*, trans. and ed. James Strachey (New York: Norton, 1989), p. 178.

12 Robert F. Kiernan, *Frivolity Unbound: Six Masters of the Camp Novel: Thomas Love Peacock, Max Beerbohm, Ronald Firbank, E. F. Benson, P. G. Wodehouse, Ivy Compton-Burnett* (New York: Continuum, 1990), pp. 39, 42.

13 Max Beerbohm, *Zuleika Dobson, Or an Oxford Love Story* (New York: Penguin, 1988), unnumbered prefatory note.

14 *Ibid.*, p. 90.

15 *Ibid.*, p. 32.

16 Rei Terada makes the case for the nonsubjective nature of feeling. Rei Terada, *Feeling in Theory: Emotion after the "Death of the Subject"* (Cambridge, Mass.: Harvard University Press, 2001).

17 Beerbohm, *Zuleika Dobson*, pp. 114, 178.

18 *Ibid.*, pp. 66, 100, 111.

19 F. W. Dupee, for example, comments, "Beerbohm's dehumanizing of his characters does perhaps ask for a bit of explaining. For me, there is only one moment in the book when it is possible to 'feel with' any of them." F. W. Dupee, "Max Beerbohm and the Rigors of Fantasy," *The Surprise of Excellence: Modern Essays on Max Beerbohm*, ed. J. G. Riewald (Hamden, Conn.: Shoe String Press, 1974), p. 183.

20 Beerbohm, *Zuleika Dobson*, pp. 103, 209.

21 *Ibid.*, p. 22.

22 Michael Levenson, *A Genealogy of Modernism: A Study of English Literary Doctrine, 1908–1922* (Cambridge University Press, 1984), p. 77.

23 Marjorie Perloff notes that the major figures of the Futurist moment retain strong affinities with their *fin-de-siècle* forebears, that Marinetti "was writing, as late as 1909, decadent versions of Baudelairean lyric," that Pound's Imagism in the early 1910s was "a free verse based on the *vers libre* of the French Symbolists." Marjorie Perloff, *The Futurist Moment: Avant-Garde, Avant Guerre, and the Language of Rupture* (University of Chicago Press, 2003), pp. 83, 163.

24 Ezra Pound, "The Serious Artist," *Literary Essays of Ezra Pound*, ed. T. S. Eliot (New York: New Directions, 1968), p. 44.

25 F. T. Marinetti, "The Founding and Manifesto of Futurism," *Let's Murder the Moonshine: Selected Writings*, trans. R. W. Flint and Arthur A. Coppotelli, ed. R.W. Flint (Los Angeles, Calif.: Sun and Moon Classics, 1991), p. 51.

26 "Long Live the Vortex!", *Blast*, 1 (June 20, 1914), 8. dl.lib.brown.edu/pdfs/1143209523824858.pdf.

27 This logic would then be one of many places in which Joseph Litvak's writing about sophistication would apply well to an analysis of modernism; he views "culture as a *contest of sophistications*, where victory often redounds to those

who best disavow their sophistication." Joseph Litvak, *Strange Gourmets: Sophistication, Theory, and the Novel* (Durham, NC: Duke University Press, 1997), p. 5.

28 Perloff, *Futurist Moment*, p. III.

29 Levenson, *A Genealogy of Modernism*, p. 134.

30 Pound, "A Retrospect," *Literary Essays*, pp. 12, 14.

31 *Ibid.*, p. 13.

32 Pound, "The Serious Artist," *Literary Essays*, p. 45.

33 *Ibid.*

34 *Ibid.*

35 The association of satire and surgery is an old one. See Mary Claire Randolph, "The Medical Concept in English Renaissance Satiric Theory," in *Satire: Modern Essays in Criticism*, ed. Ronald Paulson (Englewood Cliffs, NJ: Prentice Hall, 1971), pp. 135–70.

36 Wyndham Lewis, *Tarr: The 1918 Edition*, ed. Paul O'Keefe (Santa Rosa, Calif.: Black Sparrow, 1990), pp. 33, 45, 51.

37 Wyndham Lewis, *Blasting and Bombardiering* (Berkeley: University of California Press, 1967), p. 87.

38 Reed Way Dasenbrock, quoted in English, *Comic Transactions*, p. 80.

39 Hugh Kenner, *Wyndham Lewis* (Norfolk, Conn.: New Directions, 1954), p. 30.

40 As Douglas Mao remarks, "Tarr himself seem[s] composed more of polemic than of feeling." Douglas Mao, *Solid Objects: Modernism and the Test of Production* (Princeton University Press, 1998), p. 95.

41 Wyndham Lewis, *Tarr*, p. 300.

42 Martin Puchner, *Poetry of the Revoluton: Marx, Manifestos, and the Avant-gardes* (Princeton University Press, 2006), p. 122.

43 Wyndham Lewis, *Tarr*, p. 14.

44 *Ibid.*, p. 42.

45 *Ibid.*, p. 43.

46 *Ibid.*, p. 314.

47 Wyndham Lewis, *Men Without Art*, p. 113.

48 Wyndham Lewis, *Tarr*, p. viii.

49 *Ibid.*, p. 30.

50 *Ibid.*, p. 243. Michael Levenson's reading hinges on Tarr's failure to free himself from his own sexual drives and achieve a disinterested artistic consciousness. Michael Levenson, *Modernism and the Fate of Individuality: Character and Novelistic Form from Conrad to Woolf* (Cambridge University Press, 1991), p. 141. Peter Nicholls also comments upon Tarr's inability to negotiate the social world; see Nicholls, *Modernisms*, pp. 183 ff.

51 Kenner, *Wyndham Lewis*, p. 43.

52 Wyndham Lewis, *Tarr*, p. 299.

53 Paul Peppis, *Literature, Politics, and the English Avant-Garde: Nation and Empire, 1901–1918* (Cambridge University Press, 2000), p. 150.

54 Wyndham Lewis, *Tarr*, p. 51.

55 *Ibid.*, p. 179.

56 Ann Ardis, *Modernism and Cultural Conflict: 1880–1922* (Cambridge University Press, 2002), p. 103.

57 Wyndham Lewis, *Tarr*, pp. 191, 192.

58 For a fuller discussion of Lewis's failure to adhere to externals, see Levenson, *Modernism and the Fate of Individuality*, p. 126.

59 Wyndham Lewis, *Tarr*, p. 192.

60 *Ibid.*

61 Richard Aldington, "The Influence of Mr. James Joyce," in *Modernism: An Anthology of Sources and Documents*, ed. Vassiliki Kolocotroni *et al.* (University of Chicago Press, 1998), p. 400.

62 Hugh Kenner, *Dublin's Joyce* (New York: Columbia University Press, 1987). The quotation from the van Dorens is from Robert Bell, *Jocoserious Joyce: The Fate of Folly in* Ulysses (Ithaca, NY: Cornell University Press, 1991), p. 64.

63 R. Bell, *Jocoserious Joyce*, pp. 8, 12, 35. My view of the satiric in *Ulysses* is anticipated by both Bell and by Maureen Waters, "James Joyce and Buck Mulligan," *The Comic Irishman* (Albany, NY: State University of New York Press, 1984), pp. 95–109.

64 Joyce, *Ulysses*, 1.204.

65 *Ibid.*, 1.589–93.

66 *Ibid.*, 9.568–74

67 R. Bell, *Jocoserious Joyce*, p. 8.

68 Joyce, *Ulysses*, 1.152–53, 9.483.

69 Waters, *Comic Irishman*, p. 106.

70 Joyce, *Ulysses*, 9.472.

71 *Ibid.*, 1.21–23.

72 *Ibid.*, 9.507–11.

73 R. Bell, *Jocoserious Joyce*, p. 8.

74 Waters, *Comic Irishman*, p. 91.

75 Jerome Meckier, *Aldous Huxley: Satire and Structure* (London: Chatto & Windus, 1969), pp. 1–2.

76 Flann O'Brien, *At Swim-Two-Birds* (Normal, Ill.: Dalkey Archive Press, 1998), p. 12.

77 Aldous Huxley, *Antic Hay* (Normal, Ill.: Dalkey Archive Press, 1997), pp. 97, 99.

78 T. Miller, *Late Modernism*, p. 158.

79 Huxley, *Antic Hay*, p. 39.

80 *Ibid.*, p. 41.

81 *Ibid.*, p. 31.

82 *Ibid.*

83 *Ibid.*, pp. 108–09.

84 *Ibid.*, pp. 14, 88, 103

85 *Ibid.*, pp. 41, 67.

86 See Aldous Huxley, "The Substitutes for Religion," *Aldous Huxley: Complete Essays*, vol. ii, *1926–1929*, ed. Robert S. Baker and James Sexton (Chicago: Ivan R. Dee, 2000), p. 254. I thank Sandy Reyes for bringing this source to my attention.

87 Huxley, *Antic Hay*, p. 67.
88 *Ibid.*, pp. 62, 179.
89 *Ibid.*, p. 100.
90 *Ibid.*, p. 103.
91 *Ibid.*, p. 193.
92 *Ibid.*, p. 123.
93 *Ibid.*, p. 56.
94 Cf. "The incident occurs, but nothing can be done with it: it is merely one more symptom of an obscure malaise … There is no attempt to relate the fact of poverty to the social system which permits Gumbril and his friends their privileged fantasy-lives." Terry Eagleton, *Exiles and Émigrés: Studies in Modern Literature* (New York: Schocken, 1970), p. 41.
95 Huxley, *Antic Hay*, p. 179.
96 *Ibid.*
97 T. Miller, *Late Modernism*, p. 12.
98 Samuel Hynes, *The Auden Generation: Literature and Politics in England in the 1930s* (London: The Bodley Head, 1976).
99 A. Wilde, *Horizons of Assent*, p. 42.
100 *Ibid.*, p. 99.
101 *Ibid.*, p. 43.
102 *Ibid.*, p. 108.
103 *Ibid.*, pp. 101, 117.
104 T. Miller, *Late Modernism*, pp. 42, 63.
105 These others include Irving Howe, Fredric Jameson, and Joshua Esty. Howe describes a modernism of three phases, each defined by a different view of the self, from "an inflation of the self" to "a minute examination of its own inner dynamics" to "an emptying-out of the self." Irving Howe, *Decline of the New* (New York: Harcourt, 1970), p. 5. Fredric Jameson's *Fables of Aggression* emphasizes Wyndham Lewis's dispersal of subjectivity and the value he places on satiric laughter. Joshua Esty's *A Shrinking Island: Modernism and National Culture in England* (Princeton University Press, 2004) looks primarily at the later works of earlier modernists such as Forster, Woolf, and Eliot, and sees in their later writings a retreat from metropolitanism and an effort to shore up a notion of English culture.
106 T. Miller, *Late Modernism*, p. 14.
107 Marjorie Perloff, Preface to F. T. Marinetti, *Let's Murder the Moonshine: Selected Writings*, trans. R. W. Flint and Arthur A. Coppotelli, ed. R. W. Flint (Los Angeles, Calif.: Sun and Moon Classics, 1991), p. 5.
108 Lewis, who is a central presence in Miller's study, was a key figure in early modernism, but Miller argues that late modernism returned to aesthetic possibilities temporarily eclipsed by high modernism. T. Miller, *Late Modernism*, pp. 18, 20.
109 Levenson notes "a persistent ambiguity in early modernism: the desire for the autonomy of form and the claim that the root source and justification for art is individual expression." From this ambiguity arise two strains of

modernism, one he calls "classical" (and which is in effect a romanticism by other means), the other "antihumanist." Both strains have been called "objective," leading to critical confusion. Levenson, *A Genealogy of Modernism*, pp. 98, 119, 135.

110 Rainey, Introduction to *Modernism*, p. 2.

111 Henry Green, Interview, "Henry Green: The Art of Fiction #22," *Paris Review*, 19 (1958), 16. www.theparisreview.org/viewinterview.php/prmMID/4800.

112 Michael Gorra, *The English Novel at Mid-Century: From the Leaning Tower* (New York: St. Martin's, 1990), p. 1.

113 *Ibid.*, pp. 12, 14, 18.

114 Jameson, *A Singular Modernity*, pp. 199–200.

115 *Ibid.*, p. 165.

116 As Jameson puts it, what makes late modernism late is not only the existence of modernism but also its theorization: "what guides such practice and enables it in the first place is very precisely that moment in which the modern has been theorized and conceptually named and identified in terms of the autonomy of the aesthetic." Jameson, *A Singular Modernity*, p. 197.

117 Nathanael West, "The Dream Life of Balso Snell," in *Nathanael West: Novels and Other Writings*, ed. Sacvan Bercovitch (New York: Library of America, 1997), p. 23.

118 Quoted as an epigraph to Evelyn Waugh, *Vile Bodies* (Boston: Little, Brown, 1930), no page number given.

119 Cf. Eve Sedgwick's observation that "affects can be, and are, attached to things, people, ideas, sensations, relations, activities, ambitions, institutions, and any number of other things, including other affects. Thus one can be excited by anger, disgusted by shame, or surprised by joy." Eve Kosofsky Sedgwick, *Touching Feeling: Affect, Pedagogy, Performativity* (Durham, NC: Duke University Press, 2003), p. 19.

3 THE RULE OF OUTRAGE: EVELYN WAUGH'S "VILE BODIES"

1 Waugh's rejection of satire is quoted in Chapter 1. On modernism, see his comments on Joyce, who "started off writing very well," but "ends up a lunatic." Martin Stannard, *Evelyn Waugh: The Early Years, 1903–1939* (New York: Norton, 1987), p. 208.

2 Fredric Jameson, *Fables of Aggression: Wyndham Lewis, The Modernist as Fascist* (Berkeley: University of California Press, 1979).

3 See, among others, George McCartney, *Confused Roaring: Evelyn Waugh and the Modernist Tradition* (Bloomington: Indiana University Press, 1987).

4 An exception is Terry Eagleton, *Exiles and Émigrés: Studies in Modern Literature* (New York: Schocken, 1970).

5 Robert Murray Davis, *Evelyn Waugh and the Forms of His Time* (Washington, DC: Catholic University of America, 1989), p. 59; Jeffrey Heath, *The Picturesque Prison: Evelyn Waugh and his Writing* (Montreal: McGill-Queen's

University Press, 1982), p. 81; Samuel Hynes, *The Auden Generation: Literature and Politics in England in the 1930s* (London: The Bodley Head, 1976), pp. 58–59; Alvin Kernan, *The Plot of Satire* (New Haven, Conn.: Yale University Press, 1965), p. 160; William Myers, *Evelyn Waugh and the Problem of Evil* (London: Faber, 1991), p. 18.

6 See Frederick Beaty, *The Ironic World of Evelyn Waugh: A Study of Eight Novels* (DeKalb: Northern Illinois University Press, 1992), p. 53; Michael Gorra, *The English Novel at Mid-Century: From the Leaning Tower* (New York: St. Martin's, 1990), p. 157.

7 Wyndham Lewis, *Men Without Art* (New York: Russell & Russell, 1964), p. 11.

8 Adam Parkes has taken this scene as emblematic of the ways in which British modernism as a whole "was shaped in significant ways by an ongoing dialogue with a culture of censorship." Parkes, *Modernism and the Theater of Censorship* (Oxford University Press, 1996), p. viii.

9 The "Illustrated" works of Aristotle refer to a falsely or facetiously attributed pseudoscientific work describing the processes of human reproduction and pregnancy. In Chapter 10 of *Ulysses*, Leopold Bloom looks through a copy of Aristotle's "Masterpiece" in a bookseller's stall.

10 Cf. Gorra, *The English Novel*, p. 165.

11 William Ian Miller, *The Anatomy of Disgust* (Cambridge, Mass.: Harvard University Press, 1997), p. 184.

12 Michael Seidel, *Satiric Inheritance: Rabelais to Sterne* (Princeton University Press, 1979), p. 3.

13 Myers points out that Nina, Adam, and Ginger are each given moments of acute vulnerability in order to maintain their humanity; Alain Blayac distinguishes Waugh's "humour," tinged with sympathy, from intellectual "wit," and argues that it serves as "the touchstone and instrument of the writer's wounded affectivity"; Ian Littlewood goes so far as to claim that the emotional moments in *Vile Bodies* teeter "on the edge of sentimentality." Myers, *The Problem of Evil*, p. 18; Alain Blayac, "Evelyn Waugh and Humour," in Alain Blayac (ed.), *Evelyn Waugh: New Directions* (London: Macmillan, 1992), p. 115; Ian Littlewood, *The Writings of Evelyn Waugh* (Oxford: Basil Blackwell, 1983), p. 19.

14 Tyrus Miller, *Late Modernism: Politics, Fiction and the Arts Between the World Wars* (Berkeley: University of California Press, 1999), p. 158.

15 D. H. Lawrence, *Studies in Classic American Literature* (New York: Viking, 1964), p. vii.

16 Walter Lippmann, *Public Opinion* (New York: Free Press, 1965), p. 10.

17 *Ibid.*, p. 18.

18 *Ibid.*, p. 11.

19 Michael North, *Reading 1922: A Return to the Scene of the Modern* (Oxford University Press, 1999); Justus Nieland, *Feeling Modern: The Eccentricities of Public Life* (Champaign: University of Illinois Press, 2008).

20 Waugh, "Let Us Return to the Nineties but not to Oscar Wilde," *The Essays, Articles and Reviews of Evelyn Waugh*, ed. Donat Gallagher (London: Methuen, 1983), p. 123.

21 Patrick Collier, *Modernism on Fleet Street* (Burlington, Vt.: Ashgate, 2006).

22 Lippmann, *Public Opinion*, p. 19.

23 *Ibid.*, p. 224.

24 *Ibid.*, p. 19.

25 See Davis, *The Forms of His Time*, p. 129; Myers, *The Problem of Evil*, p. 144; Stannard, *The Early Years*, p. 205; Robert R. Garnett, *From Grimes to Brideshead: The Early Novels of Eveyln Waugh* (Toronto: Associated University Presses, 1990), p. 59.

26 The change in tone parallels the differences Freud detailed between jokes and dreams. The hallucinatory nature of dreams, like that of Agatha's psychosis, is a sensory phenomenon, whereas jokes are not. Moreover, "a dream is a completely asocial mental product" while "a joke … is the most social of all the mental functions that aim at a yield of pleasure"; a dream dispenses with intelligibility, while a joke requires intelligibility. Thus "the dream-work operates by the same methods as jokes, but in its use of them it transgresses the limits that are respected by jokes." Sigmund Freud, *Jokes and Their Relation to the Unconscious*, trans. and ed. James Strachey (New York: Norton, 1989), pp. 214–15, 222.

27 Waugh, "Fan-Fare," *Essays, Articles and Reviews*, p. 303.

28 Davis, *Forms of His Time*, p. 15

29 This last reading is the one shared by Blayac, "Evelyn Waugh and Humour," p. 116, and Garnett, *From Grimes to Brideshead*, p. 72.

30 Hynes, *Auden Generation*, p. 60.

31 Lippmann, *Public Opinion*, p. 224.

32 Hynes, *Auden Generation*, p. 62.

33 Waugh, "Ronald Firbank," *Essays, Articles and Reviews*, pp. 57, 58. The joke about the bottle-green bowler is lifted almost directly from Firbank's *The Flower Beneath the Foot*.

34 Waugh, "Ronald Firbank," pp. 58, 59. For a discussion of Firbank's influence, see James Carens, *The Satiric Art of Evelyn Waugh* (Seattle: University of Washington Press, 1966), pp. 5–10.

35 Waugh, "Let Us Return to the Nineties," p. 125.

36 Waugh, "Satire and Fiction," *Essays, Articles and Reviews*, p. 102.

37 George McCartney, "The Being and Becoming of Evelyn Waugh," in *Evelyn Waugh: New Directions*, p. 143.

38 Evelyn Waugh, *Decline and Fall* (Boston: Little, Brown, 1956), p. 159.

39 *Ibid.*

40 *Ibid.*

41 On Waugh and Futurism, see McCartney, "The Being and Becoming"; Brooke Allen, "*Vile Bodies*: A Futurist Fantasy," *Twentieth Century Literature*, 40.3 (1994): 318–28; and Archie Loss, "*Vile Bodies*, Vorticism, and Italian Futurism," *Journal of Modern Literature*, 18.1 (1992): 155–64. McCartney recognizes the attack on Marinetti in the motor-racing scene as well, but perhaps overemphasizes Waugh's intellectual alliance with Lewis. Allen recognizes Lewis as a target, while noting that the antihumanism of Lewis and

Marinetti had a technical influence on Waugh. Loss likewise sees an ambivalent attitude toward Futurism and Vorticism; for him, Waugh deploys certain Futurist strategies, such as an emphasis on motion, but cannot celebrate the machine as his predecessors do.

42 F. T. Marinetti, "The Founding and Manifesto of Futurism," *Let's Murder the Moonshine: Selected Writings*, trans. R. W. Flint and Arthur A. Coppotelli, ed. R. W. Flint (Los Angeles, Calif.: Sun and Moon Classics, 1991), p. 49.

43 Davis, for example, suggests that Waugh deploys "an aesthetic rather than a psychological conception of character." Davis, *Forms of His Time*, p. 21. See also Carens, *The Satiric Art*, p. 60; Gorra, *The English Novel*, p. 159; Kernan, *The Plot of Satire*, p. 149.

44 Gorra argues that *Vile Bodies* exhibits an awareness of the disquieting or even disgusting as well as the comic consequences of the vision of the human as mechanical. *The English Novel*, p. 162.

45 Seidel, *Satiric Inheritance*, p. 3.

46 *Ibid.*, p. 4.

4 LAUGHTER AND FEAR IN "A HANDFUL OF DUST"

1 Donat O'Donnell, [Conor Cruise O'Brien], "The Pieties of Evelyn Waugh," in James Carens (ed.), *Critical Essays on Evelyn Waugh* (Boston, Mass.: G. K. Hall, 1987), p. 50.

2 Terry Eagleton has criticized exactly this "conflict between a sense of morality and a sense style" in the early fiction, but my own aim here is analytic rather than didactic. Terry Eagleton, *Exiles and Émigrés: Studies in Modern Literature* (New York: Schocken, 1970), p. 43. See also Jeffrey Heath, *The Picturesque Prison: Evelyn Waugh and His Writing* (Montreal: McGill-Queen's University Press, 1982), p. 84.

3 George McCartney, *Confused Roaring: Evelyn Waugh and the Modernist Tradition* (Bloomington: Indiana University Press, 1987), p. 3.

4 Thomas Drewry, "Tony Last's Two Children in *A Handful of Dust*," *Evelyn Waugh Newsletter and Studies*, 25.3 (1991): 5–8.

5 Eve Kosofsky Sedgwick, *Epistemology of the Closet* (Berkeley: University of California Press, 1990), p. 132.

6 Calvin Lane identifies this death as the first moment in Waugh's fiction where he allows compassion for his characters. Calvin Lane, *Evelyn Waugh* (Boston, Mass.: Twayne, 1981), p. 60.

7 Evelyn Waugh, "Ronald Firbank," *The Essays, Articles and Reviews of Evelyn Waugh*, ed. Donat Gallagher (London: Methuen, 1983), pp. 56–57; see also "Let Us Return to the Nineties But Not to Oscar Wilde," *Essays, Articles, and Reviews*, pp. 122–25.

8 See Eagleton, *Exiles and Émigrés*, p. 47; Ian Littlewood, *The Writings of Evelyn Waugh* (Oxford: Basil Blackwell, 1983), p. 14. Eagleton claims that this tonal quality impairs Waugh's critique of upper-class manners because it puts

forward no valid alternative. Eagleton's complaint – that the satire fails to maintain a stable, didactic irony – displays a moralistic discomfort with double movement of satire.

9 Littlewood again comes close to my view: "Implicit in the book is a recognition that those attitudes of sophisticated detachment which had been part of the glamour of the social milieu to which he once aspired were, from the inside, potentially vicious." He later claims *A Handful of Dust* "deliberately puts far more strain than any previous [novel] on [Waugh's] habitual mechanisms of defense. Detachment is harder to maintain, humour more difficult to find, romanticism a more dangerous commitment." *The Writings of Evelyn Waugh*, pp. 24, 146.

10 James Hall sees the central theme of Waugh's work as "the sad history of all rebellions in manners, the slide from bold experiment to fashionable cliché." James Hall, *The Tragic Comedians: Seven Modern British Novelists* (Bloomington: Indiana University Press, 1978), p. 46.

11 Sedgwick, *Epistemology*, p. 153.

12 *Ibid.*, pp. 153, 156.

13 *Ibid.*, p. 154.

14 Evelyn Waugh, *The Letters of Evelyn Waugh*, ed. Mark Amory (New Haven, Conn.: Ticknor & Fields, 1980), p. 39.

15 *Ibid.*, p. 40.

16 *Ibid.*, p. 41.

17 For similar views, see Frederic J. Stopp, *Evelyn Waugh: Portrait of an Artist* (Boston: Little Brown, 1958), p. 93; James Carens, *The Satiric Art of Evelyn Waugh* (Seattle: University of Washington Press, 1966), p. 85.

18 It is further significant that Waugh uses neither directly quoted mental language nor free indirect discourse to render Tony's thoughts, but instead the technique Dorrit Cohn has called "psycho-narration" – narratorial language that assumes neither the voice nor the idiom of the character. This technique allows him the least obtrusive departure from his external method, since he never has to alter the voice of the narrator, providing Tony's feelings without forcing Tony to undergo uncharacteristic bouts of introspection. Dorrit Cohn, *Transparent Minds: Narrative Modes for Presenting Consciousness in Fiction* (Princeton University Press, 1978), p. 46.

19 Roland Barthes, Introduction to *Critical Essays*, trans. Richard Howard (Evanston, Ill.: Northwestern University Press, 1972), p. xiv.

20 *Ibid.*, p. xvii.

21 Wyndham Lewis, *Men Without Art* (New York: Russell & Russell), p. 112; José Ortega y Gasset, *The Dehumanization of Art and Other Writings on Art and Culture* (Garden City, NY: Doubleday, 1956), p. 11. For a comparison of Lewis and Ortega, and their common interest in promoting an antihumanist aesthetic, see Ella Zohar Ophir, "Towards a Pitiless Fiction: Abstraction, Comedy, and Modernist Antihumanism," *MFS: Modern Fiction Studies*, 52.1 (2006): 92–120.

22 Quoted in Martin Stannard, *Evelyn Waugh: The Early Years, 1903–1939* (New York: Norton, 1987), p. 377. Eagleton voices a similar complaint, objecting

that "the American exploration reveals the hollowness of English culture as 'metaphysically' rather than socially determined," thereby undermining the effectiveness of the novel's social critique. Eagleton, *Exiles and Émigrés*, p. 56.

23 Julian Jebb (ed.), *Writers at Work: Third Series* (New York: Viking, 1967), p. 109; Waugh, "Fan-Fare," *Essays, Articles and Reviews*, p. 303.

24 Waugh, *Letters*, p. 88.

25 John Ruskin, *The Stones of Venice*, vol. iii (London: J. M. Dent, 1907), p. 115.

26 Wasson's reading has corrected the assumption that Waugh endorses Tony's attachment to big houses and Victorian ideals. Yet it reads the novel as a morality tale, stabilizing Waugh as a normative, Christian satirist, and inadequately acknowledging the contradictions inherent in his method. Richard Wasson, "*A Handful of Dust*: Critique of Victorianism," in *Critical Essays on Evelyn Waugh*, 133–43. See also Brooke Allen, "The Man Who Didn't Like Dickens: Evelyn Waugh and Boz," *Dickens Quarterly*, 8.4 (1991): 155–62; Jerome Meckier, "Why the Man Who Liked Dickens Reads Dickens Instead of Conrad: Waugh's *A Handful of Dust*," *Novel: A Forum on Fiction*, 13.2 (1980): 171–87.

27 Shoshana Felman, "Turning the Screw of Interpretation," in Shoshana Felman (ed.), *Literature and Psychoanalysis: The Question of Reading Otherwise* (Baltimore, Md.: Johns Hopkins University Press, 1982), pp. 94–207.

28 Sigmund Freud, "The Uncanny," *The Standard Edition of the Complete Psychological Works of Sigmund Freud*, vol. xvii, trans. and ed. James Strachey (London: Hogarth, 1961), p. 219.

29 *Ibid.*, p. 249.

30 *Ibid.*, p. 250. Stanley Cavell and Eric Santner both point out that there is no necessary contradiction between an explanation of the uncanny that relies on the persistence of magical thinking and one that relies on castration fears, since it is in the oedipal phase that the repression of magical thinking takes place. Stanley Cavell, *In Quest of the Ordinary: Lines of Skepticism and Romanticism* (University of Chicago Press, 1988), pp. 155–56; Eric Santner, *On Creaturely Life: Rilke, Benjamin, Sebald* (University of Chicago Press, 2006), pp. 190–91.

31 Freud, "The Uncanny," p. 250.

32 On Conrad, Dickens, and Waugh, see also Meckier, "Why the Man Who Liked Dickens Reads Dickens Instead of Conrad"; Allen, "The Man Who Didn't Like Dickens"; McCartney, *Confused Roaring*.

33 Waugh, "Fan-Fare," *Essays, Articles and Reviews*, p. 303.

34 Michael Gorra in fact suggests that this passage was explicitly modeled after Joyce. Michael Gorra, *The English Novel at Mid-Century: From the Leaning Tower* (New York: St Martin's, 1990), p. 176.

35 Bruno Bettelheim, *The Uses of Enchantment: The Meaning and Importance of Fairy Tales* (New York: Knopf, 1976), p. 170.

36 *Ibid.*, p. 245.

37 For similarities between Todd and Tony, especially in their capacities as fathers, see Heath, *The Picturesque Prison*, pp. 105, 113, 118. For the original

short story see Evelyn Waugh, "The Man Who Liked Dickens," in *The Book of Fantasy*, ed. Jorge Luis Borges, Silvina Ocampo, and A. Bioy Casares (New York: Viking, 1988), pp. 304–14.

38 Freud describes a similar "splitting" in "The Sandman": "In the story of Nathaniel's childhood, the figures of his father and Coppelius represent the two opposites into which the father-imago is split by his ambivalence; whereas the one threatens to blind him – that is, to castrate him – the other, the 'good' father, intercedes for his sight. The part of the complex which is most strongly repressed, the death-wish against the 'bad' father, finds expression in the death of the 'good' father." Freud, "Uncanny," p. 232.

39 Neil Hertz, *The End of the Line: Essays in Psychoanalysis and the Sublime* (New York: Columbia University Press, 1985), p. 98.

40 *Ibid.*, p. 102.

41 Sigmund Freud, *Beyond the Pleasure Principle*, trans. and ed. James Strachey (New York: Norton, 1989), p. 42.

42 See, e.g., Allen, "The Man Who Didn't Like Dickens, p. 155. John Howard Wilson dissents, holding out hope for Tony's return to Hetton. John Howard Wilson, "A Note on the Ending of *A Handful of Dust*," *Evelyn Waugh Newsletter*, 24.3 (1990): 2.

43 Freud, *Beyond the Pleasure Principle*, pp. 43, 44.

44 *Ibid.*, p. 24.

45 *Ibid.*, p. 41.

46 Hertz, *The End of the Line*, p. 105.

47 Slavoj Žižek, *The Sublime Object of Ideology* (New York: Verso, 1989), p. 43.

48 Cavell remarks on the same phenomenon when he understands fantastic literature to rest on "discoveries of otherness or estrangement," particularly the Freudian realization of our "estrangement from our own soul." This estrangement, what Cavell in a different context calls horror, entails "the perception of the precariousness of human identity." See Cavell, *In Quest of the Ordinary*, p. 185 and his *The Claim of Reason: Wittgenstein, Skepticism, Morality and Tragedy* (Oxford University Press, 1979), p. 418.

49 Henri Bergson, "Laughter," in Wylie Sypher (ed.), *Comedy* (Garden City, NY: Doubleday, 1956), p. 84.

50 Freud, "Uncanny," p. 255. Similarly, in his discussion of "The Sandman," Freud argues *against* the doll as a source of the uncanny in the story precisely because of its satiric coloring: "Nor is this atmosphere [of the uncanny] heightened by the fact that the author himself treats the episode of Olympia with a faint touch of satire and uses it to poke fun at the young man's idealization of his mistress." Freud, "Uncanny," p. 227.

51 Cavell suggests that, following Bergson, "we might conceive of laughter as the natural response to automatonity when we *know* the other to be human," thus construing "laughter as some reverse of amazement." Hence "the perception of the comedy . . . is essential to, is the same as, the detection of the madness." Cavell, *The Claim of Reason*, p. 415.

52 Waugh, "Apotheosis of an Unhappy Hypocrite," *Essays, Articles, and Reviews*, p. 447.
53 *Ibid.*
54 Dickens was Arthur Waugh's favorite author, according to Stannard, *The Early Years*, p. 25.
55 Evelyn Waugh, *A Little Learning* (Boston: Little, Brown, 1964), pp. 71–72.
56 Evelyn Waugh, *Ninety-Two Days* (London: Methuen, 1991), pp. 120–21.

5 'COLD COMFORT FARM' AND MENTAL LIFE

1 Reggie Oliver, *Out of the Woodshed: A Portrait of Stella Gibbons* (London: Bloomsbury, 1998), p. 111.
2 Faye Hammill, "*Cold Comfort Farm*, D. H. Lawrence, and English Literary Culture between the Wars," *MFS: Modern Fiction Studies*, 47 (2001): 842.
3 Jane Tompkins, *Sensational Designs: The Cultural Work of American Fiction, 1790–1860* (Oxford University Press, 1985); Ann Douglas, *The Feminization of American Culture* (New York: Knopf, 1977).
4 Philip B. Gould, "Introduction: Revisiting the 'Feminization' of American Culture," *differences: A Journal of Feminist Cultural Studies*, 11.3 (1999): i–xii.
5 Eve Kosofsky Sedgwick, *Epistemology of the Closet* (Berkeley: University of California Press, 1990); Julie Ellison, *Cato's Tears and the Making of Anglo-American Emotion* (University of Chicago Press, 1999).
6 e.g., Nicola Humble, *The Feminine Middlebrow Novel, 1920s to 1950s: Class, Domesticity, and Bohemianism* (Oxford University Press, 2001).
7 Regina Barreca, *Untamed and Unabashed: Essays on Women and Humor in British Literature* (Detroit, Mich.: Wayne State University Press, 1994), p. 15.
8 Chris Baldick, *1910–1940: The Modern Movement*, The Oxford English Literary History, vol. x (Oxford University Press, 2004), pp. 294–95.
9 Oliver, *Out of the Woodshed*, p. 120.
10 Cited in Barreca, *Untamed and Unabashed*, p. 21.
11 Wendy Parkins suggests that in the novel "female agency simultaneously conceals and deploys middle-class authority." Wendy Parkins, "Moving Dangerously: Mobility and the Modern Woman," *Tulsa Studies in Women's Literature*, 20 (2001): 88.
12 "The comedy flows in part from the parody of Flora as an interfering upper-middle-class woman who uses her leisure to meddle in the personal lives of others." English Studies Group, Centre for Contemporary Cultural Studies, Birmingham, "Thinking the Thirties," in Francis Barker (ed.), *1936: The Sociology of Literature: Practices of Literature and Politics* (University of Essex Press, 1979), p. 18.
13 See reviews quoted by Oliver, *Out of the Woodshed*, p. 112.
14 Raymond Williams cites as Gibbons's precursors Mary Webb, Sheila Kaye-Smith along with D. H. Lawrence, Emily Brontë, George Eliot, Thomas Hardy, and the Powyses. Hammill adds the Americans Edith Wharton and Eugene O'Neill as well as the English contemporaries H. A. Manhood and

Hugh Walpole. Raymond Williams, *The Country and the City* (Oxford University Press, 1973), p. 253. See also Oliver, *Out of the Woodshed*, pp. 113–17; Hammill, "English Literary Culture," *passim*.

15 Baldick, *1910–1940: The Modern Movement*, p. 171.

16 Williams, *The Country and the City*, p. 252. Jacqueline Ann Ariail cites the description of Egdon Heath in Hardy's *The Return of the Native*; see Jacqueline Ann Ariail, "*Cold Comfort Farm* and Stella Gibbons," *Ariel* 9 (1978): 63–73.

17 D. H. Lawrence, *The Rainbow* (New York: Viking, 1973), p. 2.

18 Williams, *The Country and the City*, p. 253.

19 *Ibid.*

20 Parkins, "Moving Dangerously," 86–87.

21 K. D. M. Snell writes: "In *Cold Comfort Farm*, the apparent distance between the rural and urban worlds was magnifed." Quoted in Hammill, "English Literary Culture," 848.

22 Cf. Parkins, "Moving Dangerously," 87.

23 George Orwell, "Inside the Whale," *A Collection of Essays* (Garden City, NY: Doubleday, 1954), p. 228.

24 See English Studies Group, "Thinking the Thirties," pp. 8, 15; Hammill, "English Literary Culture," 839.

25 As Lucy McDiarmid suggests to me, "Yĕs" likely alludes to the modernist fascination with Japanese Noh drama.

26 Humble calls Flora "the epitome of middlebrow sensibilities." Humble, *The Feminine Middlebrow Novel*, p. 31. Most of the critics cited here emphasize the middlebrow, anti-modernist side of *Cold Comfort Farm* without recognizing its own assertion of aesthetic and class superiority.

27 Joseph Litvak, *Strange Gourmets: Sophistication, Theory, and the Novel* (Durham, NC: Duke University Press, 1997), p. 29.

28 Georg Simmel, "The Metropolis and Mental Life," *On Individual and Social Forms: Selected Writings*, ed. Donald N. Levine (University of Chicago Press, 1971), p. 326.

29 *Ibid.*, p. 325.

30 Georg Simmel, *The Philosophy of Money*, trans. Tom Bottomore and David Frisby (London: Routledge and Kegan Paul, 1978), p. 256.

31 "As the epitome of middlebrow sensibilities, Flora's disdain is carefully balanced: she expresses no shock at the antics of the free-living highbrows, rather a weary contempt, produced partly by over-familiarity . . . she moves in social circles in which these 'types' are encountered all too frequently. The eternal literary standards of Dickens and (elsewhere) Jane Austen are her counters against the intellectual fripperies and fashions of the highbrow, which are presented as ephemeral by contrast." Humble, *The Feminine Middlebrow Novel*, p. 31.

32 Simmel, "Metropolis," p. 327.

33 *Ibid.*, p. 325.

34 Writes Lukács: "The novel is the epic of an age in which the extensive totality of life is no longer directly given, in which the immanence of

meaning in life has become a problem, yet which still thinks in terms of totality." Georg Lukács, "From *The Theory of the Novel: A Historico-Philosophical Essay on the Forms of Great Epic Literature*," in Michael McKeon (ed.), *The Theory of the Novel: A Historical Approach* (Baltimore, Md.: Johns Hopkins University Press, 2000), p. 186. See also Walter Benjamin, "The Storyteller: Reflections on the Work of Nikolai Leskov," *Illuminations: Essays and Reflections*, trans. Harry Zohn (New York: Schocken, 1968), p. 99.

35 Lukács, *The Theory of the Novel*, p. 185.

36 Elizabeth S. Goodstein, *Experience Without Qualities: Boredom and Modernity* (Palo Alto, Calif.: Stanford University Press, 2005), p. 268.

37 Lukács, *The Theory of the Novel*, p. 186.

38 Simmel, "Metropolis," p. 339.

39 *Ibid.*

40 Oliver notes that Gibbons spent Easter 1931 at a farm in Sussex working on the novel, *Out of the Woodshed*, p. 111.

41 Marianne Torgovnick discusses the Eurocentric misreading of African art as expressionist. Marianne Torgovnick, *Gone Primitive: Savage Intellects, Modern Lives* (University of Chicago Press, 1990).

42 Simmel, "Metropolis," p. 327.

43 *Ibid.*, p. 325.

44 Sedgwick, *Epistemology*, p. 154.

45 Humble writes that in *Cold Comfort Farm* "a conflict between an Austen and a Brontë world view is played out" in which ultimately "the Brontë-plot is consigned to the past: the modern world requires the open rationalism of an Austen." *The Feminine Middlebrow Novel*, pp. 179–80.

46 Jane Austen, *Mansfield Park*, ed. Claudia Johnson (New York: Norton, 1998), p. 312.

47 Henri Bergson, "Laughter," in Wylie Sypher (ed.), *Comedy* (Garden City, NY: Doubleday, 1956), p. 63.

48 *Ibid.*, pp. 63–64.

49 *Ibid.*, p. 72.

50 Ariail, "*Cold Comfort Farm* and Stella Gibbons," 69. See also Parkins, "Moving Dangerously," 89. The Birmingham English Studies Group writes: "In the closing pages Flora Poste leaves the ordinary world which she has created on the Wings of Romance, in her lover's aeroplane," but judiciously adds, "There are hints here that the formulaic romance is being parodied." English Studies Group, "Thinking the Thirties," p. 16.

51 Parkins, "Moving Dangerously," 88.

52 Suzanne Clark, *Sentimental Modernism: Women Writers and the Revolution of the Word* (Bloomington: Indiana University Press, 1991), pp. 2–3.

53 Rita Felski, *The Gender of Modernity* (Cambridge, Mass.: Harvard University Press, 1995), p. 88.

54 Barreca, *Untamed and Unabashed*, p. 23.

55 Oliver, *Out of the Woodshed*, p. 97.

56 There is significant variation too within the interpretations of the novel's gender politics. The English Studies Group emphasizes the fact that "All of the women in this text, whether under the dominance of Aunt Ada or of Flora, are assigned to the same subordinate role within familial sexual relations." English Studies Group, "Thinking the Thirties," p. 17. Parkins sees a reversion to nineteenth-century models of female agency that were limited to the domestic sphere. Parkins, "Moving Dangerously." Ariail sees the novel as a woman writer's struggle against male predecessors. Ariail, "*Cold Comfort Farm* and Stella Gibbons."

57 Simmel, "Metropolis," p. 329.

6 NATHANAEL WEST AND THE MYSTERY OF FEELING

1 Justus Nieland reads the "affective estrangement" of *Miss Lonelyhearts* as a rejection of both "the aristocratic black humor of the surrealist avant-garde" and the "affective universality of slapstick" – and consequently of both the high modernist transcendence of material world offered by surrealism and the Enlightenment models of feeling in the public sphere encouraged by slapstick. Justus Nieland, *Feeling Modern: The Eccentricities of Public Life* (Champaign: University of Illinois Press, 2008), pp. 196, 210.

2 Nathanael West, *Nathanael West: Novels and Other Writings*, ed. Sacvan Bercovitch (New York: Library of America, 1997), p. 396.

3 Nathanael West, *The Dream Life of Balso Snell, ibid.*, pp. 25–26.

4 See especially Rita Barnard, *The Great Depression and the Culture of Abundance* (Cambridge University Press, 1995); Philip Brian Harper, *Framing the Margins: The Social Logic of Postmodern Culture* (Oxford University Press, 1994); Thomas Strychacz, *Modernism, Mass Culture and Professionalism* (Cambridge University Press, 1993); Jonathan Veitch, *American Superrealism: Nathanael West and the Politics of Representation in the 1930s* (Madison: University of Wisconsin Press, 1997). On the (dubious) distinction between a "constructive," conservative Anglo-American "high modernism" and a radical European "avant-garde," see Peter Bürger, *Theory of the Avant-Garde*, trans. Michael Shaw (Minneapolis: University of Minnesota Press, 1984), p. xv; Andreas Huyssen, *After the Great Divide: Modernism, Mass Culture, Postmodernism* (Bloomington: Indiana University Press, 1986), pp. 31, 163.

5 Max F. Schultz, "Nathanael West's Desperate Detachment," *Critical Essays on Nathanael West*, ed. Ben Siegel (New York: G. K. Hall, 1994), p. 151. Similar views include Daniel Aaron, "Late Thoughts on Nathanael West," in *Modern Critical Views: Nathanael West*, ed. Harold Bloom (New York: Chelsea House, 1986), pp. 61–68; Norman Podhoretz, "Nathanael West: A Particular Kind of Joking," in *Critical Essays on Nathanael West*, pp. 80–86.

6 Veitch, *American Superrealism*, p. xx; Barnard, *The Great Depression*, p. 168; Harper, *Framing the Margins*, p. 53; Strychacz, *Modernism, Mass Culture, and Professionalism*, p. 164.

7 Malcolm Bradbury, *The Modern American Novel* (New York: Penguin, 1983), pp. 126–27. Bradbury acknowledges the persistence of continuing formal experiment.

8 Dorothy Parker, "The Siege of Madrid," *The Portable Dorothy Parker* (New York: Viking, 1973), p. 589.

9 Jay Martin, *Nathanael West: The Art of his Life* (New York: Carroll and Graf, 1970), pp. 344–53.

10 West, *Novels and Other Writings*, p. 795.

11 *Ibid.*, p. 794.

12 *Ibid.*, pp. 791–92, 793.

13 Cf. Harold Bloom's claim that "West's humor has *no* liberating element whatsoever." Harold Bloom, Introduction to *Nathanael West: Modern Critical Views*, p. 4. Sianne Ngai's discussion of "ugly feelings" arising from "situations of suspended agency" similarly emphasizes their "noncathartic" nature and political ineffectuality. Sianne Ngai, *Ugly Feelings* (Cambridge, Mass.: Harvard University Press, 2005), pp. 1, 6.

14 West, *Novels and Other Writings*, p. 795.

15 The curious factoid that Trilling and West simultaneously attended New York's De Witt Clinton High School may suggest that their common questioning of sincerity betrays a larger generational or cultural concern. Martin, *Nathanael West*, p. 35.

16 Quoted *ibid.*, p. 336.

17 A political reading of West accepts this argument more or less at face value. Thus Barnard asserts that for West "the social realist techniques of the thirties are suspect" since they can lapse into a nostalgic "glorification" of a suffering proletariat, while Veitch maintains that West "suspected that the pretensions to innocence, the return to a populist provincialism that [Ma Joad] represented, harbored the seeds of a homegrown fascism." Barnard, *Great Depression*, p. 163; Veitch, *American Superrealism*, p. xiii. Yet one can invoke West's criterion of "truth" as an end for art that adopts any variety of modes and serves any variety of ideologies. Flannery O'Connor, in many ways a literary disciple of West's, maintained that her own brand of grotesque comedy provided a model not for leftist but for Catholic art, and precisely because of its "reality" or "truth."

18 West, *Novels and Other Writings*, p. 794.

19 Nathanael West, *A Cool Million*, *Novels and Other Writings*, p. 224.

20 *Ibid.*, pp. 223, 225.

21 Nathanael West, *Miss Lonelyhearts*, *Novels and Other Writings*, p. 119.

22 *Ibid.*, p. 118.

23 Ronal Paulson, *Don Quixote in England: The Aesthetics of Laughter* (Baltimore, Md.: Johns Hopkins University Press, 1998), p. xii.

24 Richard Rorty, *Contingency, Irony, and Solidarity* (Cambridge University Press, 1989), p. 73.

25 West, *Miss Lonelyhearts*, p. 95. Cf. Mark Conroy's deconstructive reading, which sees the novel's problems as problems of language. Mark Conroy,

"Letters and Spirit in *Miss Lonelyhearts*," in Harold Bloom (ed.), *Modern Critical Interpretations: Nathanael West's* Miss Lonelyhearts (New York: Chelsea House, 1987), pp. 111–24.

26 West, *Miss Lonelyhearts*, p. 59.

27 *Ibid.*, p. 74.

28 *Ibid.*, p. 88.

29 Steven Weisenburger argues that the painting goes beyond normative, "generative" satire to a "degenerative" mode of satire "that develops, not from the logic of 'objects' or 'targets' that shapes his earlier satires, but from narratives of violence and degeneration." Steven Weisenburger, *Fables of Subversion: Satire and the American Novel, 1930–1980* (Athens: University of Georgia Press, 1995), p. 45. See also Alvin Kernan, *The Plot of Satire* (New Haven, Conn.: Yale University Press, 1965), pp. 59–60.

30 West, *Miss Lonelyhearts*, p. 75.

31 West, *Novels and Other Writings*, p. 465.

32 West, *Balso Snell*, p. 42.

33 Kernan, *The Plot of Satire*, p. 55.

34 Although West is almost reflexively described as a writer of the grotesque, criticism has done little to explain the usefulness of the term. On West as a writer in the grotesque tradition, see Susan Edmunds, "Modern Taste and the Body Beautiful in Nathanael West's *The Day of the Locust*," *Modern Fiction Studies*, 44:2 (1998): 306–30; Bernard McElroy, *Fiction of the Modern Grotesque* (New York: Macmillan, 1989); Dieter Meindl, *American Fiction and the Metaphysics of the Grotesque* (Columbia: University of Missouri Press, 1996).

35 Fredric Jameson, *Postmodernism: Or, the Cultural Logic of Late Capitalism* (Durham, NC: Duke University Press, 1991), p. 11.

36 *Ibid.*, p. 12.

37 Sherwood Anderson, *Winesburg, Ohio* (New York: Penguin, 1960), p. 31.

38 Daniel Aaron, "Waiting for the Apocalypse," in *Critical Essays on Nathanael West*, p. 79; Martin, *Nathanael West*, p. 312; Susan Hegeman, *Patterns for America: Modernism and the Concept of Culture* (Princeton University Press, 1999), p. 156.

39 *Ibid.*, pp. 28–29.

40 *Ibid.*, pp. 31, 32.

41 Hegeman, *Patterns for America*, p. 156.

42 Tim Armstrong, *Modernism, Technology, and the Body: A Cultural Study* (Cambridge University Press, 1998), p. 238.

43 Wolfgang Kayser, *The Grotesque in Art and Literature*, trans. Ulrich Weisstein (New York: Columbia University Press, 1957), p. 183. Freud identifies the same phenomenon. Sigmund Freud, "The Uncanny," *The Standard Edition of the Complete Psychological Works of Sigmund Freud*, vol. xvii, trans. and ed. James Strachey (London: Hogarth, 1961), p. 226.

44 Wyndham Lewis, *Men Without Art* (New York: Russell & Russell), p. 116.

45 Lewis's comments on dwarves in *Men Without Art* anticipate not only the Spanish dwarf of his own *The Revenge for Love*, but also West's

(still uncreated) Abe Kusich: "Dwarfs in Spain are the objects of constant mirth, on the part of their 'normal' fellow-citizens. Everyone pokes fun at them, there is no hypocrisy, as with us, and the dwarf gets on very well indeed. He is treated as a pet animal, and enjoys himself very much." Wyndham Lewis, *Men Without Art*, p. 112.

46 Of *Miss Lonelyhearts*, Nieland observes West's "insistent presentation of characters as alienated from their affects, which are mechanical, stylized, and stagey." Nieland, *Feeling Modern*, p. 210.

7 'NIGHTWOOD' AND THE ENDS OF SATIRE

1 Matei Calinescu, *Five Faces of Modernity: Modernism, Avant-Garde, Decadence, Kitsch, Postmodernism* (Durham, NC: Duke University Press, 1987), pp. 155–56.

2 Michael Seidel, *Satiric Inheritance: Rabelais to Sterne* (Princeton University Press, 1979), p. 63.

3 *Ibid.*, p. 264.

4 Jane Marcus's groundbreaking Bakhtinian reading views the novel as an anti-authoritarian Rabelaisian epic with "deep roots in folk culture," but over-emphasizes the celebratory dimension of the novel, and ignores Bakhtin's reading of modernism as an era characterized by a reduced laughter. Jane Marcus, "Laughing at Leviticus: *Nightwood* as Woman's Circus Epic," in Mary Lynn Broe (ed.), *Silence and Power: A Reevaluation of Djuna Barnes* (Carbondale: Southern Illinois University Press, 1991), pp. 221–50. Tyrus Miller notes Barnes's "satiric attitude toward tradition" but does not apply this idea in a sustained way to *Nightwood*. Miller, *Late Modernism: Politics, Fiction and the Arts Between the World Wars* (Berkeley: University of California Press, 1999), p. 124. Justus Nieland focuses on laughter in the novel as the sign of an extra-human animality that disrupts norms of personality, "a comic repudiation of emotional propriety and the sort of immanent community implied by Bergson's comic theory." Justus Nieland, *Feeling Modern: The Eccentricities of Public Life* (Champaign: University of Illinois Press, 2008), p. 248.

5 Victoria L. Smith reads the novel's language as a symptom of Freudian melancholy. Victoria L. Smith, "A Story beside(s) Itself: The Language of Loss in Djuna Barnes's *Nightwood*," *PMLA*, 114.2 (1999): 194–206.

6 Donald J. Greiner, "Djuna Barnes's *Nightwood* and the American Origins of Black Humor," *Critique*, 17.1 (1975): 44; Louis Kannenstine, *The Art of Djuna Barnes: Duality and Damnation* (New York University Press, 1977), p. 115; Marcus, "Laughing at Leviticus," pp. 221–50; Mary Russo, *The Female Grotesque*, pp. 171–72; Sheryl Stevenson, "Writing the Grotesque Body: Djuna Barnes' Carnival Parody," in *Silence and Power*, p. 81. Andrew Field has gone so far as to call the "grotesque" the "unifying principle" of all Barnes's work. Andrew Field, *Djuna: The Formidable Miss Barnes* (Austin: University of Texas Press, 1985), p. 33.

7 Peter Stallybrass and Allon White, *The Politics and Poetics of Transgression* (Ithaca, NY: Cornell University Press, 1986), p. 44.

8 John Hawkes, D. J. Hughes, and Ihab Hassan, "Symposium: Fiction Today," *Massachusetts Review*, 3.4 (1962): 784–97; Stanley Edgard Hyman, "The Wash of the World," *Standards: A Chronicle of Books for our Time* (New York: Horizon, 1966), pp. 58–62.

9 T. S. Eliot, Introduction to Djuna Barnes, *Nightwood* (New York: New Directions, 1937), p. xvi.

10 Joseph Frank, *The Widening Gyre: Crisis and Mastery in Modern Literature* (New Brunswick, NJ: Rutgers University Press, 1963), p. 43, and many subsequent critics.

11 Marcus, "Laughing at Leviticus," p. 233, and many subsequent critics.

12 Alvin Kernan, *The Plot of Satire* (New Haven, Conn.: Yale University Press, 1965), p. 151.

13 Alan Singer, *A Metaphorics of Fiction: Discontinuity and Discourse in the Modern Novel* (Tallahassee: University Press of Florida, 1983), p. 60.

14 Seidel, *Satiric Inheritance*, p. 263.

15 Karen Kaivola, *All Contraries Confounded: The Lyrical Fiction of Virginia Woolf, Djuna Barnes, and Marguerite Duras* (Iowa City: University of Iowa Press, 1991), p. 82. Similarly, Marcus sees the novel's pattern of impotence as a "celebrat[ion of] the nonphallic penis, the limp member of the transvestite." Marcus, "Laughing at Leviticus," pp. 228, 229.

16 Cf. Merrill Cole's claim that "*Nightwood* punishes the politically well-intentioned." Merrill Cole, "Backwards Ventriloquy: The Historical Uncanny in Barnes's *Nightwood*," *Twentieth-Century Literature*, 52.4 (2006): 399.

17 Wyndham Lewis, *Men Without Art* (New York: Russell & Russell, 1964), pp. 228–29.

18 The cancellation of life presents a Schopenhauerian view of procreation, and squares with Phillip Herring's claim that Barnes viewed perpetuation of the species as sinful, or at least misguided. Phillip Herring, *Djuna: The Life and Work of Djuna Barnes* (New York: Viking, 1995), p. 207.

19 Andrea Harris, *Other Sexes: Rewriting Differences from Woolf to Winterson* (Albany, NY: State University of New York Press, 2000), p. 76.

20 Cf. Nieland, *Feeling Modern*, p. 225.

21 Walter Benjamin, "Unpacking My Library," *Illuminations: Essays and Reflections*, trans. Harry Zohn, ed. Hannah Arendt (New York: Schocken, 1968), p. 64.

22 See Meryl Altman, "A Book of Repulsive Jews?: Rereading *Nightwood*," *Review of Contemporary Fiction*, 13.3 (1993): 160–71; Lara Trubowitz, "In Search of 'The Jew' in Djuna Barnes's *Nightwood*: Jewishness, Antisemitism, Structure, and Style," *MFS: Modern Fiction Studies*, 51.2 (2005): 311–34.

23 Seidel, *Satiric Inheritance*, p. 251.

24 For example, Bonnie Kime Scott's suggestion that the narrative voice is unreliable here because it assumes Felix's point of view, and that Robin's gesture is "perhaps better seen as a religious rite," seems quite wishfully to

deny the extremity of Barnes's vision. Bonnie Kime Scott, *Refiguring Modernism*, vol. ii, *Postmodern Feminist Readings of Woolf, West, and Barnes* (Bloomington: Indiana University Press, 1995), p. 115.

25 Marcus, "Laughing at Leviticus," p. 241.

26 Kaivola, *All Contraries Confounded*, p. 83.

27 Sigmund Freud, "The Uncanny," *The Standard Edition of the Complete Psychological Works of Sigmund Freud*, vol. xvii, trans. and ed. James Strachey (London: Hogarth, 1961), pp. 226, 233.

28 *Ibid.*, p. 240.

29 *Ibid.*, pp. 240–41.

30 Marcus, "Laughing at Leviticus," and Cole, "Backwards Ventriloquy," discuss uncanny motifs in the novel.

31 Also cited by Freud, "Uncanny," p. 244.

32 Miller, *Late Modernism*, p. 139; Nieland, *Feeling Modern*, p. 219.

33 Miller, *Late Modernism*, p. 156; Nieland, *Feeling Modern*, p. 221.

34 Kenneth Burke, "Version, Con-, Per-, and In- (Thoughts on Djuna Barnes's Novel *Nightwood*)," p. 249.

35 "Nigh T. Wood" is Barnes's own phrase. Quoted in Cheryl J. Plumb, Introduction to *Nightwood: The Original Version and Related Drafts*, ed. Cheryl J. Plumb (Normal, Ill.: Dalkey Archive, 1995), p. ix.

36 For Metcalf as prototype of Jenny, see Herring, *The Life and Work of Djuna Barnes*, p. 162.

37 Note Herring's parenthetical in his account of *Nightwood*'s origin: "it was fundamentally written out of love (except for the 'Squatter' chapter)," *ibid.*, p. 165.

38 For an account of Barnes's possibly sexual relationship with her grandmother, Zadel, see *ibid.*, pp. 54 ff.

8 BECKETT'S AUTHORITARIAN PERSONALITIES

1 Fredric Jameson, *A Singular Modernity: Essay on the Ontology of the Present* (London: Verso, 2002), p. 165.

2 The Belgian philosopher Arnold Geulincx compared the mind's limited freedom to that of an eastward-walking passenger on a westward-bound ship. Richard Begam, *Samuel Beckett and the End of Modernity* (Palo Alto, Calif.: Stanford University Press, 1996), p. 50.

3 On Beckett's relation to precursors, see *ibid.*, p. 38; Neil Corcoran, *After Yeats and Joyce: Reading Modern Irish Literature* (Oxford University Press, 1997), p. 31.

4 See, among others, Begam, *The End of Modernity*, and Anthony Uhlmann, *Beckett and Poststructuralism* (Cambridge University Press, 1999).

5 Many critics treat the comic in Beckett. Ruby Cohn catalogs varieties of laughter, recognizing, according to the typology of *Watt*'s Arsene, that Beckett's laughter can be ethical (bitter), intellectual (hollow), or pure and "dianoetic" (mirthless); Hugh Kenner emphasizes the abstract or

mathematical quality of his comedy, arguing that Beckett's comedy "selects elements from a closed set, and then arranges them inside a closed field"; Andrew Gibson focuses on the comic effects that derive from the subversion of narrative conventions; Shane Weller examines the ethics of Beckett's comedy in the context of Continental philosophy; Michael North focuses on the motifs of doubling, repetition, and seriality, which "generate possibility out of repetition." Ruby Cohn, *Samuel Beckett: The Comic Gamut* (New Brunswick, NJ: Rutgers University Press, 1962), p. 287; Hugh Kenner, *Flaubert, Joyce, and Beckett: The Stoic Comedians* (Boston: Beacon, 1962), p. 94; Andrew Gibson, *Reading Narrative Discourse: Studies in the Novel from Cervantes to Beckett* (New York: Palgrave, 1990); Shane Weller, *Beckett, Literature, and the Ethics of Alterity* (New York: Palgrave, 2006); Michael North, *Machine-Age Comedy* (Oxford University Press, 2009), p. 162.

6 Paul Sheehan, *Modernism, Narrative, and Humanism* (Cambridge University Press, 2002), p. 153.

7 Tyrus Miller, *Late Modernism: Politics, Fiction and the Arts Between the World Wars* (Berkeley: University of California Press, 1999), pp. 195, 203, 190.

8 Fredric Jameson, *Fables of Aggression: Wyndham Lewis, The Modernist as Fascist* (Berkeley: University of California Press, 1980), p. 35. Jameson develops the notion of *écriture* as schizophrenia in "Postmodernism and Consumer Society," in Hal Foster (ed.), *The Anti-Aesthetic* (Port Townsend, Wash.: Bay Press, 1983), pp. 111–25.

9 Eve Kosofsky Sedgwick, *Touching Feeling: Affect, Pedagogy, Performativity* (Durham, NC: Duke University Press, 2003), p. 12.

10 *Ibid.*, p. 13.

11 Weller, *The Ethics of Alterity*, p. 131; Cohn, *The Comic Gamut*, p. 8.

12 For a thorough comparison of Molloy and Moran, see H. Porter Abbott, *The Fiction of Samuel Beckett: Form and Effect* (Berkeley: University of California Press, 1973), p. 100.

13 Cf. Cohn, *The Comic Gamut*, p. 123.

14 Abbott, *The Fiction of Samuel Beckett*, p. 102.

15 John Guillory, "The Memo and Modernity," *Critical Inquiry*, 31 (2004): 112, 114, 116.

16 Abbott, *The Fiction of Samuel Beckett*, p. 103.

17 Steven Weisenburger claims that American satire of the post-war era develops not from the context of a bourgeois society but from a bureaucratic information society. Steven Weisenburger, *Fables of Subversion: Satire and the American Novel, 1930–1980* (Athens: University of Georgia Press, 1995), p. 6.

18 Cf. Simon Critchley, *Very Little ... Almost Nothing: Death, Philosophy, Literature* (New York: Routledge, 1997), p. 162.

19 Samuel Taylor Coleridge, "Frost at Midnight," *The Complete Poems*, ed. William Keach (New York: Penguin, 1997), p. 321.

20 *Ibid.*

21 Maria DiBattista, *First Love: The Affections of Modern Fiction* (University of Chicago Press, 1991), p. 220.

22 Martha Nussbaum claims that Moran's relationship with Jacques displays "parental punishment strangely mixed with paternal care, love blocked by the need to discipline." The result is that "each instance of affection must be checked by guilty moral resolve." Martha Nussbaum, "Narrative Emotions: Beckett's Genealogy of Love," *Love's Knowledge: Essays on Philosophy and Literature* (Oxford University Press, 1990), p. 300.

23 Irwin Katz, "Gordon Allport's 'The Nature of Prejudice'," *Political Psychology*, 12.1 (1991): 130. Cf. Thomas Wheatland, *The Frankfurt School in Exile* (Minneapolis: University of Minnesota Press, 2009), p. 257. While the intellectual concerns in Beckett's France may not have been exactly those of Adorno's American setting, European émigrés such as Adorno and Arendt were fully in dialogue with French intellectuals such as Sartre.

24 Katz, "Gordon Allport's 'The Nature of Prejudice'," p. 130. T. W. Adorno, Else Frenkel-Brunswik, Daniel J. Levinson *et al.*, *The Authoritarian Personality* (New York: Harper and Row, 1950).

25 Richard Sennett, *Authority* (New York: Knopf, 1980), pp. 24, 25.

26 Adorno *et al.*, *Authoritarian Personality*, p. 759.

27 *Ibid.*

28 *Ibid.*

29 *Ibid.*

30 *Ibid.*

31 T. W. Adorno, "Trying to Understand *Endgame*," in Brian O'Connor (ed.), *The Adorno Reader* (Malden, Mass.: Blackwell, 2000), pp. 319–51.

32 T. W. Adorno, "Commitment," in Andrew Arato and Eike Gebhardt (eds), *The Essential Frankfurt School Reader* (New York: Continuum, 1982), p. 303.

33 *Ibid.*

34 T. W. Adorno, "Freudian Theory and the Pattern of Fascist Propaganda," *ibid.*, p. 124.

35 Sennett, *Authority*, p. 75.

36 Adorno, "Freudian Theory," p. 124.

37 Alan Astro, *Understanding Samuel Beckett* (Columbia: University of South Carolina Press, 1990), p. 61. Cf. Philologos, "On Language: Waiting for Youdi," *Jewish Daily Forward Online*, Nov. 12, 2004. www.forward.com/articles/4523/.

38 Cf. Uhlmann, *Beckett and Poststructuralism*, p. 48.

39 Adorno, "Freudian Theory," p. 127.

40 Sennett, *Authority*, p. 45.

41 Adorno *et al.*, *Authoritarian Personality*, p. 609.

42 Critchley, *Very Little ... Almost Nothing*, p. 157.

43 James Knowlson, *Damned to Fame: The Life of Samuel Beckett* (New York: Grove, 1996), p. 37.

44 *Ibid.*, p. 336.

45 *Ibid.*, pp. 36–37.

46 Gilles Deleuze, "Coldness and Cruelty," in *Masochism* (New York: Zone Books, 1989), p. 86.

47 *Ibid.*, p. 87. Deleuze's essay aims to revise Freud by decoupling sadism from masochism. Deleuze argues that sadism and masochism enact very different paths for libido. Yet he acknowledges that each does produce the other. As I will show, Moran indeed displays both sadistic and masochistic dimensions.

48 Cf. Cohn: "All the heroes of Beckett's French fiction invite our laughter at their savage drives – Moran's towards his son, Molloy's towards his mother, Malone's towards his creations, the Unnamable's towards his creators." Cohn, *The Comic Gamut*, p. 287.

49 Deleuze, "Coldness and Cruelty," p. 118.

50 *Ibid.*, p. 83.

51 This production of sorrow or shame from the renunciation of affection in the name of the law is rife throughout Moran's narrative: cf. *M*, pp. 102, 109, 161.

52 Deleuze, "Coldness and Cruelty," p. 126.

53 Quoted in Sianne Ngai, *Ugly Feelings* (Cambridge, Mass.: Harvard University Press, 2005), p. 179.

54 *Ibid.*, p. 190.

55 Beckett to Thomas MacGreevey, Oct. 5, 1930: "How can one write here, when every day vulgarizes one's hostility and turns anger into irritation and petulance?" Quoted in Knowlson, *Damned to Fame*, p. 124.

56 Deleuze, "Coldness and Cruelty," p. 85.

57 Adorno, "Freudian Theory," p. 120.

58 *Ibid.*

59 Gilles Deleuze, "The Exhausted," in *Essays Critical and Clinical*, trans. Daniel W. Smith and Michael A. Greco (Minneapolis: University of Minnesota Press, 1997), p. 154. Deleuze is preceded by Kenner, who sees Beckett as inheriting a tradition of inventory from Joyce's "Ithaca" chapter of *Ulysses*, a technique whereby "the more trivial the matter the more space is devoted to its analysis." Hugh Kenner, *The Stoic Comedians*, p. 82.

60 Ngai, *Ugly Feelings*, p. 260.

61 *Ibid.*, p. 261.

62 *Ibid.*, p. 294.

63 *Ibid.*, pp. 294, 297.

64 Interestingly, Adorno abhorred Chaplin's use of slapstick in *The Great Dictator* as an indulgence of sadism and a trivialization of political reality in the service of polemical art. Adorno's avoidance of the more obviously sadistic slapstick moments in Beckett indicates, perhaps, the Achilles heel that is his own moralism. For Adorno's differences with Benjamin on slapstick, see Justus Nieland, "Killing Time: Charlie Chaplin and the Comic Passion of *Monsieur Verdoux*," *Modernist Cultures*, 2.2 (2006): 190.

65 Sigmund Freud, *Jokes and Their Relation to the Unconscious*, trans. and ed. James Strachey (New York: Norton, 1989), p. 226.

66 Critchley, *Very Little … Almost Nothing*, pp. 141–44.

67 Sheehan, *Modernism, Narrative, and Humanism*, pp. 170 ff.

68 "Not to want to say, not to know what you want to say, not to be able to say what you think you want to say, and never to stop saying, or hardly ever, that is the thing to keep in mind, even in the heat of composition" (*M*, p. 28).

69 Samuel Beckett, *The Unnamable*, in *Three Novels by Samuel Beckett: Molloy, Malone Dies, The Unnamable*, trans. Samuel Beckett and Patrick Bowles (1951; New York: Grove, 1955), p. 297.

Index

Abbott, H. Porter, 165, 166
Acton, Harold, 78
Addams, Charles, xi
Adorno, Theodor W., 8, 17, 168–70, 171, 176–77, 183
aestheticism, 22, 24, 25–27, 28, 38, 42, 65–66; *see also* symbolism
affect. *See* modernism and affect; satire and affect; sentimentality
Aldington, Richard, 33
Altieri, Charles, 13
Anderson, Sherwood, 116, 132–33, 154
Ardis, Ann, 32
Armstrong, Tim, 132
Astro, Alan, 170
Auden, W. H., 7–8, 18
Austen, Jane, 94, 102, 106, 109, 110, 112–13
authenticity, 11, 16–17, 22, 46; *see also* Trilling, Lionel
    in Djuna Barnes, 154–55, 159–60
    in Evelyn Waugh, 61
    in Ezra Pound, 28
    in Nathanael West, 116, 128, 132, 134

Baier, Annette, 175
Bakhtin, Mikhail, 10, 11, 34, 98, 129, 208
Baldick, Chris, 2, 93, 96
Baldwin, James, 12
Barnard, Rita, 116, 117, 206
Barnes, Djuna, 11, 41, 43, 44, 164
    Nightwood, 138–60
        anti-procreative imagery in, 143–44, 145–49, 151–53
        characterization in, 150–51, 153, 154, 155–60
        compared to *A Handful of Dust*, 145–46, 149, 158
        compared to *Macbeth*, 151–52
        compared to *The Day of the Locust*, 158
        compared to *Ulysses*, 141

Dr. O'Connor as satirist, 140–45
        grotesque in, 139–40, 142–43, 157
        inheritance in, 139, 145–50
        parallels to Barnes's life, 158–59
        ridicule in, 139, 141, 146, 155–58
Barreca, Regina, 93, 112
Barthes, Roland, 80
Beckett, Samuel, 41, 44
    and James Joyce, 161, 162, 167
    and Marcel Proust, 162, 178
    and William Butler Yeats, 162
    as humanist, 162–64
    as late modernist, 161–62
    as postmodernist, 162–64
    Molloy, 161–83
        and detective/spy novel, 166
        and midcentury analyses of fascism, 168–69
        and sadism/masochism, 168–69, 171–73, 176, 177, 179, 182
        and slapstick, 173–74, 178–79, 180; *see also Molloy*, sudden violence in
        compared to *Cold Comfort Farm*, 175
        irritation in, 175–76
        Moran's narrative as bureaucratic report, 164–67
        obsessive-compulsive patterns in, 176–83
        parallels to Beckett's life, 171–72
        paternity in, 166–68, 168–71
        sudden violence in, 179, 180, 181
    Murphy, 161, 162, 176
    Waiting for Godot, 168
    Watt, 162, 163
Beerbohm, Max, 22, 27, 55, 56, 102
    Zuleika Dobson, 23–26
Bell, Michael, 12, 16
Bell, Robert, 34, 36
Benjamin, Walter, 105, 107, 147–48, 149
Bergson, Henri, 67
    on anaesthesia of the heart, 23, 33
    on comic rigidity, 89, 110–11, 146, 181